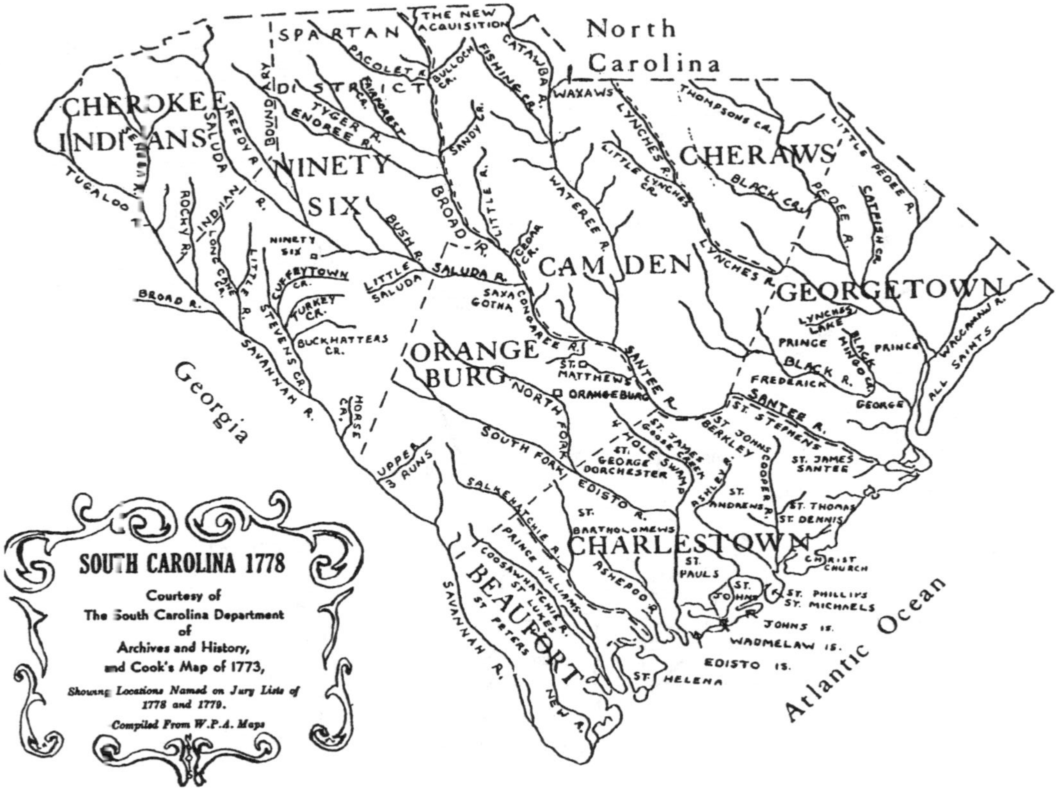
SOUTH CAROLINA 1778
Courtesy of
The South Carolina Department
of
Archives and History,
and Cook's Map of 1773,
Showing Locations Named on Jury Lists of
1778 and 1779.
Compiled From W.P.A. Maps
North Carolina
Georgia
Atlantic Ocean
CHEROKEE INDIANS
SPARTAN DISTRICT
THE NEW ACQUISITION
NINETY SIX
CAMDEN
CHERAWS
GEORGETOWN
ORANGEBURG
CHARLESTOWN
BEAUFORT
BOUNDARY
TUGALOO R.
SALUDA R.
REEDY R.
ROCKY R.
INDIAN R.
LONG CANE CR.
LITTLE R.
BROAD R.
SAVANNAH R.
STEVENS CR.
NINETY SIX
CUFFEYTOWN CR.
TURKEY CR.
BUCKHATTERS CR.
HORSE CR.
LITTLE SALUDA
BUSH R.
SALUDA R.
TYGER R.
ENOREE R.
FAIRFOREST CR.
PACOLET R.
BULLOCH CR.
FISHING CR.
CATAWBA R.
SANDY CR.
LITTLE R.
CEDAR CR.
WATEREE R.
WAXAWS
LYNCHES R.
LITTLE LYNCHES CR.
THOMPSONS CR.
BLACK CR.
PEDEE R.
CATFISH CR.
LITTLE PEDEE R.
SAXA GOTHA
CONGAREE R.
SANTEE R.
ST. MATTHEWS
ORANGEBURG
NORTH FORK
SOUTH FORK
UPPER 3 RUNS
EDISTO R.
ST. GEORGE DORCHESTER
4 HOLE SWAMP
ST. JAMES GOOSE CREEK
ST. JOHNS BERKLEY
ASHLEY R.
ST. ANDREWS
COOPER R.
ST. STEPHENS
ST. JAMES SANTEE
ST. THOMAS
ST. DENNIS
CHRIST CHURCH
ST. PHILLIPS
ST. MICHAELS
ST. PAULS
ST. JOHNS
JOHNS IS.
WADMELAW IS.
EDISTO IS.
ST. HELENA
ST. BARTHOLOMEWS
ASHEPOO R.
SALKEHATCHIE R.
PRINCE WILLIAMS
COOSAWHATCHIE R.
ST LUKES
ST PETERS
NEW R.
FREDERICK
BLACK R.
PRINCE
LYNCHES LAKE
BLACK MINGO CR.
PRINCE
GEORGE
WACCAMAW R.
ALL SAINTS

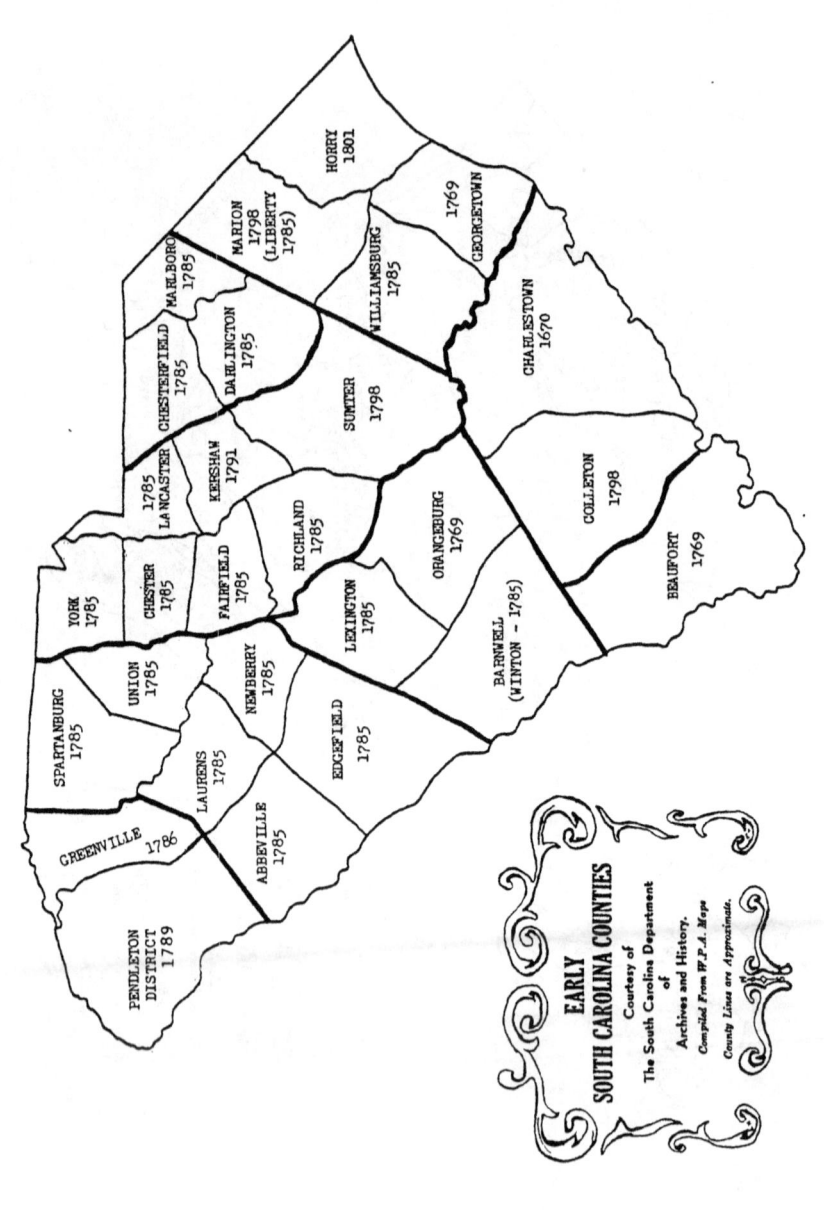

The JURY LISTS Of SOUTH CAROLINA 1778 - 1779

The JURY LISTS Of SOUTH CAROLINA 1778 - 1779

Compiled by
GE LEE CORLEY HENDRIX
and
MORN McKOY LINDSAY

CLEARFIELD

Reprinted for
Clearfield Company by
Genealogical Publishing Co.
Baltimore, Maryland
2004, 2007

ISBN-13: 978-0-8063-0906-4
ISBN-10: 0-8063-0906-7

Originally published: Greenville, South Carolina, 1975
Reprinted, by arrangement, Genealogical Publishing Co., Inc.
Baltimore, Maryland, 1980
Copyright © 1975
Ge Lee Corley Hendrix and Morn McKoy Lindsay
All Rights Reserved
Library of Congress Catalogue Card Number 80-68124

Made in the United States of America

This Book

Is

Lovingly Dedicated

To

Our Husbands

And to the

Behethland Butler Chapter

Of The

Daughters of the American Revolution

Greenville, South Carolina

TABLE OF CONTENTS

Miscellaneous Act No. 1078	1
Charlestown District	3
Georgetown District	29
Cheraws District	40
Camden District	44
Beaufort District	61
Orangeburg District	66
Miscellaneous Act No. 1123	74
Ninety Six District	76
Index	105

FOREWORD

THE JURY LISTS OF 1778 - 1779 were copied from the original handwritten lists on deposit at the South Carolina Department of Archives and History in Columbia, South Carolina. The names in this book are in the same sequence as the original lists, and every effort was made to copy the names exactly as written, including misspellings.

The handwriting was beautiful old script, but the scribes formed a few letters so similarly that some names had to be examined very carefully to be sure they were copied correctly. An alternate spelling or question mark has been added by the compilers to names that were not clearly written. However, all other words in parentheses, such as occupations or places of residence, are exactly as written on the original lists. As the original jury lists were evidently copied from tax lists* (which unfortunately no longer exist), it is possible that some errors in spelling were made in the tax lists themselves, or at the time they were copied.

South Carolina was divided into seven districts during this time period. In the jury lists, each district is divided into geographical areas, helping to pinpoint where the individuals lived. Maps are provided in the book to help locate these areas were in after the county system was organized. In Camden District, "The New Acquisition" was that area once thought to be in North Carolina, but when the boundary was re-surveyed in 1772, it was established as being in South Carolina, and is present day York County. In Ninety Six District, Spartan District included what is now Spartanburg, Union and Cherokee counties. Most of the other areas are identified by parishes, rivers, and streams.

These jury lists are the closest thing we have to a complete state census before 1790. Except for the alphabetized lists, the names are probably grouped with others who lived nearby, which give clues to neighbors and relatives. These names indicate who many of the residents of South Carolina were before the influx of settlers after the Revolution. Many of the names are also found later to be residents of Georgia and other states, as the westward migration began after the Revolution.

One of the purposes in publishing this book is to make research in early South Carolina history easier for people who do not have access to the records of South Carolina. As it has been almost two hundred years since the jury lists were drawn up, we thought the celebration of the Bicentennial Anniversary of our nation's independence an ideal time to promote interest in South Carolina's history, and to encourage others with the time, interest, and ability to do likewise.

*Ref: S.C. Circuit Court Act #1095, Article XVII, 29 July, 1769. "The Judges of the said Court of Common Pleas in Charlestown shall cause lists of jurors in civil causes, grand and petit jurors, to be made for Charlestown, and also for each of the country districts and precincts, from the next antecedent tax list of persons within such respective districts or precincts aforesaid".

SOUTH CAROLINA
AT A GENERAL ASSEMBLY begun and holden at Charles Town on Monday the fifth day of January in the year of our Lord one thousand seven hundred and seventy eight and from thence continued by divers adjournments to Saturday-the twenty eighth day of March, in the year of our Lord one thousand seven hundred and seventy eight.

AN ACT for establishing a new List of Jury-men from the Districts of Charles Town - George Town, Cheraws, Camden, Beaufort and Orangeburgh within this state.

WHEREAS by the increase of the number of Inhabitants and the Death and removal of many Persons who resided in the State it is necessary to form a new list of Jury Men for the Several Districts within this State that the Burthen of that Service may be the more equally divided amongst the People BE IT THEREFORE ENACTED by His Excellency Rawlins Lowndes Esquire President and Commander in Chief in and over the State of South Carolina by the Honourable the Legislative Council and General Assembly of the said State and by the Authority of the Same that the several persons whose names are inserted in the different Schedules or lists hereunto annexed as Jury Lists for the Several Districts of Charles Town - George Town, Cheraws, Camden, Beaufort and Orangeburgh within this state and intitled the Grand Jury List, Petit Jury List and the Special Jury list of each of the said Districts respectively are hereby deemed and declared to be qualified and obliged to serve as Jury Men for such Districts respectively according to the several Jury Lists in which their names are so inserted: That is to say, all Persons whose Names are inserted in the Petit Jury List of any of the Districts aforesaid and hereunto annexed shall be summoned returned and obliged to serve as Petit Jury Men for such District the Special Jury List of which their Names are so inserted in all cases where Tales are allowed by Law AND BE IT FURTHER ENACTED by the aforesaid that each of the several lists hereunto annexed as the Grand Jury List, Petit Jury list and Special Jury list of any Districts before mentioned is hereby deemed and declared to be the legal Grand Jury list, Petit Jury list and special Jury list respectively of such respective Districts And that at the next sitting of the Court of Common Pleas or General Sessions in Charles Town and that the next sitting of the said Courts for any of the other Districts aforesaid the Judge or Judges of the said Courts shall cause to be written at respectively on small seperate pieces of Paper of any equal Size the Names of every Person in the list hereunto annexed as the Grand Jury List of the District where such Court is so held and after having compared such Names with such Lists shall cause them to be put in a Box or Chest prepared for that purpose with proper divisions made therein according to the Directions of the Acts of the General Assembly now in force respecting Jurors and Jury list And the said Judges or Judge shall also then and there cause to be written on small seperate pieces of Paper of equal size the Names of every Person in the list hereunto annexed as the Petit Jury List of the District where such Court is so held and after comparing such Names with the said Box or Chest prepared for the holding of such Petit Jurys List of such District according to the aforesaid acts respecting Jurors and Jury lists as aforesaid And shall also then and there cause to be written on small seperate Pieces of Paper of equal size as aforesaid the Name of every Person in the List hereunto annexed as the special Jury List of the District where such Court is so held and after comparing such Names with the said List shall cause them to be put into one of the two Divisions of the said Box prepared for holding such special Jury List of such District according to the Acts aforesaid respecting Jurors and Jury Lists as aforesaid. AND BE IT FURTHER ENACTED by the Authority aforesaid That all Grand Juries and Petit Juries of the Court of Common Pleas which shall hereafter be drawn for any of the Districts aforesaid shall be drawn from the Names which shall be taken from the List of Grand Jurors and the list of Petit Jurors respectively for such Districts hereunto annexed as aforesaid and which shall be put into the Jury Box of such District as before directed by this Act shall in every other respect than what is particularly expressed and declared by this Act be drawn summoned returned and impanelled agreeable to and in such Form and manner and at such Times and Places as are directed and prescribed by an Act called "the Circuit Court Act" passed the twenty ninth Day of July one Thousand Seven Hundred and Sixty nine or any other Act in force at the Time of the passing of this Act relative to the drawing of Juries AND BE IT FURTHER ENACTED by the Authority aforesaid that all Persons whose Names are inserted in any of the Jury Lists annexed to this act are respectively liable to all Pains and Penalties that Jurors are liable to by any Law of force in this State And that all Acts and Verdicts by any Jury drawn under and by Virtue of this Act shall be as valid Effectual to all Intents and purposes as this Act or Verdict of any Jury can be by law.

Ref: - S. C. Archives - MS Act 1778 - Act No. 1078

GRAND JURORS FOR THE PARISH
OF ST. PHILIP & ST. MICHAEL

James Anderson
Ichabod Atwell
William Ancrum
Alexander Alexander
Samuel Ash
Charles Atkins
James Henry Butler
Francis Bremar
James Brian
Jacob Boomer
Peter Bouteton
Peter Bounetheau
John Benfield
John Bush
John Baddeley
John Boomer
Robert Beard
Daniel Bourdeaux
Joseph Atkinson
John Bowen
Barnard Beekman
Robert Brailsford
Thomas Bee
Isaac Holmes
David Bruce
John Bonsall
Benjamin Baker
Thomas Buckle
Nathaniel Blundell
Thomas Baldwin
James Balantine
Peter Bocquet Junior
Samuel Beekman
James Bentham
John Baker
Joseph Bee
William Banbury
John Beale
Edward Blake
Peter Bacot
John Berwick
Josiah Bonneau
John Brailsford
Francis Baker
Samuel Bonsall
Thomas Corbett
Levinus Clarkson
James Cook
John Clements
John Chambers
Joseph Creighton
Henry Crouch

John Calvert
Joseph Cox
Daniel Cannon
Alexander Chisolme
Bryan Cape
McCartan Campbell
William Creighton
Philotheos Chiffelle
James Courtone
George Cook
Timothy Crosby
Martin Clime
Robert Cochran
John Colcock
John Callahan
Benjamin Cattel
William Cattel
Samuel Cordes
Richard Cole
Robert Daniel
Thomas Doughty
William Doughty
Joseph Darrell
Joseph Dill
William Downes
Benjamin Dart
Arthur Downes
Stephen Lee
John Dorsius
Cornelius Dewees
James Donaldson
John Dutarque
James Darby
John Dart
Edward Darell
John Davis
John Duvall
William Denny
John Delka
John Dawson
John Deas
Paul Douxsaint
William Henry Drayton
John Drayton
James Edwards
Edmund Egan
John Edwards
Barnard Elliott
Thomas Eveleigh
Benjamin Elliott
Nicholas Eveleigh
William Edwards
Charles Elliott
Thomas Farr
John Fisher (Cabinet Maker)

Alexander Fraser
James Fisher (Mercht)
Lucas Florin
George Flagg
Brian Foskey
Thomas Fell
William Fair
Samuel Fley
John Fisher
Thomas Ferguson
John Grant (Sadler)
William Graham
John Paul Grimke
Joseph Glover
John Lewis Gervais
John Giles
Christopher Gruber
Frederick Grimke
Francis Gottier
William Gibbes
Theodore Gailliard
Christopher Gadsden
George Greenland
Alexander Gillon
John Guines
William Hopkins
Thomas Hutchison
Elias Horry Junior
John Hollbeck
Samuel Hopkins
Richard Hutson
William Hest
Robert Howard
Joel Holmes
John Huger
John Harleston Junior
Thomas Horry
Mathias Hutchinson
John Howe
John Hatfield
William Hort
William Halliday
William Hales
William Hinckley
George Abbott Hall
William Hopton
William Harvey
Joseph Hutchings
John Howell
Thomas Hall
Thomas Harris
Patrick Hinds
Daniel Horry
Isaac Huger
Joshua Hart
Philip Hart
Benjamin Huger

Isaac Harleston
Thomas Ham
Thomas Harvey
Thomas Heyward Junr
William Johnson
Thomas Jones
John Jeffords Junior
Alexander Inglis
Michael Kalteisen
Zephaniah Kinsley
James King
Joseph Kemmel
James Keith
James Lennox
Joshua Lockwood
William Logan
Solomon Legare
Henry Lindower
Edward Lightwood
Aaron Loocock
Charles Johnston
Felix Long
Robert Lindsay
John Lyon
Thomas Legare Junior
Joseph Leeson
William Lennox
Samuel Legare
Thomas Latham
Richard Lushington
John Lanneau
Bazille Lanneau
Thomas Legare
Henry Lyburt
William Livingston
William Loocock
William Long
Daniel Legare
Henry Laurence
Benjamin Lord
Andrew Lord
Thomas Lynch
William Lee
John Mathews
William Moultrie
William Miller
Nathaniel Morgan
Alexander Marshall
Thomas Middleton
David Milling
Charles Motte
Robert Muncreef
John Raven Mathews
Martin Miller
Isaac Mazyck
Ephraim Mitchell
Benjamin Mathewes

Jacob Motte
Stephen Mazyck
Philip Meyer
Mark Morris
William Mills
Richard Muncreef
Isaac Motte
James McCall
William McKemmy
John McCall
Arthur Middleton
Michael Muckenfuss
Thomas Moultrie
Alexander McQueen
William Mewhanny
John McQueen
Richard Mercer
Patrick Moon
Alexander Macbeth
Peter Meurset
Abraham Markley
Sampson Neyle
George Noddings
Edward North
John Neufville
James Neilson
Edward Oats
John Owen
Lewis Ogier
Darby Pendergrass
George Powell
Isaac Peace
Hext Prioleau
John Poaug
Hopkin Prise
Samuel Price
William Patterson
George Gabriel Powell
Thomas Phepoe
John Parker
John Ernest Poyas
Charles Pinckney
Samuel Prioleau Junior
Philip Porcher
Paul Pritchard
Robert William Powell
Samuel Perdriau
James Parsons
William Price
William Parker
Charles Cotesworth Pinckney
Thomas Pinckney
Henry Pendleton
Robert Philp
Nathan[1] Russell
Robert Ray
Thomas Ratcliff Junior

William Roper
John Rose
Thomas Rivers
George Rout
Robert Raper
McCully Righton
Owen Roberts
Andrew Reid
Christopher Rogers
William Reid
Robert Rowand
Jacob Read
John Russell (shipwright)
Henry Reeves
Edward Rutledge
Hugh Rutledge
William Russell
James Strickland
John Scott
James Stedman
Stephen Shrewsberry
John Stevenson
George Smithson
Andrew Stewart
Samuel Stent
William Stukes
Thomas Smith
George Smith
Paul Smyser
Abraham Spidell
John Shutterling
Thomas Shubrick
William Somarsall
Daniel Stroble
Jeremiah Savage
William Scott Junior
Hugh Swinton
Thomas Savage
Roger Smith
John Smyth
Josiah Smith Junior
John Scott Junior
George Smith Junior
Maurice Simmons
Humphry Sommers
Jonathan Sarrazin
John Scott (son of Jonathan)
Audeon St John
Thomas Singleton
William Scott
Christopher Fitzsimons
Thomas Tucker
George Tew
John Troup
Simon Tufts
Theodore Trezvant
James Toussiger

Anthony Toomer
Henry Timrod
Richard Todd
John Torrans
John Thompson
William Trusler
Philip Tydiman
Stephen Townsend
Paul Townsend
Jacob Valk
Joseph Veree
Benjamin Villepontoux
Benjamin Wilkins
William Wayne
John Mortimer Williams
Samuel Warnock
Robert Williams
James Witter
Melchior Werley
John Waring
Jacob Williman
Benjamin Wish
James Wakefield
Joshua Ward
John Wagner
Sims White
John Webb
Edward Weyman
William Wilson
Jacob Warley
Gasper Washing
William Walton
Christopher Willeman
William Williamson
John Wragg
Richard Wainwright
George Young
Plowden Weston
Thomas You
Thomas Young
Samuel Wainwright

GRAND JURORS FOR
CHRIST CHURCH PARISH

Thomas Barksdale
John Severance
Thomas Whitesides
Charvil Wingood
John White
William Cook
Peter Sanders
Thomas Hamlin
Andrew Hibben
Thomas White
George White
Thomas Barton

Joseph Wigfall
Joseph Maybank
John Murrell
George Arthur
George Paddon Bond
Daniel Jeffords
Arnoldus Vanderkorst
Joshua Toomer
Andrew Quelch
Paul Murrell
George Hamlin
Gabriel Capers
Peter Croft
George Barksdale
Clement Lamprier
Daniel Manson
Nathan Legare
Elias Wigfall
John Jeffords
Robert Murrell Junior

GRAND JURORS FOR THE PARISH
OF ST JAMES GOOSE CREEK

Thomas Walter
William Eckles
Benjamin Smith
Henry Smith
William Withers
Peter Tamplat
James Streater
Benjamin Coachman
Benjamin Mazyck
William Bull Junior
John Wright
Alexander Mazyck
John George Ripley
George Pooser
John Morgandollar

GRAND JURORS FOR THE PARISH
OF ST JOHNS BERKLEY COUNTY

Samuel Bonneau
Thomas Broughton Junior
Elias Ball Junior
John Cordes
John Harleston
Nathaniel Broughton
Samuel Cordes
William Moultrie Junior
Zachariah Villepontoux Jun[r]
Thomas Sabb
James Ravenel
Henry Ravenel
Daniel Ravenel
Stephen Mazyck Junior

Henry Ravenel Junior
Anthony Mitchell
Joseph Marion
Isaac Coutourier Junior
Joseph Greenland
Isaac Coutourier
Isaac Bradwell
Gabriel Gignilliat
Peter Videaux

GRAND JURORS FOR THE PARISH
OF ST. GEORGE DORCHESTER

Stephen Cater
Patrick Hewes
Isaac Drose
Peter Horlbeck
John Glaze
Thomas Waring Junior
Philip Gioham
Daniel Drose
Daniel Stewart
Morton Waring
John Izard
John Joor
Jervis Henry Stevens
John Christian Smith
Benjamin Waring
Thomas Waring
Benjamin Coachman Junior
Richard Waring
Nathaniel Bradwell
Richard Bohun Baker
Richard Walter
George Evans
Robert Cattel
John Allyn Walter
Christian Ridlesparger
John Byrd
George Draxler
James Harley
William Dewitt
Andrew Hall
Henry Pooser
John Fullerton
Maurice Lee
William Morgan

GRAND JURORS FOR THE PARISHES
OF ST. THOMAS AND ST. DENNIS

John Moore
Thomas Screven
Thomas Addison
Thomas Cochran
William Glen Junior
Isaac Lesesne

Hopson Pinckney
Robert Quash
Edward Thomas
Benjamin Marion
John Wigfall
Andrew Hasell
Thomas Karwon
Joseph Fogartie
Thomas Joel
Benjamin Simmons
Thomas Ashby
Ebenezer Roach
James Akin
Thomas Dearington
Robert Johnston
John Garden
John Dearington
Nathan Tart

GRAND JURORS FOR THE PARISH
OF ST. ANDREW

John Linning
Abraham Ladson
Benjamin Fuller
Thomas Fuller
Thomas Rose
Richard Park Stobo
John Holman
Nathaniel Fuller
Thomas Elliott
William Croskeys
John Dill
John Goldie
John Hearne
William Holmes
Malory Rivers
John Rivers
William Royall
Benjamin Stiles
Benjamin Stone
Archibald Scott

GRAND JURORS FOR JOHNS ISLAND

Abraham Waite
Edward Fenwicke
William Mathews
Benjamin Mathews
Daniel Holmes
Thomas Hanscomb
William Boone
George Mathews
John Holmes

GRAND JURORS FOR EDISTO
ISLAND

Andrew Townsend
Joseph Seabrook
Joseph Seabrook Junr.
Benjamin Eddings
Benjamin Seabrook
James Clark
James Murray
Joseph Fickling
John Adams
William Maxwell
Benjamin Jenkins
Joseph Jenkins
Daniel Jenkins
David Adams

GRAND JURORS FOR
WADMELAW ISLAND

George Fickling
William Smiley
Isaac Battoon
William Sams
James Laroach

GRAND JURORS FOR THE
PARISH OF ST BARTHOLOMEW

William Oswald
John Croll
Robert Bellengall
Wilson Cook
Joseph Dobbins
David Battey
Joseph Koger
James Thompson
Thos Roberts
John Logan
Isaac Ford
Robert Rose
William Hamilton
John Ward
Stephen Akeman
Joseph Chambers
James Cavaneau
James Postell Junior
Dennis Mahonny
John Van Marginhoff
John Singleton
James Stewart
Edward Forshaw
James Skirving Junior
Philip Smith
John Crosskeys
John Sanders
Isaac Haynes
Joseph Glover Junior
William Clay Snipes

Robert Caborne
John Bowler
William Bowler
Daniel Dalton
William Smith
William Smith Junior
Francis Smith
John Wells
Henry Hyrne
Thomas Hutchinson
John Elias Hutchinson
Jeremiah Miles
Thomas Hutchinson Junr
Edmond Bellenger Junior
William Gibson
Peter Girardeau
John Warren
John Bellenger
William Webb
William Godfrey
James Hamilton
Benjamin Gignilliat
John Miles
Thomas Ladson
Jacob Stevens
James Lyle
Samuel Dunlap
Samuel Beaty
Valentine Lynn
John McFarlen
George Sheapherd
James McKewn
John Lambert

GRAND JURORS FOR THE
PARISH OF ST PAUL

Andrew Leitch
George Ford
Henry Fletcher
James D. Yarborough
Henry Nichols
James Nichols
Allen Miles
William Mill
William Garner
Richard Perry
William McLaughlin
John Sommers
Jehu Wilson
John Brailsford
Edward Perry
William Dunning
Isaac McPherson
Thomas Smith
George Livingston
Robert Ladson

Melcher Garner
John Farr
Thomas Farr Junior
William Smith
William Ladson
Joseph Bee
Joseph Kann
Andrew Johnston
Andrew Kann
Joseph Smith
Christopher Peter
Thomas Osborn
William Skirving
John Mitchell
Morton Wilkinson

GRAND JURORS FOR THE PARISH
OF ST JAMES SANTEE

Isaac Legrand
John Jaudon
Capers Boone
Jacob Jenneret
Lewis Miles
Thomas Boone
Michael Boineau
John Barnett
John Drake
Elisha Barnett
Edward Jermain
Elias Ball
Levi Durand
Theodore Gaillard
Anthony Simons
Charles Gaillard

William Lewis
Richard Withers
Joseph Huggins
Peter Mouzon
Joseph Legare
Daniel McGregor

GRAND JURORS FOR THE
PARISH OF ST STEPHEN

John Peyre
Peter Guerry
Peter Coutourier
John Palmer
John Palmer Junior
Joseph Palmer
Hezekiah Maham
James Sinkler
Charles Cantey
Ja^s Guerry
John Guerry
John Coutourier
Samuel Peyre
Peter Porcher
Mathew Whitefield
Danl Cahusae?
Isaac Porcher
Isaac Dubose
Rene Richbourgh
Philip Williams
John Gaillard
Peter Sinkler
David Gaillard
Thomas Cooper

PETIT JORORS FOR THE DISTRICT OF CHARLES TOWN

PETIT JURORS FOR THE PARISH
OF ST PHILIP AND ST MICHAEL

Alexander Adamson
Ralph Atmore
James Anderson
Ichabod Atwell
William Ancrum
Robert Austin
Alexander Alexander
John Abercrombie
Emanuel Abrahams
Samuel Ash
Charles Atkins
George Ancrum Junior
John Anthony
William Axson
Solomon Aaron
James Askew

James Henry Butler
Francis Bremar
James Brian
Jacob Boomer
Peter Bouteton
Peter Bounetheau
Henry Blackenhorn
John Benfield
John Bush
John Baddeley
John Boomer
Michael Black
Robert Beard
Daniel Bourdeaux
Joseph Atkinson
John Bowen (up the path)
Henry Bookless
Barnard Beekman
Robert Brailsford

Thomas Bee
Henry Bembridge
David Bruce
John Bonsell
Benjamin Baker
John Bouniott
William Benney
James Bricken
Thomas Buckle
Nathaniel Blundell
Thomas Baldwin
James Balantine
Thomas Bourke
Joseph Badger
Joseph Beiler
David Boillatt
Peter Bocquett Junior
Samuel Beekman
James Bentham
John Baker
Joseph Bee
John Blott
William Banbury
John Bury
Jacob Bowler
Charles Burkmire
William Burrows
John Beal
Edward Blake
Peter Bacot
John Berwick
Josiah Bonneau
Pierce Butler
Francis Bayle
Alexander Bruce
John Brailsford
Joseph Ball
Thomas Bennet
David Burger
Samuel Butler
John Bryan
Thomas Corbett
Benjamin Cook
Henry Caldwell
Levinus Clarkson
James Cook
Moses Chauvet
Joseph Cartwright
Moses Cohen
John Clements
John Chambers
William Cunnington
Joseph Creighton
Sampson Clark
Isaac Cohen
Henry Crouch
William Cameron

John Calvert
George Cahoon
Joseph Cox
Daniel Cannon
John Coram
Samuel Cross
Alexander Chisolme
Brian Cape
McCartan Campbell
William Creighton
John Creighton
Benjamin Coward
Francis Cobia
Philotheos Chiffelle
James Courtone
George Cook
Timothy Crosby
Thomas Coker
Martin Clime
Robert Cockran
William Capers
John Colcock
John Callahan
Jacob Cohen
Benjamin Cattel
John Coppithorn
William Cattel
Gilbert Chambers
Thomas Coram
Benjamin Cudworth
Tobias Cambridge
Samuel Cordas
Richard Cole
James Duncan
Joseph Darling
Robert Daniel
Thomas Doughty
William Doughty
Joseph Darrell
George Duncan
Joseph Dill
William Downes
Benjamin Dart
Isaac Dacosta
Arthur Downes
Stephen Lee
Robert Dewar
James Donnavan
John Dorcius
Cornelius Dewees
James Donaldson
John Dutarque
James Donnavan (up the path)
James Darby
James Dunning
Stephen Duval (pilot)
John Dart

Philip Dewees
Benjamin Darrell
Edward Darrell
John Davis
Abraham Dacosta
Christian Dawson
John Duval
Peter Dener
William Denney
John Delka
James Duncan (Blacksmith)
John Dawson
John Deas
Paul Douxsaint
Isaac DaCosta Junior
William Henry Drayton
Benjamin Dores
John Drayton
James Edwards
Edmond Egan
William Easton
George Ehney
John Edwards
Thomas Eustace
John Eberley
Joshua Eden
Barnard Elliott
Thomas Eveleigh
William Edwards (Sadler)
Charles Elliott
John Fabre
Thomas Farr
John George Fardo
Mungo Finlayson
James Fisher (Merchant)
John Fisher
Alexander Fraser
Lucas Florin
George Flagg
John Fyfe
Bryan Foshey? Foskey?
Thomas Fell
William Fair
Samuel Fley
John Fisher (Cabinet Maker)
Anthony Farrasteau
Thomas Ferguson
James Fogartie
Jacob Frick
Robert Frogg
Christopher Fitzsimmons
Francis Grott
Daniel Gratton
John Walter Gibbes
James Graves
John Grant (Sadler)
James Gross (Barber)

William Greenwood
Seth Gilbert
William Gowdy
William Graham
John Grant (Shoemaker)
Joseph Gaultier
John Paul Grimke
James Gillaudeau
John Gourley
William Gibbes
John Lewis Gervais
John Giles
Othneil Giles
Christian Gruber
Frederick Grimke
Francis Gottier
Theodore Gaillard Junior
Claudius Gilleaud
John Groaning
Christopher Gadsden
George Greenland
Samuel Gruber
Alexander Gillon
John Gaboriel
John Guines
Francis Henricks
William Hopkins
Thomas Hutchinson
Philip Hawkins
Elias Horry Junior
John Horlbeck
William Hutchins
Samuel Hopkins
John Hampton
Richard Hutson
William Hest
Thomas Hammet
Edward Hare
Robert Howard
Joel Holmes
John Newton Hartley
Donald Harper
John Huger
John Harleston Junior
Dalzel Hunter
Mathias Hutchinson
John Howe
John Hatfield
Thomas Harper
William Hort
William Holliday
William Hales
William Hinckley
Charles Harris
George Abbott Hall
Peter Horn
Sir Edmond Head

William Hopton
Joseph Hutchings
John Howell
Francis Huger
Thomas Hall
Thomas Harris
Patrick Hinds
Daniel Horry
Isaac Huger
Joshua Hart
Philip Hart
Benjamin Huger
Isaac Harleston
Thomas Ham
Thomas Higgins
Richard Ham
Thomas Harvey
Thomas Heyward Junior
James Jennings
Samuel Jones (Tanner)
Joseph Jones (Shopkeeper)
William Johnson
Thomas Jones
Ralp Izard
Thomas Irvey
John Irnst
John Jeffer
Israel Joseph
Samuel Jones
Charles Johnston
Alexander Inglis
Alexander James
John Imrie
Michael Keller
John Kerkner
David Kaufman
Michael Kalteisen
Robert Knox
Zephaniah Kinsley
James King
Joseph Kimmel
James Keith
George Kean (Bricklayer)
James Lennox
Joshua Lockwood
William Logan
Peter LePoole
Solomon Legare
Nicholas Langford
Henry Lindour
Edward Lightwood
Aaron Loocock
Felix Long
Richard Latham
Robert Lindsay
Rawlins Lowndes
John Lyon

Thomas Legare Junior
John Luich
Joseph Leeson
Robert Larry
William Lennox
Samuel Legare
Markes Lazarus
Thomas Latham
Thomas Liston
Richard Lushington
John Lanneau
Bazil Lanneau
Thomas Legare
Henry Lybert
William Livingston
Charles Linning
James Lynch
William Loocock
John Lahiff
William Long
Daniel Legare
Henry Laurens
Benjamin Lord
Andrew Lord
George Layfield
William Laurence (Carver)
Thomas Lynch
William Lee
John Mathewes
Alexander Moultrie
John Minot
William Moultrie
George Morris
Samuel Miller
William Miller
John McCall (Taylor)
Nathaniel Morgan
Walter Mayne
William Massey
Samuel McCorkel
Alexander Marshal
Thomas Middleton
John Miot
Henry McNally
Samuel Maverick
James Mackie
Jacob Moses
David Milling
John McCall Junior
Charles Motte
James McClenehan
William Mason
David Maul
Lachlan Martin
Robert Muncreef
John Raven Mathewes
Martin Miller

Isaac Mazyck
Ephraim Mitchell
Jacob Motte
Stephen Mazyck
Philip Meyer
Mark Morris
John Michael
William Mills
Richard Muncreef
Philip Mentzing
Myer Moses
Isaac Motte
James McCall
William McKimmy
John McCall (Merchant)
William McGillivery
Adam Minick
Edward McReady
Henry Middleton
Arthur Middleton
Michael Muckenfuss
John Mathewes (Cordwainer)
Thomas Moultrie
Alexander McQueen
Robert McCloklan
William Mewhanny
John McQueen
Henry Marque
Richard Mercer
Patrick Moon
Philip Moses
Barnard Moses
Alexander McBeth
Peter Meurset
Abraham Martley
William Nisbett
Sampson Neyle
George Noddings
Edward North
Frederick Nann
Philip Neizar
George Nedhammer
John Neufville
Edward Neufville Junior
William Nicoll
John North
James Neilson
Edward Oats
James OHair
Thomas Oliver
John Owen
James Oliphant (Jeweller)
Lewis Ogeir
Hugh Pollock
Martin Pesnegar
Darby Pendergrass
George Powell
Isaac Peace
Job Palmer

Hext Prioleau
John Poaug
Hopkin Prise
Paul Pritchard
Samuel Price
William Patterson
George Gabriel Powell
Thomas Phepoe
John Parker
John Ernest Poyas
Charles Pickney
Samuel Prioleau
Samuel Prioleau Junior
Philip Prioleau
Philip Porcher
Robert William Powell
Samuel Perdriau
James Parsons
William Price
William Parker
Charles Cotsworth Pinckney
Thomas Pinckney
John Philip
Peter Prow
Robert Philp
Abraham Pearce
Henry Pendleton
William Print
Nathaniel Russell
Robert Ray
Thomas Radcliffe Junior
William Roper
John Rutledge
John Rose
Charles Ramadge
Thomas Rivers
George Rout
Robert Raper
McCully Righten
John Robertson (Vintner)
Martin Rimley
James Roche
Owen Roberts
Andrew Reid
Peter Ross
Christopher Rogers
John Richardson
William Reid
John Ralph
Robert Rowand
Jacob Read
Charles Reiley
Jacob Remington
John Russell (Shipwright)
John Ruberry
Henry Reeves
Alexander Russell
Edward Rutledge
Hugh Rutledge

Charles Roberts
Alexander Rose
Andrew Rutledge
William Russell
Christopher Sheets
Samuel Stone
William Stone
James Strickland
Thomas Stuart
John Scott
Augustine Stillman
James Stedman
Stephen Shrewsberry
Peter Storr
John Stevenson
George Smithson
Paul Snyder
John Sansum
Labastion Spencer
John Smith
Jacob Sass
William Stoll
Andrew Stuart
David Saylor
Samuel Stent
David Smith (Baker)
William Samways
William Stukes
Thomas Smith
George Smith Junior
Paul Smyzer
Abraham Spidell
Christian Sigwald
John Shutterling
Thomas Shubrick
Humphry Sommers
William Sommersall
Daniel Stroble
James St John
Jeremiah Savage
John Scott (son of Jonathan)
William Scott Junior
Hugh Swinton
John Spicesegar
Ed^d Shrewsberry
Thomas Savage
Roger Smith
John Smyth
Josiah Smith Junior
John Scott Junior
Maurice Simmons
Bracey Singleton
Samuel Scottou
James Sharp
Pott Shaw
Jonathan Sarrazin
Audeon St John

John Stattler
Thomas Singleton
William Scott
William Savage
James Snead
David Swanson
Isaac Seymour
Matthew Shepherd
Nicholas Smith
Peter Smith (Carpenter)
Thomas Tucker
George Tew
John Troup
Simon Tufts
Theodore Trezvant
James Toussiger
Anthony Toomer
Henry Timrod
Stephen Thomas
Richard Todd
William Touch
John Turner
Lewis Timmon
Daniel Tharin
Philip Thorn
John Torrans
John Thompson
Benjam Elliott
William Trusler
Philip Tydiman
Stephen Townsend
Paul Townsend
Peter Timothy
John Tuke
David Taylor
Joseph Turpin Junior
John Richard Tallman
Edward Trescot
Jacob Valk
John Vineyard
Peter Valton
Joseph Verree
Benjamin Villipontoux
William Valentine
Philip Will
Benjamin Wilkins
William Wilkins
John Wragg (Tradd Street)
James Wilkins
James Wright
William Wayne
John Mortimer Williams
John Wakefield
John Wyatt
Samuel Warnock
Robert Williams
John Wood

14

John Wells Junior
James Wier
James Wright (Baker)
James Witter
Richard Ellis
John Watson
Melchior Werley
John Waring
Jacob Willeman
Benjamin Wish
James Wakefield
Joshua Ward
John Wagner
Sims White
John Webb
Edward Weyman
William Wilson
Jacob Warly
Gasper Washing
William Walton
Christopher Willeman
William Williamson
John Wragg
Richard Wainwright
John Wilson
John Ward (Taylor)
Plowden Weston
James Green Williams
Jacob White
John Welsh
Samuel Wainwright
Benjamin Waller
Lebbeus Whitney
George Young
Thomas You
Joseph Yates
Thomas Young
Richard Yeadon
Nicholas Eveleigh

PETIT JURORS FOR CHRIST CHURCH PARISH

Thomas Barksdale
John Severance
Edward Whiteside
Thomas Whiteside
Charvil Wingood
John White
William Cook
Peter Saunders
Thomas Hamlin
John Milner
Andrew Hibben
Arnoldus Vanderhorst
John Boon
James Eden

Thomas White
George White
Isaac Legare
Joseph Whilden
Peter Murrell
Joseph Wigfall
Joseph Maybank
John Murrell
Samuel Vaney
George Arthur
George Paddon Bond
James Bollough
Daniel Jeffords
John Jeffords
Thomas Severance
James Evans
William Player
John Hartman
John Eden
George Sinclare Capers
Thomas Player
Elias Evans
John Dorrell
Thomas Barton
Robert Murrell Junior
Joshua Toomer
Nathaniel Arthur
Alexander McNellidge
Andrew Quelch
John Whiteside
Allen Bolton
Jonathan Dorrell
Valentine Darr
John Inglish
William Bonhoist
Joseph Frazer
Elisha Whilden
George Hamlin
Gabriel Capers
Peter Croft
Thomas Joy
Benjamin Joy
George Barksdale
John Bollough
William Bennet
John Sandford Dart
John Hatter
Clement Lamprier
Daniel Manson
Nathan Legare
Elias Wigfall
Samuel White
Paul Murrell
Samuel Lacey

PETIT JURORS FOR THE PARISH OF ST JAMES GOOSECREEK

John Morgandollar
George Pooser
James Jenkins
Robert Hurst
Joseph Wood
Thomas Walter
Samuel Lynes
George Brown
William Eckles
Richard Broughton
Andrew Broughton Junior
Thomas Black
Benjamin Smith
Henry Smith
John Young
John Glen
Daniel Glen
John Wood
William Withers
George Philhour
John Fulmer
Michael Koubensack
Conrod Kickeley
John George Ripley
Peter Tamplat
James Streater
Henry Onsild
John Readhemer
Benjamin Coachman
Elisha Tamplat
Henry Branton
Christian Finley
Thomas Ellis
Stephen Mazyck
Benjamin Kempster
Keating Simmons
James Rockford
Benjamin Mazyck
William Bull Junior
John Wright
Richard Gough
Alexander Mazyck

PETIT JURORS FOR THE PARISH
OF ST JOHNS BERKLEY COUNTY

Samuel Bonneau
Thomas Broughton Junior
Elias Ball Junior
Frederick Brindley
John George Brindley
Nathaniel Savineau
John Cordes
Lance Smith
James Cordes
John Cox
Thomas Broughton

Blake Seay White
William Moultrie Junior
Peter Witten
Heugh McWalter
Paul Marion
William Lee
Zachariah Villepontoux Jr
Thomas Sabb
William Taek (Tack?)
Isaac Gourdine
James Oliver
James Ravenel
Henry Ravenel
Daniel Ravenel
Stephen Mazyck Junior
John Weare
Thomas Edmanson
Henry Ravenel Junior
Anthony Mitchell
John Matthews
Peter Benoist
John Hopkins
Richard Norman
Alexander Hamilton
William Flint
John Cook
Philip Coutourier
Edward Smith
James Marion
Job Marion
Joseph Marion
Benjamin Marion Junior
Henry Coram
Isaac Coutourier Junior
Joseph Greenland
William Axon
Isaac Coutourier
Isaac Bradwell
John Christopher Martin
Gabriel Gignilliatt
Henry Boyd
Peter Videau
Francis Marion (Colonel)
John Harleston
Nicholas Parkinson
Nathaniel Broughton
Samuel Cordes

PETIT JURORS FOR THE PARISH
OF ST GEORGE DORCHESTER

Jacob Miners
George Keckerley
Stephen Cater
Patrick Hewes
Isaac Drose
Peter Horlbeck

John Glaze
Thomas Waring Junior
Philip Givham
Daniel Drose
John Walter
Daniel Stewart
Andrew Perdrieau
Francis Postell
Morton Waring
John Ezard
Alexander Wright
John Joor
Jervis Henry Stevens
John Christian Smith
Thomas Hutchinson
Benjamin Waring
Jacob Axson
Jesse Baker
Zachariah Blackledge
Thomas Waring
Benjamin Coachman Junior
John Swift
James Stewart
Edward Stacey
William Burgess
Richard Waring
Nathaniel Bradwell
Richard Bohum Baker
Richard Walter
Nathaniel Bradwell Junior
John Bradwell
Jacob Walter
George Evans
Robert Cattell
John Allyn Walter
Joseph Joor
Simon Irons
Christian Ridlesparger
Isaac Uttsey
Jacob Linder
Lewis Grossman
Jonathan Hughes
Thomas Pendarvis
Thomas Pendarvis Junior
David Rumph Junior
Jesse Ritter
John Adam Meyers
Christian Smith
John Hoff
John Noak
John Byrd
Caleb Hughes
Joseph Russell
George Draxler
Michael Derr
Philip Jesman
James Harley

David Rumph
Samuel Riggs
John Bruner
William Stead Junior
William Riggs
John Brothers
Elisha Hall
William Dewitt
Thomas Clark
James Ryan
George Muckinfuss
Andrew Hall
James Harrey
Thomas Caton
Gasper Stroble
William Mellard
John Caton
Henry Pooser
James Minis
John Dandridge
James Dewitt
Thomas Kelly
Thomas Box
Samuel Owens
John Auting
Barnard Libinder
Christian Roath
Thomas Lewis
Felix Brunes?
James Maine
Philip Bower
John Fullerton
Maurice Lee
William Morgan

PETIT JURORS FOR THE PARISH
OF ST THOMAS & ST DENNIS

John Moore
Thomas Screven
Thomas Addison
Thomas Cochran
John Heskett
William Glen Junior
Philip Mack
Isaac Lesesne
Hopson Pinckney
Robert Quash
Richard Singletary
Edward Thomas
Benjamin Marion
Thomas Butler
John Wigfall
Andrew Hasell
Thomas Karwon
Joseph Sanders Junior
Samuel Bullock

Abraham Roulain
Samuel Wells
Jermiah Brower
William Wells
Peter Bouchett
Thomas Joel
Benjamin Simmons
Thomas Ashby
Anthony Ashby
Vincent Guerin
Joseph Bell
Robert Collins
Ebenezer Roche
John Mourdah
James Atkin
John Singletary
Thomas Dearington
Richard Dearington
Robert Johnston
John Garden
James Jaudon
Charles Chovin
John Dearington
Thomas Prior
Joseph Walnock
William Hamlin
Henry Keyler
Nathan Tart
Thomas Akin

PETIT JURORS FOR THE
PARISH OF ST ANDREW

John Linning
Matharin Guerin Junior
William Chapman
Philip Henry
Abraham Ladson
Benjamin Fuller
Thomas Fuller
Jacob Verner
Jacob Inkles
Thomas Rose
Thomas Mell
Francis Rose
Samuel Jones
Richard Park Stobo
John Frazer
John Holman
John Godfrey
Nathaniel Fuller
Thomas Elliott
Edmond Bellenger
Edward Legge
Daniel Bedon James Island
William Bennet
Thomas Burchall

Solomon Milner
William Croskeys
John Chinners
John Dill
John Goldie
William Gibbes
John Hearne
William Holmer
William King
Francis Pearce
Malary Rivers
George Rivers
Col^o Robert Rivers
Samuel Rivers
John Rivers
William Royall
George Russell
Joseph Rivers
Benjamin Stiles
Joseph Starling
Henry Samways
John Stent
Paul Stent
Samuel Stent
William Starling
John Scott
Benjamin Stone
Archibald Scott
John Witter
Thomas Witter

PETIT JURORS FOR JOHNS
ISLAND, COLLETON COUNTY

Abraham Waight
Isaac Waight Junior
Edward Fenwicke
Daniel Hall
Henry Slade
George Frey
John Stanyarne
William Mathewes
Samuel Palmarin
Benjamin Mathews
Patrick Coil
John Freir
James Witter Senr
Daniel Holmes
Solomon Freir
Thomas Hanscomb
James Smith
William Stanyarne
Thomas Ladson
William Boone
Thomas Humphris
George Mathewes
William Sandiford
John Holmes
Abraham Waight Junior

PETIT JURORS FOR EDISTOE
ISLAND ST JOHNS COLLETON
COUNTY

Andrew Townsend
Ralph Baily
Joseph Seabrook Junior
William Evans
Abraham Bush
Thomas Hext
John Seabrook
William Rennolds
Benjamin Eddings
Benjamin Seabrook
Jeremiah Eaton
James Clark
John Seabrook Junior
Arch^d Whaley
John Cowen
Ephraim Mikell
Benjamin Jenkins Junior
James Murray
William Hannaham
Robert Maxey
Joseph Fickling Junior
John Desberry
John Wilson
Hugh Cowen
Florence Flinn
Joseph Fickling
Winburn Laughton
John Theus
Samuel Eaton
Joseph Scott
Thomas Hannahan
Joseph Parnerton
James Beckett
John Adams
Joseph Maxey
William Maxwell
William Whippy
John White
John Hannahan
Daniel Evans
Robert McKenzie
Paul Hamilton
James Fickling Junior
Benjamin Jenkins
Joseph Seabrook
George McNarney
Nathaniel Morgan
Charles Flinn
Joshua Cox
Joseph Whippy
Moses Bollough
Thomas Westcot
Joseph Eddings

Joseph Jenkins
Thomas Whaley
William Bonsal
William Stanyarne
Daniel Jenkins
David Adams

PETIT JURORS FOR WADMELAW
ISLAND ST JOHNS COLLETON
COUNTY

Daniel Townsend
William Lowry
George Fickling
William Smiley
Isaac Batton
Hugh Wilson
William Sams
Jeremiah Fickling
George Fickling Junior
Thomas Hicks
James Laroach
Robert McGilverey
John Freeman
Henry Livingston
Mathias Bricket

PETIT JURORS FOR THE
PARISH OF ST BARTHOLOMEW

William Oswald
John Driffle?
John Caskin
James Buchannan
Patrick Johnston
John Crole
Robert Bellingall
James Lewis Culliatt
Wilson Cook
Joseph Dobbins
David Batty
Joseph Roger (Koger?)
John Lemocks
William Bridges
Edward Wood
James Thompson
Jasper Harlock
Thomas Roberts
John Logan
Isaac Ford
Maurice Williams
Robert Rose
Felix Hussar
Abraham Bush
William Hambleton

John Bishop
John Ward
John Timman
William McColough
Richard Chitteh
Christopher Jordan
Hugh Campbell
David Williamson
David Forshaw
Joseph Rumney
Stephen Akeman
Joseph Chambers
Peter Youngblood
James Cavana
James Postell Junior
John Todd
Thomas Crole
Michael Razor
George Cling
Dennis Mahony
George Kenneg (Kenney?)
Samuel Riley
John Van Marginhoff
William Findley
John North
John Singelton
James Stuart
Jacob Smiser
John Sullivan
John Mollett
Alexander Wilson
David Culliatt
Edward Forshaw
David Campbell
Joseph Oswald
James Miller
Lazarus Briers
John Cone
Patrick Fitzpatrick
Benjamin Chapple
Samuel Eastlake
James Skirving Junior
Philip Smith
John Croskeys
John Sanders
George Smith
John Harman
Isaac Hayne
Joseph Glover Junior
William Clay Snipes
Charles Shepheard
Josiah Miles
Robert Caborne
William Cunningham
John Bowler
John Webber
James Wilson

William Bowler
Joseph Stephens
William Carter
John Armstrong
John Godfrey
Daniel Dalton
Charles Smith
Robert Jordan
Samuel Blenco
Robert Little
William Smith Junior
James Whaley
Benjamin Perriman
William Smith
Francis Smith
John Wells
Matthew Wells
Thomas Miller
Henry Hyrne
Thomas Hutchinson
John Hughes
Peter Smith
Lachlan McIntosh
John Elias Hutchinson
Jermiah Miles
Thomas Hutchinson Junr
John Cato Fields
Hubart Chamberlain
Edmond Bellenger Junior
William Gibson
Peter Girardeau
John Warren
Edward Legge Junior
John Bellinger
William Webb
William Godfrey
John Cockran
James Hamilton
Henry Wilson
John Lambright
Thomas Harrison
Joseph Rheme
Cornelius Snees
David Stephens
Benjamin Gignilliatt
John Miles
Samuel Fletcher
Thomas Ladson
John Smiley
Jacob Stevens
James Lyle
David Miller
John Varlin
Samuel Dunlap
William Mills
Samuel Wright
Samuel Baty

Vallentine Lynn
John McFarlen
George Shepheard
John Curtis
Nathaniel Cothen
Solomon Harper
Ed^d Robertson
Isaac Copeland
Hugh Watson
George Warren
William Smith
Henry Smith
George Carter
Jacob Carter
Hance McCullough
James McKewn
Solomon Gray
John Lambert

PETIT JURORS FOR THE
PARISH OF ST PAUL

Andrew Leitch
Samuel Bell
George Ford
Hillman Hutchins
Henry Fletcher
Thomas Stevens
Philip Bowers
Joseph Dandridge
George Hennzar
James D Yarborough
William Chisolme
James Gilchrist Simpson
Henry Nichols
James Nichols
William Spoon
Allen Miles
William Mell
William Garner
Francis Perry
Richard Perry
William McLaughlin
John Sommers
Zachariah Flurry
Jehu Wilson
John Jackson
John Brailsford
Edward Perry
James Stevens
William Dunning
Michael Cobia
Albert Duylmire
Isaac McPherson
John Wilson

George Livingston
William Swinton
Robert Ladson
Roger Parker Saunders
James Christie
George Bell
Philip Garner
Melcher Garner
Peter Slann
Joseph Eddings Junior
Due Chapman
John Farr
Nathaniel Farr
Thomas Farr
Robert Miles
William Smith
Charles Chapman
Francis Young Junior
Henry Liebenhentz
John Berkley
William Hudson
John Jervis
Hampton Lilebridge
Philip Culp
Francis Fountain
William Ladson
Patrick Dollard
Joseph Bee
John Veitch
John Fabian
Joseph Slann
Abraham Hayne
Hawkins Martin
Andrew Johnston
Andrew Slann
Michael Peter
Francis Shaffer
Jacob Shaffer
John Ash
Thomas Melickamp
John Simmons
Kensey Burden
Joseph Smith
Thomas Smith
Christopher Peter
William Bellamy
Thomas Osborn
William Skirving
Thomas White
Malcolm Smith
John Mitchell
Christopher Motte
Robert Rivers
William Bee
Francis Rivers
Thomas Scott
John Livingston

Thomas Hext
Henry Molholland
James Freeman
George Haig
Morton Wilkinson

PETIT JURORS FOR THE
PARISH OF ST JAMES
SANTEE

Isaac Legrand
John Jaudon
Capers Boone
Joseph Logan
Michael Boineau Junior
Samuel Dupre
Jacob Jenneret
Richard Joy
Lewis Miles
Thomas Boone Senr
Michael Boineau
Richard Blake
Peter Deschamp
John Barnett
John Drake
Peter Norman
Elisha Barnett
Daniel Sinkler
John Bennet
William Fulford
Edward Jermain
John Egan
John Blake
Hugh Anderson
William Pring
James Chappel
Benjamin Stone
Elias Ball
Thomas Egan
Levi Durand
Theodore Gaillard
Anthony Simons
Charles Gaillard
James Rivers
Benjamin Webb
Stephen Sullivan
Francis Jones
William Lewis
Richard Withers
Arch^d McClennan
Hendrick Snider
John Dooz (Door?)
Robert Walker
Christ. Rich
John Wells

Henry Hughs
Joseph Deschamp
William Anderson
John Basketfield
Robert Hunter
Joseph Huggins
Peter Mouzon
Joseph Legare
Daniel McGregar

PETIT JURORS FOR THE
PARISH OF ST STEPHEN

John Peyre
Thomas Cordes
John Black
Peter Guerry
William Buford
Peter Coutourier
Benjamin Walker
William Greenland
John Palmer Junior
Joseph Palmer
Hezekiah Maham
James Sinkler
John Palmer
Peter Palmer
Thomas Greenland
Charles Canty
James Guerry
John Guerry
John Coutourier
Isaac Barns
Daniel Williams
Francis Villepontoux
Samuel Peyre
Peter McDonald
Peter Porcher
Peter Guerry Junr
John Baily
Samuel Davis
Matthew Whitefield
Peter Robert
Adam Lewis
Daniel Cauhusac
Joseph Sand. Thomson
Ezekiel Buckler
Henry Gilman
Isaac Porcher
David Dubose
Isaac Dubose
Rene Richbourgh
Philip Williams
Nicholas Ray
Jacob Bonkost

Joshua Griffin
John Gaillard
Robert Denly
Peter Coutourier
Peter Sinkler

Francis Vanvelsin
Peter Taylor
John Markell
David Gaillard
Thomas Cooper

SPECIAL JURORS FOR THE DISTRICT OF CHARLES TOWN

SPECIAL JURORS FOR THE
PARISH OF ST PHILIP AND
ST MICHAEL

Alexander Adamson
Ralph Atmore
James Anderson
Ichabod Atwell
William Ancrum
Robert Austin
Alexander Alexander
John Abercrombie
Emanuel Abraham
Samuel Ash
Charles Atkins
George Ancrum Junior
John Anthony
William Axson
Solomon Aaron
James Askew
James Henry Butler
Francis Bremar
James Brian
Jacob Boomer
Peter Boutiton
Peter Bounetheau
Henry Blankenhorn
John Benfield
John Bush
John Baddeley
John Boomer
Michael Black
Robert Beard
Daniel Bourdeaux
Joseph Atkinson
John Bowen (up the path)
Henry Bookless
Barnard Beekman
Robert Brailsford
Thomas Bee
Henry Benbridge
David Bruce
John Bonsat
Benjamin Baker
John Bonniott
William Bennie

James Bricken
Thomas Buckle
Nathaniel Blundell
Thomas Baldwin
James Balantine
Thomas Bourke
Joseph Badger
Joseph Beeler
David Boillate
Peter Bocquet Junior
Samuel Beekman
James Bentham
John Baker
Joseph Bee
John Blott
William Banbury
John Bury
Jacob Bowler
Charles Burkmire
William Burrows
John Beale
Edward Blake
Peter Bacot
John Berwick
Josiah Bonneau
Pierce Butler
Francis Bayle
Alexander Bruce
John Brailsford
Joseph Ball
Thomas Bennet
David Burger
Samuel Butler
Thomas Corbett
Benjamin Cook
Henry Caldwell
Levinus Clarkson
James Cook
Moses Chauvet
Joseph Cartwright
Moses Cohen
John Clements
John Chambers
William Cunnington
Joseph Creighton
Sampson Clark
Isaac Cohen

Henry Crouch
William Cameron
John Calvert
George Cahoon
Joseph Cox
Daniel Cannon
John Coram
Samuel Cross
Alexander Chrisolme
Brian Cape
McCartan Campbell
William Creighton
John Creighton
Benjamin Coward
Francis Cobia
Philotheos Chiffelle
James Courtone
George Cook
Timothy Crosby
Thomas Coker
Martin Clime
Robert Cochran
William Capers
John Colcock
John Callahan
Jacob Cohen
Benjamin Cattel
John Coppithorn
William Cattel
Gilbert Chalmers
Thomas Coram
Benjamin Cudworth
Tobias Cambridge
Samuel Cordes
Richard Cole
James Duncan
Joseph Darling
Thomas Doughty
William Doughty
Joseph Darrell
George Duncan
Joseph Dill
William Downes
Benjamin Dart
Isaac Dacosta
Arthur Downes
Stephen Lee
Robert Dewar
James Donnavan
John Dorcius
Cornelius Dewees
James Donaldson
John Dutarque
James Donnavan (up the path)
James Darby
James Dunning

Stephen Duval (Pilot)
John Dart
Philip Dewees
Benjamin Darrell
Edward Darrell
John Duval
Abraham DaCosta
Christian Dawson
Peter Dener
William Denny
John Delka
James Duncan (Blacksmith
John Dawson
John Deas
Isaac DaCosta Junior
William Henry Drayton
Benjamin Dores
James Edwards
Edmond Egan
William Easton
George Ehney
John Edwards
Thomas Eustace
John Eberley
Joshua Eden
Barnard Elliott
Thomas Eveleigh
Benjamin Elliott
Richard Ellis
Nicholas Eveleigh
William Edwards (Sadler)
Thomas Farr
John George Fardo
Mungo Finlayson
James Fisher (Merchant)
John Fisher
Alexander Fraser
Lucas Florin
George Flagg
Bryan Foshy
Thomas Fell
William Fair
Samuel Fley
John Fisher (Cabinet Mak
Anthony Farresteau
Thomas Ferguson
Jacob Frick
Robert Frogg
Christopher Rogers
Francis Grott
Daniel Gratton
John Walter Gibbes
James Graves
John Grant (Sadler)
James Gross (Barber)
William Greenwood

Seth Gilbert
William Gowdy
William Graham
John Grant (Shoemaker)
Joseph Gaultier
John Paul Grimke
James Gilladeau
John Gourley
William Gibbes
John Lewis Gervais
John Giles
Othniel Giles
Christian Gruber
Framcos Goltier
Theodore Gaillard Junr
Claudius Gilland
John Grouning
George Greenland
Samuel Gruber
Alexander Gillon
John Gaboriel
John Guines
Francis Henrick
William Hopkins
Thomas Hutchinson
Elias Horry Junior
John Horlbeck
William Hutchins
Samuel Hopkins
John Hampton
William Hext
Thomas Hammet
Ed^d Hare
Robert Howard
Joel Holmes
John Newton Hartley
Donald Harper
John Huger
Dalzel Hunter
John Howe
John Hatfield
Thomas Harper
William Holliday
William Hales
William Hinckley
Charles Harris
George Abbott Hall
Peter Horn
Joseph Hutchings
John Howell
Francis Huger
Thomas Hall
Thomas Harris
Patrick Hinds
Isaac Huger
Joshua Hart

Richard Ham
Thomas Ham
Thomas Harvey
Thomas Heyward Junior
Samuel Jones (Tanner)
Joseph Jones (Shopkeeper)
William Johnson
Thomas Jones
Thomas Jervey
John Jrnst
John Jeffer
Irael Joseph
Samuel Jones
Charles Johnston
Alexander Inglis
John Imrie
Michael Keller
John Kerkner
David Koffman
Michael Kalteisen
Robert Knox
Zephaniah Kinsley
James King
Joseph Kimmel
James Keith
George Kean (Bricklayer)
James Lennox
Joshua Lockwood
William Logan
Peter Lepoole
Solomon Legare
Edward Lightwood
Aaron Loocock
Felix Long
Richard Latham
Robert Lindsay
Rawlins Lowndes
John Lyon
Thomas Legare Junior
John Luich
Joseph Leeson
Robert Larry
William Lennox
Samuel Lagare
Thomas Latham
Thomas Liston
Richard Lushington
John Lanneau
Thomas Legare
Henry Lybert
William Livingston
Charles Linning
James Lynch
William Loocock
John Lahiff
William Long

Daniel Legare Junior
Henry Laurens
Benjamin Lord
Andrew Lord
George Layfield
William Lee
John Mathewes
Alexander Moultrie
George Morris
Samuel Miller
John McCall (Taylor)
Nathaniel Morgan
Walter Mayne
Samuel McCorkel
Alexander Marshal
John Miott
Samuel Maverick
James Mackie
Jacob Moses
David Milling
John McCall Junior
Charles Motte
James McClanahan
Martin Miller
David Maul
Lacklan Martin
Robert Muncreef
John Raven Mathews
Isaac Mazyck
Philip Meyer
Mark Morris
John Michael
William Mills
Richard Muncreef
Philip Mentzing
Meyer Moses
James McCall
William McKimmy
John McCall (Merchant)
William McGilleviry
Edward McCready
Arthur Middleton
Michael Muckinfuss
John Mathews (Cordwainer)
Robert McClocklan
Henry Margew
Richard Mercer
Patrick Moon
Barnard Moses
Philip Moses
Alexander McBeth
Peter Muirset
Abraham Merkley
William Nisbett
George Noddings
Edward North

Frederick Nann
Philip Neizer (Baker)
George Nedhammer
John Neufville
Edward Neufville Junior
William Nicoll
James Neilson
Edward Oats
James OHare
John Owen
James Oliphant (Jeweller)
Lewis Ogier
Hugh Pollock
Martin Pesnigar
Darby Pendergrass
George Powell
Isaac Peace
Job Palmer
Hext Prioleau
John Poaug
Hopkin Prise
Samuel Price
William Patterson
John Earnest Poyas
Samuel Prioleau Junior
Philip Prioleau
Robert William Powell
Samuel Perdriau
William Price
William Parker
John Philips
Peter Prow
Robert Philp
William Print
Nathaniel Russell
Robert Ray
Thomas Radcliffe Junior
William Roper
John Rose
Thomas Rivers
George Rout
McCully Righten
John Robertson (Vintner)
Martin Rimley
James Roche
Andrew Reid
Peter Ross
John Richardson
William Reid
John Ralph
Robert Rowand
Charles Reiley
Jacob Remington
John Russell (Shipwright)
John Ruberry
Alexander Russell

Charles Roberts
Alexander Rose
Andrew Rutledge
William Russell
Christopher Sheets
Thomas Stuart
John Scott
James Stedman
Peter Storr
John Stevenson
George Smithson
Paul Snyder
Sabastian Spencer
John Smith
Jacob Sass
William Stoll
Andrew Stewart
David Saylor
Samuel Stent
David Smith (Baker)
William Samways
William Stukes
Thomas Smith
George Smith Junior
Paul Smyser
Abraham Spidle
Christian Segwald
John Shutterling
William Sommersall
Daniel Stroble
John Scott (son of Jonathan)
William Scott Junior
Hugh Swinton
John Spisegar
Ed^d Shrewsberry
Thomas Savage
Roger Smith
John Smyth
Josiah Smith Junior
Maurice Simmons
Bracey Singleton
Samuel Scottow
James Sharp
Jonathan Sarrizin?
Audeon St John
Thomas Singelton
James Snead
David Swanson
Peter Smith (Carpenter)
Thomas Tucker
George Tew
Simon Tufts
Theodore Trezvant
James Toussiger
Anthony Toomer

Henry Timrod
Stephen Thomas
Richard Todd
William Touch
Lewis Timmon
Daniel Tharin
Philip Thorn
John Torrans
John Thompson
William Trusler
Philip Tydiman
Paul Townsend
John Tuke
David Taylor
Joseph Turpin Junior
John Richard Tallman
Edward Trescot
Jacob Valk
John Vineyard
Peter Valton
Joseph Verree
Benjamin Villepontoux
William Valentine
Philip Will
Benjamin Wilkins
William Wilkins
John Wragg (Tradd Street)
James Wilkins
James Wright
William Wayne
John Mortimer Williams
John Wakefield
John Wyatt
Samuel Warnock
John Wood
John Wells Junior
James Weir
James Wright (Baker)
James Witter
Melchior Werley
John Waring
Jacob Willeman
Benjamin Wish
James Wakefield
John Wagner
Sims White
John Webb
Edward Weyman
Wm Wilson
Nicholas Langford
Jacob Warley
Gasper Washing
William Walton
Christopher Willeman
John Wragg

Richard Wainwright
John Ward (Taylor)
Powden Weston
Henry Lindour
James Green Williams
John Walsh
Samuel Wainwright

Benjamin Waller
Lebbeus Whitney
George Young
Thomas You
Richard Yeadon
Charles Ramadge

GRAND JURORS FOR THE
PARISH OF PRINCE GEORGE

Alexander Anderson
John Allston
George Brown
Anthony Bonneau
Thomas Ballow
Lewis Bochette
Stephen Brown
Richard Brooks
Robert Brown
Joseph Brown
John Cogdell
William Cuttino
Childermas Croft
William Poole Coachman
George Croft
Benjamin Elliott Junior
Elias Foissin
George Ford
Stephen Ford Junior
Stephen Ford Senior
Joseph Grier
John Grier
James Grier
Samuel Grier
Robert Gibson
William Godfrey
Thomas Hendlen (Georgetown)
Thomas Henning
Mark Huggins
Thomas Hasell
Robert Heriot
William Heriot
George Heriot
George Joor
William Luptan
Paul Lepear
Peter Lesesne
Thomas Mitchell
John Postell
Benjamin Porter
John Rogers
James Robertson
Job Rothmakler
Samuel Smith (Georgetown)
William Stitt
Samuel Wragg
Joseph Wragg
Thomas Wilson
John Withers
John Stewart
Micaijah Williams

Anthony Martin White
Paul Trapier Senior
Paul Trapier Junior
William Smart
Randolph Theus
Christ^r Taylor
Benjamin Tucker
Daniel Tucker
William Vaux
Thomas Smith
John Dunnam
Joseph Henning
Alexander Buchanan
Arch^d McDowal
James Bell
Peter Horry
John Buchanan
Hugh Horry
Daniel Lesesne
Alexander McGregor
John Shrine
William Benson
John Woodberry
Peter Belin
Charles Gee
James Gordon
Thomas LaBruce
Thomas Butler
Percival Pawley Senior
James Coachman
Anthony Pawley
William Allston Junior
William Allston (son of Joseph)
John Morral
Samuel Clegg
Percival Pawley Junior
Joseph Labruce
John Magill
Francis Allston
David Graham
William Waties?
James Elks
Joseph Allston
Benjamin Young
Edward Mitchell
John Green
Benjamin Trapier
Rhoddom Rawlins
Jonah Clark
William Verreen
William Henry Lewis
Thomas Harris
John Allston Junior
William Spears

Michael Bellune
Thomas Frink
Jabesh Frink
Nathaniel Dwight
Samuel Frink
John Bellamy
Benjn Gauze
Jonah Woodberry
Alex^r Wilson
Henry Durant
George Durant
Dennis Hankins
Thomas Bell
Alex^r Dunn
Daniel Morral
Samuel Price
John Pyatt
Thomas Starrat
Samuel Dwight
Charles Gauze
Richard Singleton
John Baxter
Samuel Brown
John Wilson
John Doxier
William Allston Senior
Joshua Avant
Lewis Boatwright
Abraham Buckholts
William Britton
Henry Britton
James Cassels
Henry Davis Junior
Benjamin Davis
Henry Davis Senr
William Dawsey
Ebenezer Dunnam Senr
Ebenezer Dunnam Junior
Charles Fledger
Joseph Greaves
Abraham Giles
Francis Goddard
James Garrell
William Herring
John Hambleton
James Johnson (Catfish)
Thomas Jenkins
James Johnston (Baker)
William Bellune
William Davis
Benjamin Davis
John Smith Senr
Nathan Evans
James Ford Junior
Luke Whitefield
Malachi Murphy

William Bathy
George Graham
John Graham Senr
Gilbert Johnston
Isaac Ludlam
James Johnston (Little Peedee)
William Moore
William Middleton
Benjamin Port
John Rae
Anthony Sweet
Thomas Snow

GRAND JURORS FOR THE
PARISH OF PRINCE FREDERICK

Francis Britton
Anthony White
Richard Brockinton
Elisha Screven
John Brockinton
James Commander
Edmond Carr
Daniel McGinney
William Lester
William Paulling
Thomas McCants
Benjamin Screven
William Thomson
Benjamin Handlen
William Handlen
John Winter
Robert Winter
James Stacks
George Snow
William Barton
John Barns
Richard Green
William Wilson
Meredith Hughes
Henry Hughes
Robert Davidson
John Futhey
John James
John Hamilton
Roger McGill
Hugh Ervin
William Davidson
Francis Green
Paul Jaudon
Thomas Boone Junior
John James Gotear
Samuel James
Joseph Jolly

James Lindsay
Nelson Grimes
George White
Moses Brown
William Cooper
William Scott
Robert Pettierew
William Orr
William McCautry
Alex^r McKnight
Roger Gordon
Robert Paisley
David Wilson
Robert McCautry
Philip Owens
Henry Futhy
Thomas Handlen
Samuel Nesmith
Anthony White Junior
Thomas Cooper
Thomas Paisley
Robert Witherspoone (of Williamburgh Township)
James Semple
Jesse Williams
John McRee
William Snow
John Dobbein
John Dobbein Junior
James Snow
Nathaniel Snow
Philip Britton
Philip Britton Junior
James Lane
William Cole
James Durand
William McConnell
John Burrows
Hugh McCullough
William Hamilton
Robert Dick
George Burrows Junior
Arthur Burrows
John Dick
James Blackley
Isaac Neilson
Robert Frierson
George Burrows
John Frierson
Daniel Michau
William Dixon Junior
Nathaniel Montgomery
Isaac Michau
Paul Michau
Oliver Cromwell
Robert Sutton

John Durant
Archibald McDonald
William Young
Richard Teysor
William Campbell
Isaac Rambert Senior
Thomas King
Isaac Rambert Junior
Robert McConnell
Arthur Bradley
William Frierson
Edward Plowden
Alexander Scott
Thomas Frierson
John McCauley
Joseph Mackee
Hugh Montgomery
William Plowden
James Blakeley Junior
William Dixon
Joseph Scott
Alexander McCrea Senr
Alexander McCrea Junior
George Watson
John Scott
John Witherspoon (of blk river)
Gavin Witherspoon (of Ditto)
Moses Miller
James Bradley Junior
James Witherspoon
William Presley
Benjamin Duke
Arthur Cunningham
Archibald Campbell
David Witherspoon
John McElveen
William Law
Isaac Mathews
William Newman
John Mathews
John Watts
Adam McDonald
John McDonald
William McDonald
Alexander Chovin
William Michau
Peter Lequex
Peter June
William Mathews
William Gamble
Samuel McGill
Samuel Knox
William Guess
James Fleming
Joseph Burch
Robert Baxter

31

Aaron Baker
Bartley Clark
William Dueitt
John Ervin (of Peedee)
William Fletcher
James Gregg
Joseph Gourley
William Gordon
Hugh Giles
James Baxter
John Baxter (of PeeDee)
James Keith
Benjamin Keith
Daniel Myers
Thomas McCall
David Perkins
Thomas Potts
John Potts
Richard Rennells
Robert Spring
Robert Scott
Nathan Savage
George Thomson
George Tomlinson
Gavin Weatherspoone (of PeeDee)
John Weatherspoone (of Ditto)
Robert Wilson Junior
John Gregg

PETIT JURORS FOR
THE PARISH OF
PRINCE GEORGE

Alexander Anderson
John Allston
George Brown
Anthony Bonneau
Thomas Ballow
Lewis Bochette
Stephen Brown
Richard Brooks
Robert Brown
Joseph Brown
John Cogdell
William Cuttino
Childermas Croft
William Poole Coachman
George Croft
Benjamin Elliott Junior
Elias Foissin?
George Ford
Stephen Ford Junior
Stephen Ford Senr
Joseph Grier

John Grier
James Grier
Samuel Grier
Robert Gibson
William Godfrey
Thomas Hendlen (of Georgetown
Thomas Henning
Mark Huggins
Thomas Hasell
Robert Heriot
William Heriot
George Heriot
George Joor
William Luptan
Paul Lepear
Peter Lesesne
Thomas Mitchell
John Postell
Benjamin Porter
John Rogers
James Robertson
Job Rothmakler
Samuel Smith (Georgetown)
William Stitt
Samuel Wragg
Joseph Wragg
Thomas Wilson
John Withers
John Stewart
Macaijah Williams
Anthony Martin White
Paul Trapier Senior
Paul Trapier Junior
William Smart
Randolph Theus
Christopher Taylor
Benjamin Tucker
Daniel Tucker
William Vaux
Thomas Smith
John Dunnam
Joseph Henning
Alexander Buchanan
Archibald McDowall
James Bell
Peter Horry
John Buchanan
Hugh Horry
Daniel Lesesne
Alexander McGregor
John Shrine
William Benson
John Woodberry
Peter Belin
Charles Gee
James Gordon

Thomas Labruce
Thomas Butler
Perceval Pawley Senr
James Coachman
Anthony Pawley
William Allston Junior
William Allston (son of Joseph)
John Morral
Samuel Clegg
Percival Pawley Junior
Joseph Labruce
John Magill
Francis Allston
David Graham
William Waties
James Elks
Benjamin Young
Edward Mitchell
John Green
Benjamin Trapier
Rhoddom Rawlins
Jonah Clark
William Verreen
William Henry Lewis
Thomas Harris
John Allston Junior
William Spears
Michael Bellune
Thomas Frink
Jabesh Frink
Nathaniel Dwight
Samuel Frink
John Bellamy
Benjamin Gauze
Jonah Woodberry
Alexander Wilson
Henry Durant
George Durant
Dennis Hankins
Thomas Bell
Alexander Dunn
Daniel Morral
Samuel Price
John Pyatt
Thomas Starrat
Samuel Dwight
Charles Gauze
Richard Lingeton
John Baxter
Samuel Brown
John Wilson
John Dozier
William Allston Senr
Joshua Avant
Lewis Boatwright
Abraham Buckholts

William Britton
Henry Britton
James Cassels
Henry Davis Junior
Benjamin Davis
Henry Davis Senr
William Dawsey
Ebenezer Dunnam Senr
Ebenezer Dunnum Junior
Charles Fledger
Joseph Greaves
Abraham Giles
Francis Goodard
James Garrell
William Herring
John Hambleton
James Johnston (catfish)
Thomas Jenkins
James Johnston (baker)
William Bellune
William Davis
Benjamin Davis
John Smith Senr
Nathan Evans
James Ford Junior
Luke Whitefield
Malachi Murphy
William Bathy
George Graham
John Graham Senr
Gilbert Johnston
Isaac Ludlam
James Johnston (Little PeeDee)
William Moore
William Middleton
Martyn Middleton
Benjamin Port
John Rae
Anthony Sweet
Thomas Snow
Christopher Brown
Thomas Burnham
Jesse Ballard
Anthony Crook
Jacobus Collio
John Day
Thomas Ilas
Samuel Elliott Junior
David Flowers
George Fleeson
John Glegg
John Goff
Epaphras Nott
Thomas Newhall
John Packrow
Joshua Pearson

William Porter (Prince Geo)
William Robertson
William Roberts
Alexander Rioch
John Rains
William Shackelford
Thomas Seabrook
Henry Salkes
William Stewart
Stephen Tomplate
Simeon Theus
Thomas Wilson Junior
Wilson Wilson
Alexander Shene
Mark Huggins Junior
William Wood
William Shrine
Peter Rambert
John Graham
Richard Burrows
John Jones
William McCollough
Thomas Martin Sanders
Peter Rambert Junior
Joseph Cook
John Lee
John Rambert
Abraham Schad
Stephen Clyatt
Richard Mansfield
John Henry
Samuel Hasford
Robert Bell
Clemard Greggs
Bernard Shlagal
Horatio Moore
Jeremiah Verreen
James Bell Junior
Jacob Stanaland
James Smith
Joseph Allston
John Self
John Singleton
Robert McCrackin
John Tamplatt
Moses Roberts
Adam Muckleduff
Jacob Moore
William Jordan
Adam Jordan
Charles Bond
Abraham Bond
James Row
Thomas Muckleduff
George Smith
Richard Green

Daniel Woodberry
Thomas Durant
Joseph Williamson
Constantine Newton
Stephen Peak
Jacob Anderson
William Knox
John Stephens
Mathew Brinson Senr
John Sessions
Samuel Hairgrove Junior
Samuel Cox
Nicholas Prince
John Cox
Thomas Livingston
Samuel Hairgrove Senr
Darby Paddon
Samuel Latimore
William Parker
Thomas Todd
Solomon Sessions
Thomas Blunt
Jonathan Avant
William Baker
John Bradley
Peter Buckholts
Edward Bird
Jesse Boatwright
Joseph Britton
John Bellune
James Barron
William Bearfeet
Samuel Cox
John Crofts
Francis Davis
Abraham Dew
James Davis
Fowler Dawsey
Joseph Foxworth
Job Foxworth
Thomas Grice
Thomas Ganey
James Godbolt
John Greaves
Benjamin Garrel
David Herring
John Holder
William Jones
Joseph Jenkins
Robert Jordan
Samuel Jenkins
William Keen
Zerobabel Litman
Michael Mixon
Isaac Murray
Luke Prior

Andrew Berry
Gideon Parish
Henry Flowers
John Powers
John Godbold
Joseph Hur
John Smith Junior
Thomas Godbolt
Elisha Tilghman
Benjamin Harrelson
Charles Pate
Charles Moody
John Cribb
James Alford
James Smith
Joshua Barfield
John Hollon
Moses Martin
William Kirby
Edward Howlen
Edward Owens
Michael Going
Henry Clark (Prince George)
Harrison Lucas
James Crawford
Walter Owens
William Whitefield
William Stackhouse
Othneil Tryweak
Exekiel Highet
George Sweeten
Moses Mannon
Frans Mixon
Daniel McQuin
James Munnerling
John May
William Mixon
David Owens
Joshua Perkins
John Philips
John Rogers
Thomas Rogers
Samuel Tindall
Conner Timmons
John Wood
John Walley
William Williams
Richard Woodberry
John Graham Junior
Joseph Graham
Joseph Duet
Jacob Fryer
Richard Rigell
William Anderson
Thomas Magus

PETIT JURORS FOR
THE PARISH OF
PRINCE FREDERICK

Richard Brockington
Elisha Screven
Joseph Tamplatt
Thomas Blackwell
James Commander
Edmon Carr
Charles Wilson
Thomas North
Henry Clark (P. F.)
Daniel McGinney
William Lester
William Graham
Isaac Bates
William Paulling
Nicholas Punch
Thomas McCants
Nathaniel McCants
Samuel Nesmith
Benjamin Screven
William Thomson
William Shepheard
William Gibson
David Campbell
Benjamin Handlen
William Handlen
John James Junior
John Winter
Robert Winter
Peter Paddey
John James Gotare
Samuel James
Joseph Jolly Junior
William McKelvian
John Parker
James Linsey
Hugh Opry
John Gotear
James McCutchen Junior
Alexander Scott Junior
Nelson Grimes Junior
Hugh Grimes
John Grimes
Nelson Grimes
Hugh Askins
George White
Moses Brown
James Brown
William Cooper
William Scott
Robert Petticrew

William Orr
William McCottry
Alexander McCants
Robert Hanner
Alexander McKnight
Roger Gordon
Robt Paisley
David Wilson
Robert McCottry
James McDonald
Philip Owens
Henry Futhy
Thomas Handlen (P. F.)
Samuel Nesmith
Anthony White Junior
Thomas Cooper
Thomas Paisley
George Nettles Junior
William Porter (PF)
James Owens
Reuben Watts
William Rhodes
James Semple
Jesse Williams
John McCrew
Sampson Baker
William Snow
John Dobbin
James Snow
Nathl Snow
Jesse Simon
Phillip Britton
Philip Britton Junior
Josiah Cockfield
John McDowell
William Graw
James Stacks
George Snow
William Barton
John Barnes
Robert Wilson Junior
Richard Green
William Wilson
Meredith Hughes
Robert Davidson
John Futhy
John James
Joseph Gregg
Archibald Jolly
John Hamilton
Roger McGill
Matthew Nugent
James Joseph Harrell
John Dehay
Samuel Eady
James Eady Senr

William Grimes
William McRee
Hugh Erwin
Nathl McCullough
William Davidson
George Ramsey
Francis Green
Paul Jaudon
Thomas Boone Junior
James Lane
Cornelius Nelson
Willm Wesberry
Samuel Jaudon
William Cole
James Durant
John Crawford
Joseph Jolly
William McDowell
Christopher Small
Thomas Johnstone
George Stillings
Elias McPherson
John Ward
Francis Britton
Francis Futhy
Anthony White
William McConnel
John Burrows
Hugh McCollough
William Hamilton
Thomas McCrea
John Jones
James McCollough
John Knox
James Scott
Robert Dick
George Burrows Junr
Danl Callehan
Arthur Burrows
John Dick
Samuel Paxton
John McKnight
James Blakeley
Isaac Nelson
Robert Frierson
George Burrows Senr
John Frierson
William Moore
John Moore
William Heathley
Danl Michaw
William Dixson Junior
Nathl Montgomery
Isaac Michaw
Paul Michaw
Oliver Cromwell

Robert Sutton
John Durant
Archibald McDonald
William Young
Richard Teysor
James Bare
William Campble
Isaac Rembert Senr
Thomas King
Henry White
Isaac Rembert Junior
William Boone
Robert McConnell
William McKnight
Arthur Bradley
Alex^r McCracken
Abraham Whitworth
Danl Rhodes
William Frierson
Alex^r Scott
Willm Taylor
Edward Plowden
Andrew Patterson
Thomas Frierson
James McConnell
John McCaulley
Patrick Coppley
William Hanner
Semeon Simmons
Silas Simmons
John Simon
Robert Scott
Thomas McConnell
Joseph Mickie
Hugh Montgomery
William Plowden
John Dobbin Junior
George McConnell
John McCollough
James Blakeley Junior
William Dixon Senr
John Dickson
Joseph Scott
Alexander McCrea
Alexander McCrea Junr
John McCrea
George Watson
John Scott
Moses Scott
George Green
John Witherspoone (Black River)
Gavin Witherspoone (of ditto)
James Witherspoone Senr
Moses Miller
Levi Chapman
John Raphel

James Bradley Junior
Alex Swinton
Nathan Savage
George Thomson
John Thomson
James Witherspoon Junior
John Green
William Pressley
William Lindsey
Joseph Alex^r Glass
Benjamin Duke
Joseph Mollery
Arthur Cunningham
Archibald Campble
John Leger
Barnabass Windess
Thomas Steel
Robert Witherspoone (Williamsburgh)
Samuel Wilks
Henry Mouson
William Marsden
David Witherspoone
John McElveen
William Law
Isaac Matthews
John Arnet
Alex^r Arnet
John Gibson
John June
William Newman
Drury Turner
George Tomlinson
Robert Thornley
John Timmons
William Gamble
William Frierson Junior
Ebenezer Gibson
John Matthews
George Dickey
John Watts
William Murrell
Adam McDonald
John McDonald
William McDonald
Alexander Chovin
William Michau
Peter Lequeux
Peter June
Paul Villepontoux
William Matthews
Thomas Lansdale
William Gamble
David Lemon
Samuel McGill Junior
Samuel Knox
William Guess

37

James Fleming
James Allison
Evan Vaughn
John Witherspoone (Of PeeDee)
Gavin Witherspoone (Of Ditto)
John Wells
Charles Bearfield
Jospeh Burch
James Bigem
John Baxter Junior
James Baxter
Robert Baxter
Aaron Baker
Jacob Buckholts
Stephen Britton
Noble Barnard
John Coleman
Henry Colcote
Bartley Clark
Jonathan Chadwick
William Dewitt
John Ervin (of Pee Dee)
William Fletcher
Charles Finkley
Isaac Foster
James Gregg
John Gregg
Jospeh Gourley
William Gordon
William Green Junior
Hugh Giles
Henry Hughes
John Brockington
Peter Lane
William Brown
John Hudson
Lewis Harrell
Harlock Huxford
James Harrison
Samuel Hazelton
William Hewson
Thomas Hudson
Joshua Hickman
Gavin James
David Jamison
William James
James Keith
Benjamin Keith
James Megee
Dan Myers
Thomas McCall
John McCants
Peter Newell
David Perkins
Thomas Potts
John Potts

Peter Pye
Richard Rennells
Robert Spring
Aaron Spring
Robert Gamble

SPECIAL JURORS FOR
THE DISTRICT OF
GEORGE TOWN

Joseph Henning
John Shrine
John Woodberry
Charles Gee
James Gordon
John Allston
Anthony Bonneau
Richard Brooks
Joseph Brown
John Cogdell
William Cuttino
George Croft
Wilson Wilson
Alexander Shene
William Shrine
Abraham Schad
Thomas Burnham
Jesse Bellard
Anthony Crook
Jocobus Collio
Thomas Dias
Thomas Hendlen
Thomas Henning
Mark Huggins
Thomas Hasell
Robert Heriot
William Heriot
George Heriot
William Luptan
Peter Lesesne
Thomas Mitchell
Benjamin Porter
James Robertson
Job Rothmakler
Samuel Smith
David Flowers
George Fleeson
John Glegg
John Goff
Epaphras Nott
Thomas Newhall
John Packrow
Joshua Pearson
William Porter

Alexander Rioch
John Rains
Simeon Theus
William Smart
Randolph Theus
Christopher Taylor
Paul Trapier Senior
Daniel Tucker

William Vaux
Samuel Wragg
Thomas Wilson
Micaijah Williams
An^y Martyn White
Paul Trapier Junior
Joseph Wragg
Thomas Wilson Junior

CHERAWS DISTRICT

GRAND JURORS FOR THE CHERAWS DISTRICT

Thomas Lide
John Andrews
John Heustes
Benjamin Rogers
William Lide
Charles Irbey
Willm Ellerbee
Philip Pledger
Thomas Ellerbee Junior
William Blassingham
John Speed
John Kimbrough
John Mitchell
John Balfour
Danl Sparks
John Jackson
Abel Kolb
Eli Kershaw
Samuel Wise
Charles McCall
Thomas Evans Senr
William Thomas
Wm Terrell Junior
Joseph Pledger
John Pledger
Wm Dewitt
Edward Jones
Aaron Daniel
Joshua Edward
Magnus Cargill
Robert Blair
Robert Gray
Samuel Benton
Wm Henry Mills
Charles Mason
Abel Edwards
John Holloway
Jonathan Brown
Benjamin Hicks Senr
Robert Lide
John McMuldrough
Anthony Pouney
John McCall
Nathl Saunders
Joseph Dabbs
Emanuel Cox
Thomas Ayres
John Allran
John Hodge Senr

George Hicks
Josiah Pearce
George Fruwicks
Thomas James
Henry Clarke
William Pegues
Abel Wilds
Henry Council
John Manderson
Alex^r Mackintosh
Robert Reynalds
Peter Allstone
Claudius Pegues Senr
Peter Roach
Robert Clarey
John Westfield
Alex^r Gordon
Claudius Pegues J^r
John Mikell
Samuel Baccoat
Thomas Powe
Moses Spight
James Dozer
George Myers
Simon Connell
W^m McDowell
John Pigot Senr
Clement Brown
Benjamin Davis
Thomas Rowe
Elias Dubose
Isaac Dubose
John Blakeney
Charles Evans Junior
Charles Sparks
Thomas Conn
John Brockington
George Pawley
Daniel Dubose
Benjamin Hicks Junior
Thomas Hicks
James Hicks

PETIT JURORS FOR THE CHERAW DISTRICT

Thomas Lide
John Andrew
John Heustees
Benjamin Rogers
William Lide

Charles Irbey
William Ellerbee
Phillip Pledger
Thomas Ellerbee Junior
William Blassingham
John Speed
John Kimbrough
John Mitchell
John Belfour
Daniel Sparks
John Jackson
Abel Kolb
Ely Kershaw
Sam Wise
Charles McCall
Thomas Evans Senr
William Thomas
William Terrell Junior
Joseph Pledger
John Pledger
William Dewitt
Edward Jones
Aaron Daniel
Joshua Edwards
Magnus Cargell
Robert Blair
Robert Gray
Lamuel Benton
William Henry Mills
Charles Mason
Abel Edwards
John Holloway
Jonathan Brown
Benjamin Hicks Senr
Robert Lide
John McMuldrough
Anthony Pouncy
Thomas Lord
John McCall
Nathaniel Sanders
Joseph Dabbs
Emanuel Cox
Thomas Ayers
John Alran
John Hodge Senr
George Hicks
James Hicks
Josiah Pearce
George Fruweeks
Thomas James
George Pawley
Henry Clarke
William Pegues
Abel Wilds
Henry Consill
John Manderson

Alexander McIntosh
Robert Reynalds
Peter Allston
William Strother
Claudius Pegues Senr
Peter Roach
Robert Clarey
John Westfield
Alexander Gordon
Claudius Pegues Junior
John Mickell
Samuel Bacot
Thomas Powe
Moses Spight
James Dozer
George Myres
Simon Connall
William McDowell
John Pigott Senr
Clement Brown
Benjamin Davis
Thomas Rowe
Elias Dubose
Isaac Dubose
John Blakeney
Charles Evans Senr
Charles Evans Junr
Daniel Dubose
Charles Sparks
Thomas Conn
John Brockington Junr
John Aikins
Mathew Rushing
Robert Westfield
William Carter
Thomas Boatwright
William Bishup
Abraham Cook
William Bell
Joseph Parsons
Thomas Davis
George King
Ethildred Clary
Stephen Tomkins
Thomas Hicks
John Gear
John Donaldson
Richard Street
John Evans
John Oneale
Mackey McNett
Edward Lowther
John Downes
Thomas Harry
John Edwards
Joseph Mason

Josiah Evans
William Edwards
William Standard
Simon Lundy
Daniel Lundy
Jacob Johnson
Joshua Lucas
John Lucas
Richard Gooden
John Husband
Joshua Terrill
James Thursby
William Hardick
Francis Gallaspie
Richard George
John Hodge Junior
Philip Singleton
Mathew Griffith
Isham Hodge
William Lang
William Hodge
Joshua David
John Dewitt
George Manderson
William Furniss
Evan Prethro
Joshua Douglass
Nathaniel Douglass
Lewis Malone
Benjamin Henderick
John Wilds
Enock Evans Sen[r]
Thomas Coaker
Thomas Williamson
Daniel Luke
Thomas Dean
Thomas Evans Junior
Moses Fort
Mark Hollaway
John Hollaway
John Weatherford
William James
John Marsh
James Jones
John McMuldrough Junior
Hugh McMuldrough
James Jamieson
Joseph Wood
Charles Dewitt
William Williamson
James Williamson
West Williams
William Wadkins
Joseph Allison
Thomas Vining

Joshua Stroud
Alexander Craig
Moses Pearson
Isaac Navill
Jonathan John
George Cherry
Aaron Pearson
Benjamin Kolb
William Hicks
Samuel Brown
Richard Hodge
Edward Drake
Benjamin Hicks Jun[r]
Thomas Ammon
Thomas Cothan
Thomas Connor Jun[r]
Barnabas Hannagan
Joseph Fuller
Benjamin Beverley
John Frazer
Charles Cottingham
Trushum Thomas
Burgas Williams
Jonathan Cottingham
Samuel Wines
John Smith
Thomas Pearce
Thomas Brown
James Mathews
William Prestwood
Thomas Mathews
Joseph Thompson
Stephen Parker
Elisha Parker Junior
James Norris
James Blassingham
Abel Waddle
John Heath
Benjamin Jackson
James Hays
Edmond Irbey
Jermiah Brown
James Sheilds
William Barland
Elisha Parker Sen[r]
James Knight
Robert Aikens
John Hughes
Amos Windham
Elijah Fruit
John Garner
William Cook
Josiah Dortrey
Thomas Hickson
Zachariah Nettle

Thomas Harrison
Shadrack Williamson
Stephen Gardner
John Spivey
John Phillips
Arch^d McBride
William Barran
Shadrach Adkison
Daniel Polk
Absolam Sessions
Charles Baxter
James Nicholson
Robert Nettle
John Riggs
Enoch McDowell
Henry Jackson
George Hickman
Samuel Hickman
William Hickman
Michael Russell
James Russell
Thomas Kenneday
Peter Dubose Senr
Andrew Dubose Senr
James Perkins
Joseph Chandler
Richard Curtis Senr
Edward Sessions
Saml Wadkins
Thomas Doyle
Levi Brown
Hampton Sullivant
Joseph Dubose
James Gallaway
Absolam Gallaway
Michael Mixon
Samuel Mixon
Theophelus Norwood
Jonathan Williams
John Hardy
Abraham Alquier
Isham Hatcher
Joshua Jones
Thomas McManus
John Cartledge
John Hughbanks
Enoch Rentfrow
Thomas Fail
John Spruel
Stephen Jackson
Jason Meadows
John Benson

Thomas Scottwins
Joseph Griffith
Benjamin Martin
Ephraim Horn
Robert Parlin
Thomas Ellerbee Senr
David Perkins
John Shoemake
James Holmes
John Jordan
John Thomas
Mathew Holden

SPECIAL JURORS FOR
THE CHERAW DISTRICT

John Mitchell
John Belfour
Abel Kolb
Thomas Evans
William Dewitt
Magnus Cargill
Will Henry Mills
Charles Mason
Abel Edwards
Thomas James
Abel Wilds
John Manderson
John Mickell
Thomas Powe
John Oneale
Mackey McNett
John Downs
Thomas Harry
William Edwards
John Lucas
John Dewitt
William Furniss
Evan Prethra
Joshua Douglass
Nathaniel Douglass
John Wilds
Enock Evans Senr
Thomas Evans Junr
Edmond Irbey
Jeremiah Brown
John Hughes

CAMDEN DISTRICT

GRAND JURORS TO THE
EASTWARD OF WATEREE

John Belton
John May
James Postell
John Hope
John Cooke Senr.
Jasper Sutton
John English
George Ross
Robert English
John Adamson
Burrwell Boykin
William Boykin
Samuel Boykin
John Payne
James Cary
Nathl Cary
William Lang
Elias Fort
William Sanders Senr.
George Oglevie
Ely Kershaw
Thomas Charlton
Joseph Kershaw
John Wyly
Thomas Cassity
John Millhous
James Brown
Henry Ruzeley
John Chesnutt
William Kershaw
Samuel Wise
Jared Neilson
Robert Dingle
Samuel Burnett
Rich. Richardson (Colonel)
Edward Richardson
John Gambell
James Frierson Junr.
James Frierson Senr.
Willm Byers
Willm Martin
Thomas Maples
James McDonald
John Cantey Junr.
Henry Montgomery
William Montgomery
Samuel Bennet Junr.
Joseph Cantey
James Harper
William Little
Robt. Snead
Thos. W. Jenkins

John Chisholm
Gabl. Fitzgerald
Claud^s Richbough
Henry Richbough
Jam^s Gibson
Rob Hambleton
Richd Dennis
Richd Richardson Junr.
John James Junr.
Willm McConico
Joshua Stone
Richd Harwin
William Pearson
William Smith
Thomas Sumter
James Richbough
Henry Blanchard
Robert Dingle
Alexander Purvis
Samuel Little
Matthew Singleton
John Singleton
John James Senr.
Isham Moore
Henry Clark
John Rodgers
Henry Hainsworth
Josiah Roberts
Wood Furman
John Postell
William Richardson
John G. Guignard
John Wheeler
Peter Mellett
Robert Dearington
David Reynolds Junr.
James Rembert
James Davis
Stewart Dickey
George Evans
Thomas Houze
Nathl Pace
Willm Gillum
James Sanders (of high hill)
James Atkinson
Samuel Bradley
Henry Cassells
Moses Gordon
David Wilson
Roger Wilson
William Wilson
Sylvester Dunn
Robert Carter
Jos. McKay
James Bradley

GRAND JURORS TO THE EAST SIDE OF THE WATEREE

William Roberts
John Armstrong
James Ratcliff
Richard Ratcliff
Robert Henderson
Willm Mill
John Huggins
Aaron Frierson
William Player
Ephraim Harrison
John Harrison
James Armstrong
John Story
Samuel Nelson Senr.
James Conyers Senr.
Thomas Singletary
William Fullwood
John Anderson
Hugh Bennett
Robert Lowry
John Tomlinson
Willm McCoy
Edwd Dickey
Mathew Bennett
Chas Story
John McFadden
John Burgess

GRAND JURORS TO THE EASTWARD OF THE WATEREE, WAXAW

George White
Robert Crawford
John Dabey
John Mackey
Jacob Taylor
Daniel Harper
Henry Foster
Andrew Knox
Richard Causart
William Massey
Benjamin Perry
George Wade
William Tillman
James Perry
James Cook
John Marshall

GRAND JURORS BETWEEN BROAD & CATAWBA RIVERS

Robert Ellison
William Kirkland
John Woodward
Joseph Kirkland
Henry Hunter
Thomas Woodward
George Hencock
James Anderson
John Winn
James Hart
John King
And^w Allison
Joshua English
Joshua Dinkins
Thomas Starks
William Whitaker
James Whitaker
Henry Hunter
James Harrison
Isaac Love
Richard Brown
Nazza Hunter
Simon Hirons
Joel Threewitts
Henry Chappell
Isaac Rayford
John Boyd
Joel McLemore
Howel Hay
Robert Rives
John Cook
Joseph Martin
Timothy Reeves Junr
Robert Hill
John Dorharty
John Witherspoone
David Hay
John Allston
Herman Hensler
William Strother
Drury Wyche
John Pearson
William Meyers
James Taylor
Joseph Loyd
John House
William Reeves
William Howell
Malachi Howell
Jacob Myers

Francis Goodwin
Ebijah Rimbert
William Grimes
John Russell
John Allison
John Taylor
Joseph Mickell
Robert Belton
Philip Skaven
John Kennerly
Benjamin Everett
John Geiger
Nathan Centar
Thomas Taylor
Robert Hicks
Patrick Cunningham
Robert Goodwin
James Daniel
Philip Pearson
John Siley
John Price
Robert Gill
John Walker
James Knox
Samuel Adkins
Peter Culp
John Laly
James Patten
William McKenney
Hugh McDaniel
Thomas Gater
John Titchcoat
William Embry
Thomas Hughs
Daniel Price Senr
John Lee
Alexander Twiner
Eliazer Mobley
Philip Walker
William McDonald
Amos Tims
Michael Dickson
Robert Patton

GRAND JURORS FOR
THE NEW ACQUISITION

Henry Williams
William Biers
Joseph Carell
Sam Watson

Thomas Neel
John Patton
William Hill
Nathaniel Henderson
John Fondring
John Ross
Alex Love
Francis Ross
William Bratton
Samuel Swan
Abraham Smith
Robert Leeper
Joseph Howe
James Hays
Thomas Cook
James Hannah
Peter Kirkindall
John Miller
Charles Gillon
William Barrow

PETIT JURORS TO THE
EASTWARD OF THE WATEREE

Charles Spears
Douglass Starks
Thomas Kemp
William Wyly
Nicholas Swilly
Hugh Thomson
Will Douglass
Andrew Foster
George Payne Senr.
John Cook Jun.
John Brown
Thomas Lenore
Creed Childers
Will Brummett
Will Gardner
Joseph Payne Senr.
Nathan Thomson
Robert Morris
William Tomlinson
Aaron Ferguson
Chas. Fisher
Jos. Ferguson
Benj. Ferguson
John Fields
John Wooderson
Will. Bond
Abraham Belton

Samuel Tomlinson
Malichi Murphy
Isaac Pidgeon
Thomas English
John Hutchins
James Bettie
Augustine Prentwood
Lodwick Hudson
Richd Sutton
Samuel Wyly
Thomas Fulton
Barnard Johnston
Willm Faulkner
James Ingram
Edwd Narrimer
James Love
Alexander Ingram
Chas. Kimball
Jesse Minton
Benjamin Kimball
William Johnston
Nicholas Robinson
Richd Middleton
Samuel McCluir
William Downes
John Stroud
Gilbert Nellons
Andrew Baskins
Willess Whitaker
James Roe
John Davis
John Cousins
Henry Bless
James Smith
Thomas Osta
David Rogers
Drury Spurlock
Josiah Brunson
Geo. Frierson
John Parroik
Key Tapley
John Leviston
Richd Regell
Mark Fortune
James Bowman
Robert Bowman
Will. Burchmore
Thomas Wise
John Wise
John Cass
John Paisley
John Coburn

Arthur White
John Rafield
John Williams
James Wood
James Cummins
Lewis Sweeten
John Richbough
Willm Richbough
Moses Green
Miles Potter
Brenchley Corbett
William Rigill
Anthony Lee
Edward Broughton
Joseph Terry
Willm Ragins
Chas Strange
Nathl Roads
Samuel Nelson
Chas Cantey
John Bostwick
Malcolm Kerr
James McCauley
Patrick Brock
James Bennett
Randall Platt
Robert Reiley
Ezekiel Glasgow
Thos. W. Jenkins Jun.
Mathew Bowman
John Verbee Senr.
Ebenezer Bagnell
Henry Vernon
Chas Ammonet
Jesse Nettles
Thomas Neale
Thomas Woodward
Bellington Taylor
William Wright
Isaac Lenore
Willm Barden
John Foster
Willm Hampton
Isaac Jackson Junior
Henry Vaughan
Richd Wells
Joseph Singleton
John Moore
Josiah Gale Senr.
Frederick Atkinson
Nathan^l Bradford
Charles Brunsun
Josiah Furman

John Harvin
Samuel Hatfield

PETIT JURORS TO THE
EAST SIDE OF WATEREE

Thomas Wright
Mathew Brunson
Hill Howard
Isaac Brunson Junr.
Asberry Sylvester
Abraham Pettypool
Robert Moses
William Moore
Thom^S Bradford
Willm Dinkins
William Rees
John Rees
Isaac Jackson Senr.
James McCormick
Thomas Robert
Hope Bridgway
William Williams
Moses Knighton Junr.
Nathan Ellis
John Barden
John Postell Junr.
John Bradford
Hugh Rees
Willm Bracey
Isaac Brunson Senr.
James Brunson
Moses Brunson
Thomas Compton
Samuel Tines
Chas Skinner
Timothy Dargan
Roger Roberts
John Deas
John Ja^s Gibson
Willoughby Adams
Fenneous Gibson
John Perry
Silus Perry
John Westberry
William Bennett
John Golden
Will. Brown
John Mitchell
Will Westberry
Burrell Brown
Robert Brown
William Davis
Francis Spivey
Roger Bradley
James Carter
Benj^a Cassells

Henry Cassells Junr.
Samuel McKay
John Shaw
James Montgomery
Elisha Mackay
James Holloway
Samuel Commander
John McKay
John Newman
John Hickson
Richard Benbow
Thomas Bradley
Ja^s McClurg
Mathew Bradley
George Bird
John Fleming
John Dickey
Robert Hambleton
John Gordon
Willm Thomson
Willm Newell
Willm Cassells
Willm E. Herring
James Gordon
John Law
Willm Mixon
Mathew Carter Senr.
John Robinson
Lewis McLendon
Jacob Evans Senr.
Thomas Newman
Samuel Radcliffe
Robert Williams
William Stokes
Dennis McLendon
George Wright
John Mixon
Jacob Evans Junr.
Robert Lewis
James Bourdeaux
William Floyd
Benjamin Singletary
Jacob Wooters Senr.
Evan Benbow
Hugh Gamble
Willm Anderson
Philomon Cubbage
Willm Edwards
Robert Erwin
Richd Tomlinson
Paul Fulton
Samuel Chandler
Stephen Motte
Sutton Bird
Chas Warnock
Ja^s Conyers Junr.
Ja^s McCullough
George Chandler

David Brunson Senr.
Michael Singletary
Stephen Bonneau
Adam McKelveen
William Carson
John Nelson
Samuel Bradford
Rush Hudson
Alexander McKee
William Swadell
Joshua Roads
John Brown
Ab^m Wemberly
Samuel Webb
William Ferguson
James Hamson
Willm Starks
George Pea
Ephraim Pettypool
Abner Petty
Richd Clanten
Geo. Durin
Charles Mackey
Hump^y Barnett
Sam Beltan
Alexander Burnsides
John Dobbins
Richd Burnet
Peter Haward
Geo. Platt
Patrick Leyton
David Miller
Willm Daniel
Dennis Quinley
Willm Hickman
James Toland
John Lowry
Middleton McDonald
Willm Thomson
George Sommervill
Mathew Berkley
William Peach
Edwd Kennington
Benj^a Lloyd
Willm Ray
John Robertson
John Evans
Francis Bettis
Jacob Free
Fred^k Rush
Abraham Rush
Benjamin Hail
Jacob Whitner
Jonas Griffin
Willm Clark
Willm Welsh

John Murphy
Robt Mchaffy
John Countryman
Danl Horton
John Rutlidge
Richd Anderson
John Horton
David Robinson
James McNamus
John Clark
Murry Read
Robt Gardner
Peter Baker
David Griffith
Jeremiah Lewis
Willm Neland
John Neland
Joseph Williams
John Parkins
Geo. Underwood
James Rochel
Josiah Evans
Willm Tamerlinson
James Marshall
Lewis L. Bryant
Robert Dixon
John Allin
Willm Norris
Luke Petty
John Ellerbee
Willm Maddox
Hugh Summerville
Robert Lee
Willm McGarah
John Robertson
Thos Addison
John Baker
Alston Clark
George King
Arthur Hicklin
Andrew Nutt
Frederick Kimball
George Curry
William Spivey
Willm Fisher
Robt King
Robt Cochran
Henry King
Chris^r Mathenshed
John Hood
James McCulloch
John Peters
Walter Shropshire
John Dickson
Zachary Demsoill
James Braden

Joseph Coats
Adam Thomson
Willm Scott
Geo. Sanders
John Drakeford
Joseph Messel
John Dukes
Hugh Beard
John Biddal
Benj^a Coward
Willm McKee
Willm Marlow
David Clanton
James Fleming
Peter Turley
Richard Burge
Conrod Arrant
Jacob Wisner
William Brewer
William Horton
Danl Williams
Micajah Granger
John Davis
Robt Hatley
Willm Nutt
Robert Strawbridge

PETIT JURORS BETWEEN
BROAD AND CATAWBA RIVERS

Alexander McQuaters
James Owens
Hugh McKewen
Robt McCrary
John McMullin
Gasper Bierly
Barnaby Pope
David McGraw
Lewis Pope
Patrick Smith
Henry Crumton
Willm McMorris
Edwd McGraw
Joseph Gibson
Thomas Richardson
Willm McGraw
John Miller
Major Atkinson
Geo: Lightner
Isaac Rixpoper
Thomas Habert
Jessy Ford
William Babb
William Frazer
Joseph Gibson

John Robertson
Philip Rayford
Robert Rabb
John Grigg
Richard Nuley
William Newman
Thomas Marpole
John Chapman
John Phillips
Alexander Rasbrow
Miles Busby
Jacob Ingleman
Richard Gladney
John Potts
Moses Matthews
James Wallis
Philip Hinson
Alex^r Robinson
John Robinson
Nazeres Whitehead
Thomas Lewis
Joseph Hardredge
Henry Page
Micajah Piggott
Samuel Armstrong
James Masser
Samuel Gladney
David Thomson
Hugh Smith
Archibald Pall
Robert Martin
Moses Hallis
John Philips
Samuel Gamball
John Hutchison
James Russell
John Elliott
Joseph Owens
John Greaves Junr.
Priestly Tidwell
Benj^a Owen
Richd Winn
Thomas Stone
John Agnew
John Martin
Zebukun Quant
Daniel Oquin
Theophilus Hill
Benj^a Pidgeon
Daniel Harkins
Andrew Lister
John Richardson
Willm Whitaker Junr.
Richard Whitaker
Arthur Brown Ross

David Martin
Alex^r Smith
Richard Stratford
Joshua Cherry
Roger Gibson
Robert Love
John Yarbrow
Thomas Muse
William Aldridge
Mathias Fellaw
Saul Ratlive
Nicholas Peay
Thomas Hill
Canan Keason
John Ellison
Edward Heard
John Bell Senr
John Bell Junr
Willm Hamilton
Willm Young
Ralph Jones
Francis Kirkland
Isham Dansby
David Pauet
Dennis Corral
William Pannel
Charles Nix
William Jones
John McKenney
John White
John McClanahan
Elisha McKins
John Leonard
Samuel McKenny
Bird Wall
Alexander McKown
William Hamelton
David Baird
William Neeley
John Tombelton
Peter Robertson
John McGlomory
William Hamilton
Robert Martin
William McCammon
John Ellis
James Neeley
Michael Patton
James Greer
Augustion Culp
William Seaugon
Davice Leonord
George Sliker
William Simpson

William Farice
James Canmore
John Steel
Robert Elliott
Abros Cruse
Richard Crosby
John Crosby
John Going
Abra Smith
David Farice
Thomas Medile
Samuel Doan
Andrew Miller
Nicoles Thompson
Elisha Dye
William Cloud
John Tidwill
Joseph Helms
William McCaa
James Barber
Joseph Barber
Isaac Sedge
John Lewis
John Reeves
Moses Reeves
William Collins
John Linn
Cleman Mobley
Samuel Mobley
George Holsey
Benjamin Mobley
Robert Nelson
William Hill
Francis Colman
Robert Alcorn
William Collins
John Turner
John Nixon
Thomas Taylor
Samuel Hamilton
Lewis Botner
John Wilson
Martin Sliger
Henry Brown
William Addison
Daniel Baker
William White
Willm Ledenham
Edmond Knowles
Bright Averit
Jacob Killingsworth
John Kennedy
Timothy Reeves

Eroch Lennox
Benj^a Sims
William Godwin
Ludwell Evans
Joseph Tatum
William Scott
William Smith
Martin Statler
John Wyche
John May
Thomas Dortch
Joel Williams
James Pearce
Hartwell King
Henery Carter
Gabriel Parker
And^w Salisbury
John Simons
Brazel Wilson
John Threewits
John Holsinger
James Gill
John Hambleton
William Sanders
Samuel Wright
Mathew Howell
Thomas Jeffreys
William Wilson
John Turner
Thomas House
James Martin
Samuel Boone
Mich^l McCarty
Jacob Carrell
Benj^a Blanchard
Willm Rawlinson
Thomas Williams
Henry Mitter
Richard Jefferys
Henry Seusetrunk
Hargrove Harther
Joseph East
Richard Evans
William Denly
John Cooke
Nathl King
Patineau Howell
Aberhart Neatz
Stephen Smith
Thomas Moore
Fer^k Dubbert
Chris^r Ansmenger
William Boyd
George Lewis

John Miles
Henry Wympie
Andrew Domini
John Gill
John Foust
Hans Reapson
Benjamin Carter
Hugh Gaston
Jacob Carter Senr.
Moses Bond
Joseph Walker
George Gill
James Biggem
Thomas Camron
James McCluer
John Morrow
John McCluer
John Yarbrough
David Boyd
John Gill Junr.
Robert Kilsaw
Alexander Pagam
Christopher Straight
John Morton
James McQuiston
David McQuiston
John Walker
Mathew Paten
James Harbeson
James Smith
Edmond Strange
John Blake
John Gaston
John Wear
Thomas Garrott
Robert Laird
Benjamin Street
William Sandefen
John Kell
James Begum
Rice Hughs
Moses Smith
Michael Strange
John Morris
William Ferguson
William Rocuhen
Robert Martin
Adam McCooll
John Anthony
Thomas Akin
William Anderson
Benjamin Love
Thomas Brown
Joseph McCooll

Robert Love
Mathew Patterson
William Gaston
(Blank) Brown
John Sadler
John Love
Daniel Givens
Valentine Bell
Joseph Tomster
Reuben Lacy
Patrick McGriff
John Brown
Henry Harding
John Terry
Moses Thompson
Joel Adams
William Fox
Absolom Griffin
Richard Adams
Thomas Walling
Quinton McRight
John Mottely
William Jones
Caleb Dowd
Vanner Tucker
Luke Gibson
Daniel Muse
Joseph Bradley
Henry Horn
William Simmons
Robert Craig
James Armstrong
Nocholas Warick
James Wilson
Daniel Ford
John Jones
Richd Bell
John Rambert
Joseph Joiner
Jacob Dissaker
Thomas Bond
Jacob Jones
John Blanton
James Dabney
David Humphreys
Paul Powers
Samuel Rowan
John Wells
William Tucker
William Harlow
Henry Croft
Jacob Lewis
Henry Miley
John Armstrong

Peter Crim
Robert Duke
Bryan McClendon
Thomas Muse
John Tolleson
Nimrod Mitchell
James Hoy
Thomas Davis
John McKinnie
Edward Bennett
Nathl McDill
Joseph Francklin
Peter Ansminger
James Mann
Willm Trapp
James Brown
John Leigner
John Franklyn
Micajah Rice
Francis Miles
Andrew Cromer
Willm Sanders
Peat Reapsom
Jacob Cradrick
John Foust
Chris^r Rensler
Casper Rone
William Foust
Willm Edwards
Burrit Foust
Jonathan Hodge
Nicholas Grubb
Gasper Wershing
David Wescot
Rowland Williamson
Robert Tweedy
Henry Snead
Thomas Pope
John Gee
Willm P. Howell
John Gooding
Gasper Foust
Wright Nickason
And^w Paterson
Robert Howell Jun.
Robert Lyell
John Jones
Howell Gregory
John Marshall
Arthur Howell
Edward Hollis
Robert Livingston

John McCaxs	John Smith
Fran^S Henderson	Daniel Gagas
Jonathan Jones	William Jones
William Henderson	John Carsan
William Milling	Samuel Barber
Peter Nance	Moses McCown
Alexander Rosebrough	James Hemphill
Laird Burns	Gervis Dauhady
William Boyd	Thomas Ford
Timothy McClintick	Robert Tidwell
William Lewis	John Watson
Samuel Porter	Alexander Walker
Jacob Carter	Edward Cross
James Muckelhany	Joseph Brown
Nathaniel Sampel	James Miles
James Ferguson	Aaron Lockhart
Benjamin Culp	Edward Lacy
John Smith	Daniel Travise
Henry Bishop	Robert Tindal
John Porter	Samuel Jemster
Hugh Whitesides	Clayton Rogers
William McFadden	Francis Kirkpatrick
Hugh Morton	Isaac Sadler
Samuel Wair	Joseph Bishop
James Blair	James Kirkpatrick
John McFadden	Joseph Robinson
John Gill	Thomas Stokes
Isaac Smith	James Gore
Andrew McCain	Thomas Rodens
Henry Culp	William Thomas
Michael Hurts	John Wood Senr.
James Crawford	John Lyon
Jacob Cooper	Philip Gresham
James Ferguson	William Clark
William Weare	Daniel Thomas Senr.
James Robertson	Thomas Franklyn
William Taylor	James Sanders
Nich^S Bishop	Francis Jenkins
John Campbell	John Davis
Thomas Morton	George Bell
Robert Millen	James Sharp
James McCommon	James Huey
John Walker	John Covin
John Fleming	Thomas Crosby
Adam Ferguson	James Thomas
John McCally	William Jeter
John Gaston	Anderson Thomas
John Land	John Rowe
John Brown	John McColpin
George Harris	John Moultrey
John Keer	James Moore
Alexander Adams	Hugh Stuart

Charles Spradlin
Richd Woodley
Edward Nixon
John McDaniel
William Hicklin
Samuel Penny
Samuel Chesnut
Hugh Young
George Chery
James Strong
James Wilson
James Turner
John Huston
John Fulton
James Brown
Moses Cockrill
Stephen Terry
William Stroud
William Lowerry
William Hood
James Martin
David Glen
Joshua Collins
John Caskey
David Grimes
William McCollester
George Powell
John Delashmet
James Rogers
Richard Walker
Joseph Lord
Hance Waggoner
Ephraim Mabry
Thomas Shannon
Henry Tunderburg
John Godfrey
Amenus Liles
Michael Loner
Jacob Cannamer
Jacob Barker
William Morgan
Chrispen Morgan
Edward Mobley
James Crawford
Robert Gorrell
William Adair
Thomas Huston
Joseph Gaston
James Lemon
Hazel Hardage
John Ferguson
Hugh Cooper
Philip Walker

Alexander Walker
Philip Walker
John Read
John McCown
James Wiley
William Wiley
Samuel Fulton
Paul Ferguson
Robert Walker
Robert Walker Junr.
Alexander Brown
John Hunter
Robert Gaston
John Sarvise
Robert Cowin
James Wilkins
John Mills
Hugh Ross
James Ferguson
John Oulem
Mathew Rayford

PETIT JURORS TO THE
EASTWARD WATEREE WAXAWS

Hugh Davison
Thomas Patterson
Felix Kenneday
Drury Cook
George Greer
George Douglass
And^w Mackelwain
Samuel McClanahan
Samuel Dunlap
Cornelius Anderson
John McKennie
John Dunlap
John Thomson
Arch^d Causart
Alexander Thomson
John Stevenson
Thomas McMeen
William Caston
William Hood
Laurence Carron
Isaac Barr
William Beard
Henry White
Charles Miller
William Barnet
William Davis
James Barnet
James Crawford

Robert Carn
Joseph White
Robert Dunlap
John Arnold Pendar
William Nelson
William White
William Adams
George Dunlap
William Linn
John Foster
Archibald McCorkall
Robert Ramsay
John White
Hugh White
John Greer
John Riskparret
Joseph Lee
Glass Caston
Arch^d Davis
James Simpson
William Simpson
Thomas Adams
Timothy Anderson
James Dunlap
Andrew Shaver
Adam Beard
John Mongomery
William Nisbet
Nathl Cooper
John Strain Senr.
William Montgomery
Joseph McMeen
James Moore
John Robertson
John Kenneday
Robert Montgomery
John Coffee
James Walker
James Johnston
William Brawn
John Thomson
Robert Lockhart
John Lockhart
John Strain
Henry Coffee
John Belk
Andrew Boyd
Willm Guttery
William Barton
John Baker

PETIT JURORS FOR THE
NEW ACQUISITION

Matthew Russell
David Watson
David Dickson
John Watson
Robert Ferguson
Thomas Barr
John Latimer
William Laughlin
Hugh Brison
Charles Moorhead
James Willson
Hugh Allison
Peter Peterson
Isaac Enlos
Willm Kincaid
Daniel McElverin
Henry Karr
John Hope
Thomas Harrison
Richard Price
Charles Copeland
James Henery
Simon Kuykendall
Robert McElfee
James Bridges
John Mullenax
James Irvin
John Barren
John West
Thomas James
William Watson
William McWee
William McVervey
William Dunlap
William Hall
Newberry Stockton
William Love
John Venables
Alex Hamphill
Francis Adams
James Watson
Samuel Burns
Benjamin Enlos
John Jordan
Robert Black Senr.
Abraham McCarter
Samuel Swann
James Dickey
John Gordon
Will Copeland
Drury Robinson
William Glenn

Thomas Bridges
Willm Nook
Hezi^k Collins
Jacob Julian
Wilkinson Turner
Thomas Tate
Joboll Cocklerus
Saml Wood
Jacob Hufstitler
Isaac Collins
Theophilus Feavor
Thomas Gilham
Robert Logdridge
John Smith
Hugh Sheerer
Samuel Barnett
Patrick Robinson
John Hogg
William McDow
Henry Wright
James McDow
Matthew Floyd
William Minton
John Thompson
David Bocter
George Gibson
John Peters
Matthew Cowen
Thomas Mannon
John Moffett
James Smith
Willm Dobbins
William Logan
William Henery
Alex^r Henery
Joseph Gayton
David Neell
Samuel McMurray
James Armstrong
James Ramsey
William Patrick
James Adams
James Campbell
Robert Lowry
James Thompson
William Davis
Robert Johnson
Hugh Eager
Robert Ferguson
Arch^d Barren
Patrick Duncan
Thomas Barren
John Duncan
Francis Gutherre

Damery Winbourn
James Allcorn
Joseph Clark
Moses Camp
James Wilson
John Dover
John Ellis
Moses Latham
Henry Smith
Barney Hanley
Robert McCurdy
Abram Sommerford
James Scott
William Learny
Gauvin Gibson
Samuel Denton
Moses Jones
James Tampleton
Benjamin Marl
James Pavell
Joseph Clark
John Cain
Nathl Bocter
James Pinkerton
James Lessly
Joseph Black
Joseph Collins
James Willson
Mathew Dickson
Samuel Gordon
Robert Petterson
William McCulleign
James Craig
James Clinton
John Armstrong
Saml Craig
John Cantsler
William Adams
Andrew Campbell
James Lewis
David Moore
Joseph McKinney
James Armor
Godfrey Adams
John Pierr
Arch^d Thomson
John Patton
James Rush
James Wilkinson
Jos Gabby
James Camble
John Stallions
Alex^r Stuart

Willm McDowell
John Anderson
Joseph Smith
Abraham McCorth
Patrick Smith
James Barren
Hugh Berry
Moses Ferguson
William Neily
Robert Lusk
Samuel Lusk
Hugh McCellen
James Armstrong
Thomas McCulloch
Edward Lee
Isaac Keelock
Robert Morris
John Young
John Gordon
James Armstrong
John Sellars
James Tipling
David Gordon
Richd Sadler
John Swan
Robert McClellen
Ezekiel Stanley
John Cimbert
Robert Adams
Robert Thomas
William Stewart
David Garnison
James Duff
James McWaters
William Glover
William Ross
James Ross
John Breeson
James Wilkinson
James Ross
Thomas Willson
Matthew Dickson
Hugh Pence
John Glover
William Byers
Willm Watson
William Williamson
Willm Hillhouse
James Fears
Robert Neely
Matthew Neely
Hugh Neely
John Davis
Willm Smith

Robt Fleconing
James Armstrong
John Downing
Thomas Black
Repentance Townsend
Alex^r Fleming
Willm Hannah Senr
James Moorldoon
Elijah Fleming
John Patterson
John Turner
John Fearis
Robert Latimore
James Samuel
Alex^r Eakings
Hump^y Cunningham
Robert Patrick
Robert Kerr
James Beard
William Irvin
Walter Carson
Robert Cowen
Andrew Love
Samuel Corry
John McNabb
Michael McGarth
John Bishop
Robert Glover
Samuel Byers
Daniel Harsham
Thomas Kilpatrick
James Kilpatrick
David Hambleton
James Calp
John Dickey
Ezek^l Gillam
Ebenezer Bell
David Adarion
Richard Ball
James McKealy
John McClean
John Charnahoon
David Stephenson
Andrew McNabb
James Williamson
George Sadler
John Kellough
Benjamin Phillips
Philip Sandford
Thomas Bratton
William Kelly
John Dannes
Jas Hemell
James Murphy

David Leech
Richard Sadler
William Givins
John Carroll
John Fanning
Robert Black
James Willson
Samuel Robinson
John Rigg
Willm Robinson
Ja^s Wallace
Saml Reany
Edward Leary
Ja^s McNabb
David Byers
John Garvan
John Chambers
Thomas Garvan
John Moore
Thos Bratton
John Sadler
John Murphy
James Moore
Robert Kellough
Jam^s Gibson
Joseph Waddle
Matthew Bigger
Joseph Bigger
William Takings
William Howe
David Howe
Hugh Neel
Thomas Patton
Daniel Shaw
John Price
Robert Gabby
John Hall
Alex^r McWhorter
William Berry
Robert Fearis
John Workman
James Bogs
Arch^d Steel
John Howe
John Cooper
Andrew Armour
John Kincaid
Alex^r Cannady
John Smith
James Pursley
James Davis
James Ferguson
Robert Dowdell
Abra^m Fanning
Jeroham Wood
Hugh Wilson

Matthew Rogers
William Neilson
William Ratchford
John Wallace
Ralph Croft
Nicholas Wissentunt
William Hargrove
Adam Young
James Carsan
Peter Dancer
Jonathan Belton
Peter Smith
John Durock
James Jamayon
Robert Dickey
Willm Bell
Thomas Morris
Henry Good
Robert Brown
Saml Gay
Thom^s Clandenor
Danl Croft
Robert Ash
John Wallace
John Kelly
John McNight
George Hodge
James Love

SPECIAL JURORS FOR
CAMDEN DISTRICT

Willm Wyley
Andrew Foster
George Payne
Robert English
Thomas Lenore
John Adamson
Creed Childers
Joseph Payne Senr
Thomas Jones
Burwell Boykin
John Payne
Nathan Thomson
James Cary
Robert Morris
Willm Lang
Willm Tomlinson
Nathl Cary
John Wooderson
Willm Bond
Abraham Belton
Samuel Tomlinson
Malachi Murphy

Geo Oglevie
Ely Kershaw
Thomas Charlton
Thomas English
Thomas Pemble
John Hutchins
George Gantter
James Bettie
Augustine Priestwood
Will Boykin
Joseph Kershaw
John Wyley
Samuel Wyley
James Brown
Thomas Fulton
Willm Kershaw
Willm Whitaker Senr
Willm Whitaker Junr
James Whitaker

Roger Gibson
Alexander Smith
Arthur Brown Ross
Josiah Scott
Joshua Denkins
John Martin
John Blanton
Samuel Andrew
Samuel Russell
David Martin
Robert Alexander
Benj^m Pidgeon
Richd Stradford
Thomas Oglethorpe
Joshua English
Samuel Wise
John Chesnut
Richd Whitaker
Willess Whitaker

BEAUFORT DISTRICT

GRAND JURORS
FOR ST. HELENA

David Adams
Richard Adams
Anthony Albergottie
Andrew Aggnew
Richard Russell Ash
William Adams
William Adams Junr
Lewis Bond
William Barns
Nathaniel Barnwell Junr
James Black
Thomas Brooks
John Barnwell Senr
John Bernars Barnwell
William Boone
Daniel Brabant
John Bull
George Barksdale
Launcelot Bland
John Barnwell Junr
Tho^S Chaplin
Charles Capers
John Cowen
John Devant
Isaac Devant
James Doharty
Daniel DeSaussure
Jacob Deveaux
Andrew Deveaux
William Deveaux
Gideon Dupont
John Delebare
Edmund Ellis
John Edwards Junr
William Fripp
James Frazer
Richd Woodward Flowers
John Fripp
William Fripp Junr
Nathaniel Green
John Givens
William Graham
Edward Gardner
Daniel John Green
John Gray
Charles Givens
Richard Guerard
David Guerard
Benjamin Guerard
William Hazzard

Thomas Hughes
George Hipp
John Jenkins
Joseph Jenkins
John Johnston
James Joyner
John Joyner Senr
John Joyner Junr
John Kean
Joseph Lloyd
Francis Martinanget
Joseph Mikell
William Migget
Cornelius McCarty
Allen McKee
William Norton
Joseph Oswald
Philip Parmenter
Isaac Parmenter
Robert Porteous
Joseph Powell
William Rich
John Rose
Benjamin Reynolds
Richard Proctor
Thomas Rutledge
Henry Talbird
Tunis Tebout
William Hazzard Wigg
Isaac Waight
John Chaplin
William Chaplin
James Cuthbert
Jacob Cowen

GRAND JURORS FOR
PRINCE WILLIAM'S PARISH

John Roberts
Elias Jaudon
Robert Ogle
Patrick Bower
William Ferguson
Charles Brown.
John Frampton
Stephen Bull (of Sheldon)
William Davis
Joseph Ainger
John Davis
James Smith
Philip Hext
Andrew Postell

Joseph Brailsford
Ulysses McPherson
Thomas Hutson
Major Pierce Butler
Robert Philp
Jacob Tahler
John Keating
Henry DeSaussure
John McTier
William Harden
Col^o Benjn Garden
Thomas Page
Job McPherson
John Weekley
Darias Dalton
John McPherson
Jacob VanBebben
Philip Ulmer
Adam Ulmer
Benjamin Gignilliatt
John Lightwood
Isaac Cuthbert
William Stoutenburgh
Thomas Heyward Senr
John Prioleau
Edward Garvin
John Cox (Merchant)
John Cox (Planter)

GRAND JURORS
FOR ST. PETER

James McGowen
David Raymond
James Moore
John Moore
William Brisbane
Francis Bradbury
John Lewis Bourquin
Philip Martinanget
John Vauchier
David Geroud
Joachim Hartstone
Adrain Meyers
John Lewis Buche
John Buche
James Brisbane
Richard Pendarvis
Jonathan Bryan
Cornelius Dupont
Charles Dupont
John Fenwick
Joseph Lawton
Aquilla Miles
Charles Palmer

Samuel Porcher
Paul Porcher Senr
William Ross
Robert Brown
James Gignilliat
John Smith
James Thompson
William Stafford
Paul Porcher Junr
John Grimball Senr
Henry Gendrat
Thomas Cater
Basil Coupar
John Chisholm
David Keal

PETIT JURORS
FOR ST. HELENA

David Adams
Richard Adams
Anthony Albergottie
Andrew Aggnew
Richard Russell Ash
William Adams
William Adams Junr
Lewis Bona
William Barns
Nathan Barnwell Junr
James Black
Thomas Brooks
John Barnwell Senr
John Bernars Barnwell
William Boone
Daniel Brabant
John Bull
George Barksdale
Launcelot Bland
Thomas Bell
John Barnwell Junr
Thomas Chaplin
William Chaplin
Charles Capers
John Cowen
John Chaplin
Richard Capers
James Cuthbert
Jacob Cowen
James Devant
John Devant
Isaac Devant
James Doharty
Lewis DeSaussure
Jacob Deveaux
Andrew Deveaux

William Deveaux
Gideon Dupont
Daniel DeSaussure
John Delabare
Edmond Ellis
John Edwards Junior
Philip Everhart
William Fripp
Charles Floyd
James Frazer
Richard Woodward Flowers
John Fenden
William Fearris
John Fripp
William Fripp Junr
Nathaniel Green
Daniel John Green
John Givens
William Graham
John Gray Junior
James Gray
Edward Gardner
John Grive
John Grayson
John Gray
Charles Givens
Richard Guerard
David Guerard
Benjamin Guerard
William Hazard
John Hall
Thomas Hughes
George Hipp
John Jenkins
Joseph Jenkins
John Johnston
John Jeter
James Joyner
John Joyner Senr
John Joyner Junr
John Kean
Joseph Lloyd
Nathaniel Libbie
Jacob Miller
George Moss
Francis Martinanget
Joseph Mikell
William Migget
Cornelius McCarty
Allen McKee
William Norton
Joseph Oswald
Philip Parmenter
Samuel Parmenter
Isaac Parmenter
Michael Perriclare

Robert Porteous
Joseph Powell
Richard Proctor
Meredith Rich
William Rich
John Rose
John Rhodes
Robert Richards
Benjamin Reynolds
James Reynolds Junior
John Reynolds
Thomas Rutledge
Joseph Steel
Joshua Snowden
David Stone
Daniel Savage
George Stevens
Daniel Stevens
Joseph Scott Senior
Abraham Sheecutt
Thomas Taylor
Henry Toomer
Henry Talbird
Joseph Tippen
Samuel Thorp
Tunis Teabout
William Weston
Abraham Walcott
James Welch
William Hazzard Wigg
William Waight
James Thomas Williams
Hilderson Wigg
Benjamin Walls
Isaac Waight
Paul Fripp
William Deveaux
Charles Devant
John Ellis

PETIT JURORS FOR
PRINCE WILLIAM PARISH

John Roberts
Elias Jaudon
Robert Ogle
Patrick Bower
William Ferguson
John Frampton
Charles Brown
Stephen Bull (of Sheldon)
William Davis
Joseph Ainger
Matthias Smith
John Davis

James Smith
Philip Hext
Andrew Postell
Joseph Brailsford
Ulysses McPherson
Thomas Hutson
Major Pierce Butler
Robert Philp
Jacob Tahler
John Keating
John Bellinger Kellsall
George Mont (Mout?)
Henry DeSaussure
John McTier
William Harden
John Garnier Williamson
Col⁰ Benjamin Garden
Miles Reyley
Thomas Page
Jacob Plotts
Charles Plotts
Job McPherson
John Weekley
Andrew Auglay
William Hazle
Darias Dalton
John McPherson
Jacob Van-Bebber
Philip Ulmer
Adam Ulmer
William Weekley
Benjamin Gignilliatt
Robert Rutherford
Peter Ulmer
James Fallows
Lewis Stape
Edward Ferguson
Isaac Cuthbert
Thomas Heyward Senr.
John Heyward
John Prioleau
William Stoutenburgh
Edward Garvin
John Cox (Planter)
John Cox (Merchant)
Robert Reid
William Maltby
John Parmenter
James Gray
Richard Keating
Stephen Swann
John Gilbert
Seth Prior
William Thompson (Merchant)
John Lightwood

PETIT JURORS FOR THE
PARISH OF ST. PETER

James McGowen
Anthony Godfrey
David Raymond
Benjamin Cary
James Moon
John Moore
William Brisbane
Mathew Patterson
Lewis Winkler
William Kirk
George Spencer
Thomas Shandley
Peter Grineau
John Lewis Vineau
Francis Bradbury
John Lewis Bourquin
George Keal
Gideon Kirk
Jacob Seaberman
George Mingledorf
Philip Martinanget
John Wilkins
George Hunter
James Ross
David Keal
John Bazaquie
David Sausey
John Vauchier
David Geroud
Joachim Hartstone
Charles Frouchet
Melchior Leichtenstinkinstiger
Adrian Meyers
John Lewis Buche
John Buche
James Brisbane
Samuel Wilkins
Richard Pendarvis
John Linder Jr.
Jonathan Bryan
Melchoir Humbart
John Linder Senior
John Stafford
Willoughby Pugh
Cornelius Dupont
Charles Dupont
Peter Palmerine
Gabriel Wallzer
George McCullough
Casper Springer
Joseph Glencrost
Thomas Gibbons
John Audebert
Garton Backley

Abraham Brealer
John Booker
Robert Brown
Sampson Batt
William Carr
John Chisholm
Thomas Cater
Basil Coupar
Thomas Daniels
Josiah Daniels
Nathan Davis
James Forsyth
Abraham Gendrat
Henry Gendrat
Thomas Garnett
John Grimball Senior
James Gignilliatt
Theodore Gay
Joseph Garnett
Jacob Hollbrook
John Jones
Nathan Johnston
Zachariah Knight
Peter Kettles
John Kettles
George Roberts
John Fenwick
Joseph Lawton
Robert Marlow
Samuel Manner
James Dupuis
Jesse DeLoach
Lewis Morgan
Aquila Miles
Charles Palmer
James Pelot
Samuel Pelot
Park Pepper
Samuel Porcher
Paul Porcher Senior
Paul Porcher Junior
Robert Roberts
Elias Robert
Alexander Wray
James Smart
Martin Shuman
John Smith
Joshua Stafford
William Ross
Edward Stafford
Richard Stafford
William Stafford
Joseph Smith
John Strobhart
Jacob Strobhart
James Thompson
Peter Valcar

Jesse Webb
Samuel Wilkins
William Lewis
Howell Wall
David Wonderly

SPECIAL JURORS FOR
BEAUFORT DISTRICT

James Black
John Bull
Tunis Teabout
John Johnston
Daniel Stevens
William Waight
James Frazer
Edward Gardner
John Kean
Daniel John Green
Andrew Deveaux
John Bernars Barnwell
Nathaniel Barnwell
William Hazzard Wigg
James Cuthbert
George Barksdale
Thomas Rutledge
John Rose
Anthony Albergottie
Andrew Aggnew

ORANGEBURG DISTRICT

GRAND JURORS FOR
ORANGEBURG DISTRICT
ST. MATTHEW

John Burdell
Philip Frierson
Benjamin Campbell
Samuel Tate
Rowland Evans
George Shauler
George Spinney
Edmond Mathews
Samuel Dubois
Francis Rocke (Roche?)
Jacob Chris Zahn
John Benecar
John Oliver
William Fludd
Adam Snell
John Meyers
John Griffith
Valentine Shoemaker
Jacob Whitman Senr
George King Senr
Joseph Palmer
William Thomson (Colonel)
Christopher Kenline
Thomas Sabb
Aaron Little
Joseph Mickler
William Stent
James Boldridge
Charles Collins
Casper Brown
Henry Wetstone
Daniel Kelley
George Barst
Conrad Holman
Henry Stark
David Dickson
William Simpson
Jared Fitzpatrick
Malcolm Clark
George Ancrum
Gersham Kelley
William Heatley Senr
John MacWilliams
Morgan Sabb
William Reid
Paul Farquand
Charles Heatly
William Heatly Junr
John Caldwell

John Monk
Robert Hails
Thomas Elfe

GRAND JURORS
FOR SAXE GOTHA

Jacob Frydig
George Hill
William Arthur
Godfied Drayer
George Kinewinder (Stinewinder?
Jacob Saylor
John James Haig
George Shipley
William Tucker
Christian Kayser
Nicholas Mickler
Jacob Geiger
Henry Patrick
John Murff
William Goodwin
Harman Geiger
Mathew Libecap
Andrew Raigler
Charles Benoist
William Geiger
John Adam Summers Junr
Adam Summers Senr
Michael Lightner
Jacob Bigley
Samuel Kennerly
Thomas Kennerly
James Lyton Ritchard
Jonas Beard
Ralph Humphries

GRAND JURORS
BELOW ORANGEBURG

David Crum
William Hill
Peter Sandle Senr
Andrias Frederick
Abraham Isenhood
Nich^l Shuller
Peter Moorer Senr
Nich^l Weever
Sabastian Fontius

GRAND JURORS
FOR ORANGEBURGH

Henry Snell Senr
Jacob Woolfe Senr
John Amaker
Jacob Wymor
John Jennings Senr
Simon Shingler
Christopher Rowe
Casper Ott
Lewis Golson
John Herisperger
Jacob Rumph Senr
John Robinson
John Bolziger
Henry Rickenbaker
Jacob Amaker
Jacob Stroman Senr
Jacob Stroman Junr
Donald Bruce
Jacob Hurger Senr
Henry Felder Senr

GRAND JURORS BETWEEN
THE FORKS OF THE EDISTO

John Salley
Henry Young Senr
William Pou
John Pou
Phillip Jennings

GRAND JURORS BETWEEN
THE SOUTH FORK OF
EDISTO AND SAVANNAH RIVER

Bartlet Brown
Robert Lee
Patrick Macklemurry
Isaac Bush
Thomas Castlelow
John Parkinson
Ezekiel Williams
Joseph Harley
John Hampton
Thomas Young
Jacob Buxton
Britten Williams
John Newman
Miles Riley
Robert Lark
John Clayton
Thomas Philpot

George Robinson
Henry Ferguson
Robert Hankinson
John Grant
Joseph Johnson
Steph^n Smith
Jacob Swighard
James Moore
William Robinson

PETIT JURORS
FOR ST. MATHEW

Jacob Myers
Jacob Hungerbealer
Thomas Simpson
Thomas Murry
Henry Bull
Anthony Disto
Edward Willingham
Thomas Pledger
Nathaniel Bullin
John Barrell
Alexander Guerin
Hugh Brown
Thomas Powell
John Barker
Peter Peck
George Haley
Frederick Pisler
Lewis Kern
Daniel Keller
Jacob Karr
Henry Coon
Aaron Way
Jacob Geegleman
Peter Hagler
John Ulmer
Frederich Parter
Jacob Denzler
Jacob Zigler
George Smith
John Myers
John Keller
Henry Denzler
John Ulrick Denzler
George Irish Senr
Henry Beegler
James Brown Junior
Martin Beegler
Jacob Hungerbealer
Conrad Peck
Isaac Delessline
Thomas Curtis
William Park

John Rest
Godfrid Road
Benjamin Wood
Henry Winningham
Lewis Thomson
Jacob Park
Martin Stoutenmyer
Jacob Hoover
Henry Sowerhaven
Paul Sheirer
Christian Harner
John Miller
John Mark
Wily Hoover
Joseph Burline
Jacob Kaller
John Hoffman
Stephen Stiffelmyer
Conrod Sammet
Joseph Pesner
Andrew Garish
Jacob Zigler
Jacob Bare
Jacob Rickett
Frederick King
Thomas Morrow
Jesse Evit
Mordaica McFarlan
John Burdell
Philip Frierson
Benjamin Campble
Samuel Tate
Rowland Evans
George Shooler
George Spinney
Edmond Mathews
Samuel Dubois
Francis Roche
Jacob Christopher Zohn
John Bennea
John Oliver
William Flood
Adam Snell
John Meyers
John Griffith
Valentine Shoemaker
Jacob Whiteman Senr
George King Senr
Joseph Palmer
William Thompson (Col^n)
Christopher Kenline
Thomas Sabb
Aaron Little
Joseph Mickler

William Stent
James Boldridge
Charles Collins
Casper Brown
Henry Wetstone
Daniel Kelley
George Barok
Conrod Holman
Henry Stark
David Dickson
William Simpson
Jared Fitzpatrick
Malcolm Clark
George Ancrum
Gersham Kelley
William Heatley Senr
John McWilliams
Morgan Sabb
William Read
Paul Farquand
Charles Heatley
William Heatley Junr
John Caldwell
John Monk
Robert Hails
Thomas Elfe

PETIT JURORS
FOR ORANGEBURGH

James Taylor
John Spring
Michael Gable
Joseph Cook
Joseph Hoober
Ulrick Oth
Melchoir Smith
John Kopstate
Jacob Woolfe Junr
John Denzler
James Tilly
David Tily
George Hoffman
Jacob Heickler
John Henry Denzler
John Strock
Henry Gissendaner
Christian Woolfe
Michael Housliter
George Hessey
John Derames
Henry Rowe
Jacob Fielder
Jacob Neebling
Casper Barba

Christian Inabnit
Michael Zimmerman
Adam Buckend
Peter Oth
Casper Sustruck
Frederick Ulmer
Henry Busserd
John Ticktell
John Shiders
William Bruner
Henry Felder Junior
John Stroman
Nick^S Hurter
Peter Staley
William Bonete
Jacob Harlong
Conrad Kriter
John Bare
Henry Zorn
James Carmichael
Robert Smith
Benedink Collar
James Patterson
Abraham Miller
Peter Imboden
Frederick Felder
Jacob Wonemaker Junr
John Hook
Anthony Robison
Jacob Rumph Junr
John Miller Junr
John Inabnit
John Miller Senr
Casper Menz
Bolrer Stroman
Samuel Felder
George McMickle
Thomas Wild
Frederick Purtz
Nich^l Till
Solomon Cannedy
John Lizard
Peter Roth
Henry Snell Senr
Jacob Wolfe Senr
John Amaker
Jacob Wymor
John Jennings Senr
Simon Shingler
Christopher Rowe
Casper Oth
John Herisperger
Jacob Rumph Senr
John Robinson
John Bolziger

Henry Rishenbaker
Jacob Amaker
Jacob Stroman Senr
Donald Bruce
Jacob Burgess
Bastian Zimerman
Jacob Stroman Junr

PETIT JURORS
BELOW ORANGEBURGH

Alexander Syfrid
Adam Syfrid
Nich^l Zorn
Michael Duck
William Fary
John Simons
Samuel Griffith
Tobias Harzop
Philip Zchnder
Conrod Boumgartner
John Sandle
Barn^d Harzog
Fred^k Knoble
Philip Karr
Jacob Ott Junior
Henry Reace
Peter Murer Junr
George Utzey
Frederick Myer
John Felder
John Imfinger
William Roth
Frederick Rissel
Charles Hotho
Hardy Williams
Jacob Hotho
William Seat
Christopher Metz
Robert Berry
Joseph Tucker
John Clayton
Jacob Karner
Archibald Murry
Henry Judy
Thomas Hill
William Connor
George Renerson
John Tucker
Andrew Rostig
George Harzog
Richard Berry
Emanuel Miller
David Crum

William Hill
Peter Sandle Senr
Andrees Frederick
Abraman Isenhood
Nich[l] Shooler
Peter Moorer Senr
Nicholas Weaver
Sabastian Fontius

PETIT JURORS BETWEEN
THE NORTH AND SOUTH
FORK OF EDISTO RIVER

Robert Cannon
John Cannon
Henry Shilling
Peter Griffith
Thomas Griffith
William Jenkins
Philip Pou
John Smith
Samuel Inabnit
Gideon Jennings
George Ford Junr
Thomas Ford
Evan Jones
Thomas Leomas
Joshua Standley
Benjamin Standley
Henry Williams
Henry Tetstone
Samuel Pickens
Abraham Peacock
Heronimus Zinn
James Morris
James Fair
Joseph Durner
Ephraim Purket
Michael Odam
Jacob Hurr
John Howard
Christian Plotts
John Tucker Junr
William Wernal
Edmond Jones
Charles Torney
Edward Myles
Isaac Odam
Absalon Eilands
Andrew Commins
John Sally
Henry Young Senr
William Pou
John Pou
Phillip Jennings Junr

John Patrick
John Yohn
William Jones

PETIT JURORS TO
SAVANNAH RIVER

John Collings
John Wood
Samuel Way
Richard Sanders
Edward Southwell
John Akeridge
John Brooker
Moses Odom
Joab Roundtree
James Astelew
Richard Vince
Owen Odam
Richard Kirkland
William Murphy
Richard Ogelsbie
Ase Williams
George Will[m] Clamm
John Roberts
John Wyld
Hugh Short
Isaac Davis
Moses Collins
William Wise
Isaac Sterling
Elijah Oglesby
John Laresey
Bartlet Brown Junr
William Brient
Blanchard Colding
Archibald Eagle
Samuel Colding
William Weekley
John Bush
Richard Odom
William Grim
Henry Sumeral
Sampson Griffin
Joseph Bell
William Everit
Jesse Sumeral
Daniel Green
Thomas Holly
Thomas Hughes
Jacob Forman
John Powell
Joseph Braswell
Frederick Brient

John Williams
Richard Rodgers
Green Hill
Maramadick Ganaway
John Reynolds
George Foreman Junior

PETIT JURORS BETWEEN
THE SOUTH OF EDISTO
AND SAVANNAH RIVER

Bartled Brown
Robert Lee
Patrick Macklemurry
Isaac Bush
Thomas Castlelew
John Parkinson
Ezekil Williams
John Hampton
Thomas Young
Jacob Buxton
Britten Williams
John Newman
Miles Riley
Robert Lark
John Clayton
Thomas Philpot
George Robinson
Henry Ferguson
Robert Hankinson
John Grant
Joseph Johnson
Stephen Smith
Jacob Swighard
James Moore
William Robinson
Joseph Harley

PETIT JURORS
FOR SAXA GOTHA

Jeremiah Channin
Lowrinds Grime
George Buergert
Andrew Romney
_____ld Kirsh
_____lieb Stabler
Frederick Knodle
_____istoff Slagel
Frederick Herig
John Howert
George Likes
Andrew Keigler Junr
George Seagler

Martin Wackter
George Unger
George Seawright
Henry Keaber
Mickel Raver
James Tucker
Leonard Bough
Christopher Libebrand
Michael Oswald
John Yearg
Robert Caldwell
James Spence
Mathias Vinegart
Dennis Hase
William Caldwell
Thomas Smoke
George Trayer
Godfrey Trayer Junr
John Kinsler
John Melcheroof
John Klekley
Valentine Coone
Mathias Sun
John Aberhart
Abraham See
Andrew Spence
David Friday
Frederick Briggs
Thomas Cotton
James Beams
George Traft
Frederick Williams
Thomas Edwards
Nicholas See
Jacob Harman
Jacob Haugenbough
Jacob Theiler
Jacob Richman
Andrew Kicker
Ulrick Boozer
Jacob Gallman
Christian House
John Jacob Geiger
George Slappy Junr
George Slappy Senr
Philip Poole
William Oee
John Gallman
Jacob Moake
Casper Slappy
Francis Goodwin
Godfrey Hearsman
Anthony Boughman
Philip Gill
Francis Brezina
Samuel Boyakin

John Chesnut
John George Stroub
Henry Snelgrove
Henry Sommers
Jacob Wernn
Nicholas Sommers
Andrew Holman
Jacob Haldewanger·
Francis Sommer
Ulrick Slisse
Barth^W Minigh
Michael Bayer
Peter Mightler
George Dokins
John Swightenberg
Michael Earkle
Jacob Slisse
Michael Viller
Thomas Long
James Adey
John Richard
John Follmer
Archb^d Dunbar
John Swikard
George Wisse
James Hollanshead
John Commelander
John Geiger
George Swikard
Jacob Bughter
John Hipp
Stephen Elizer
Jacob Burkerd
John Strub
Benedict Nunemaker
Simon Yunginger
Casper Libhard
Abraham Geiger
James Twerner

George Baucknacht
Joseph Kennerly
Thomas Beigley
Thomas Ramcy
John Gartman
Barth^W Gartman
Thomas Bee
Jacob Stake
John Quatlibaum
James Kenvily
Jacob Fridig
George Hill
William Arthur
Ralph Humphries
Godfrid Drayer
George Stinwinder
Jacob Saylor
John James Haig
George Shipley
William Tucker
Christian Kayser
Nich^s Mickler
Jacob Geiger
Henry Patrick
John Murff
William Goodwin
Harman Geiger
Mathews Libecap
Andrew Kaigler
Charles Benoist
William Giger
John Adam Summers
Adam Summers Senr
Michael Lightner
Jacob Bigley
Samuel Kennerly
James Lyton Richard
Jonas Beard
Micha^l Vinegart
Robert Spence

SPECIAL JURORS FOR ORANGEBURG DISTRICT

Samuel Rowe
Frederick Felder
Henry Felder Senr
Samuel Felder
Jacob Felder
Henry Rowe
Jacob Woolf Junr
Christopher Rowe
John Stroman
James Carmichael
Robert Smith
John Shider
James Taylor
Donald Bruce
John Jennings Senr
Jacob Woolf Senr
David Woolf
John Lyzard
Jacob Ott Senr
James Paterson
Philip Jennings
Henry Shilling

John Pou
Samuel Inabnet
George Hessey
Henry Rickenbaker
Jacob Wymore
William Robison
Jacob Rumph Senr
John Bolziger
Peter Roth
John Derams
Henry Gissendaner
John Hooke
Jacob Wonamaker
Emanuel Miller
Joseph Hoober
John Ott
Ulrich Ott
John Kopstate
Casper Mentz
Jacob Moorer
John Moorer

In the Council Chamber the 28th day of March 1778

Assented to

Raw[s] Lowndes

Mo Bee
Speaker for the
General Assembly

Hugh Rutledge
Speaker of the
Legislative Council

State of South Carolina AT A GENERAL ASSEMBLY begun and holden at Charles Town on Monday the fourth day of January in the Year of our Lord One thousand seven hundred and seventy-nine; and from thence continued by divers Adjournments to Saturday - the twentieth - day of February - in the year of our Lord One Thousand seven hundred and seventy-nine.

AN ORDINANCE for appointing a new Jury List for the District of Ninety-six, and to empower and direct the Judges out of the same to draw a Grand and Petit Jury to serve at the next Court of General Sessions to be holden for the said District next after the passing of this Ordinance, and for other purposes therein mentioned.

WHEREAS the Jury Lists hitherto made out for said District has been very imperfect, not more than one fifth part having ever been on the Jury List, of those by Law qualified to serve, rendering the service thereby unequal and burdensome on those whose Names were inserted therein, while at the same time many reputable and proper Persons who have been Settlers and Inhabitants in the said District, and others who have arrived at full age since the last Lists were made out, altogether excape doing any duty in that respect, and the Judges, from the Causes aforesaid, have been prevented, at the last holding of the Court in that District, to draw a Grand and Petit Jury for the next Court, as by Law they were required to do. AND WHEREAS it would be extremely hurtful to the public, as well as to Individuals who have or may have Business depending at the said Court, to be delayed for want of a Jury to transact the necessary Business of the said Court on the day appointed by Law: For Remedy whereof, BE IT ORDAINED by the Honorable The Senate and House of Representatives of the State of South-Carolina now met and sitting in General Assembly and by the Authority of the same, That the several Persons whose Names are inserted in the Schedule of List hereunto annexed, intitled "A List of Grand Jurymen," shall be drawn by Ballot, impannelled, summoned and obliged to serve on all Grand Juries at the Circuit Courts to be holden hereafter for the District of Ninety six. AND the several Persons whose Names are inserted in the schedule or List hereunto annexed, intitled "A List of Petit Jurymen and Jurymen in Civil Causes," shall be drawn by Ballot, impannelled, summoned and obliged to serve on all Petit and other Juries and Inquests whatsoever, for the said District of Ninety-six: AND that the several Persons whose Names are inserted in a Schedule or List hereunto annexed intitled "A List of Special Jurymen" shall be summoned, returned and obliged to serve as Talesmen in all Cases where Tales are allowed by Law for the said District of Ninety-six. AND BE IT FURTHER ORDAINED by the authority aforesaid, That as soon as may be after the passing of the Ordinance, any one or more of the Judges of the Court of General Sessions shall cause to be written on small pieces of paper, of an equal size and Bigness, the Names of all the Persons hereby appointed to serve as Juryman, and having first diligently compared them with the List or Schedule hereunto annexed, shall cause them to be put in a Box or Chest to be prepared for that purpose, with proper Divisions made therein, which shall be marked on the Cover, to demoninate to what Jury they belong, and any one, or more of the said Judges, out of the Persons appointed to serve on Juries as aforesaid, shall cause to be drawn a Grand and Petit Jury and Jury for Civil Causes, to serve at the next Court to be holden for the said District of Ninety-six, which drawing shall be at the Court Room in the State House in Charles Town on or before the first day of March next, between the hours of Ten in the Forenoon and two in the afternoon, by a child under the age of Ten years, agreeable to the usual practice of drawing Juries. AND BE IT FURTHER ORDAINED by the Authority aforesaid, that the Juries so drawn shall be summoned, returned and impannelled to serve at the said Court for the District of Ninety-six, to be holden on the twenty sixth day of April next, and shall be held, reputed, taken and deemed in Law to all Intents and purposes whatsoever as competent and legal; AND all their Acts and Verdicts, of as full force, validity and effect, as if the Jury had been drawn at the same time and place prescribed by any former Law, Rule, Usage or Practice of the said Court, any Law, Usage or Custom to the contrary thereof in any wise notwithstanding. AND BE IT FURTHER ORDAINED by the Authority aforesaid, That from and after the first drawing of the Jury in manner and form as aforesaid, for holding the next Court at Ninety six, on the twenty sixth day of April next, the Jury thereafter from Time to Time, out of the List hereby established, shall be drawn, summoned, returned and impannelled agreeable to, and in manner and form, and at the Times and places directed and prescribed by the act called The Circuit Court Act, or any other acts in force relative thereto, anything herein contained to the contrary notwithstanding, and shall be intitled to all Priviledges, and subject and liable to all the Duties, Fines, Pains and Penalties, which are allowed enjoined and inflicted by the Laws of this State, on Jurymen. AND WHEREAS the Court House at Camden was lately burnt, and the Judge or Judges going that Circuit, cannot by Law hold the Courts for Camden District at any other places; BE IT THEREFORE ORDAINED by the authority aforesaid that the said Judge or Judges, until a Court House is built for the said District, shall and may hold the said Courts at such place or places in the Town of Camden as he or they shall think proper, and if at any time hereafter any other of the Court Houses in the several Districts of this State should be burnt or destroyed, it shall and may be lawful for the Judge or Judges going Circuit, to hold the Court for such District respectively, until a new Court House can be built, at any other House they may think proper, at or near the place where the Court House for such District now stands. AND WHEREAS the Jury List for the District of Cheraws, hath, this same defect in the Jury Box, been so intermixed, that Juries cannot be regularly drawn or impannelled agreeable to Law: BE IT THEREFORE ORDAINED by the authority aforesaid that the Judge or Judges who shall next go on the Northern Circuit, is and are hereby authorized and required, from the Jury List established for the said District, by an act passed the twenty eighth day of March last, to make and prepare a new Jury List, and distribute the same into the different Divisions of the Jury Box aforesaid, from which Lists, Juries for the said District shall in future be drawn.

Ref: - S. C. Archives - MS Act 1779 - No. 1123

NINETY-SIX DISTRICT

GRAND JURY LIST FOR NINETY-SIX DISTRICT

LONG CANES AND
PLACES ADJACENT

LeRoy Hammond
Patrick Calhoun
Andrew Williamson
Andrew Pickens
William Calhoun
William Hutton
Alexander Noble
James Noble
William Carson
Charles Williams
Michael Deval
James Patterson
William Hanvey
Thomas Lee
John Anderson
Reuben Weed
John Downing
Robert Melvil (Turkey Creek)
James Crawford Senr.
William Pratt
Robert Fraser
William Cannon
Andrew Liddle
John Johnston
John Ewing Calhoun
Francis Johnston
Thomas Langdon
Aaron Steel
Hugh McCay
James Liddle
John Miller
William Luckie
Thomas Hamilton
Joseph Turnbull
James Ponder
William Russel
William Baskens
John Varner
Hugh Read
Alexander Ramsey
John Possey
Harrison Possey
Joseph Swearengain
James Alexander
James Caldwell
Matthew Thomson
William McKinley

John Middleton
George Pettigrew
Robert Anderson
Alexander McAlpin
William Harris
Moses Davis
William Robinson
William Hutchison
Joseph Calhoun
John Cowan
Thomas Barksdale
James Carter
Robert Carter
John Martin
Samuel Winbush
Edward Keating
James Gordon
Andrew Robertson
John Foster Junr.
James Loosk
Capt. Andw Hamilton
Thomas Weems
Jesse Campbell
Robert Norris
Thomas Edwards
Willis Breaseal
Robert Messer
Archibald Hamilton
Alexander Chavas
John Lesley
Samuel Watt
William Woods
David Pressley
Benjamin Harrison
William McGaw
James Scott (Long Canes)
Arthur Dickson
Joseph Pickens
William Wilson
Samuel Kerr
John Pickens junior
Benjamin Davis (Savannah River)
John Barksdale
Archibald Murray

CUFFEE TOWN AND TURKEY CREEK

John Purves
John Scott
Benjamin Tutt
Richard Tutt
Hugh Middleton
Robert Wallace
William Perrin
James Harrison
John Adams
James Adams
James Letcher
Thomas Butler
Henry Key
Elisha Robinson
John Griffith
Drury Pace
Robert Garrett
Henry Ware
John Garrett
Henry Dalton
Charles Williams (Turkey Creek)
Samuel Scott
Samuel Anderson
Patrick Gibson

ABOVE NINETY SIX COURT HOUSE

John Wardlaw
Isaac Mitchell
Ezekiel Smith
William Hallems
Samuel Norwood
Jeremiah Joyner
Joshua Moore
John Roseman
John Cobb
George Read
Adam Crain Jones
James Campbell
Benjamin Edins
Hugh Wardlaw
Richard King
Thomas Leach
Nathaniel Bullock
Benjamin Mitchell
John Bowie
Adam McKee
William Canedy

BELOW NINETY-SIX COURT HOUSE

John Towles
Thomas Berry
Nathaniel Spraggins
Nathaniel Abney
John Berry
William Abney
Thomas Eastland
Francis Brown
Richard Alleson
Richard Buckalie
James Chaney
John Chaney
George Chaney
Bailley Chaney
Samuel Savage
John Edwards
Benjamin Cook

NEAR NINETY-SIX COURT HOUSE

Richard A. Rapley
Dennet Abney
John Bullock
Thomas Anderson
Culbert Anderson
Samuel Ramsey
William Brown
Richard Moore
Matthew Mirthlan
John Mamilton
Thomas Kealing Smith
James Harkins
Isham Green
Frederick Glover
Thomas Wilson
Robert Merriweather
William Merriweather
Gilbert Smithers
Robert Dickey
Andrew Caldwell
Obed Holloway
Field Perdue
David Hunter
Jacob Withrs
William Robertson (Ninety-six)
Nathan Simes
William Bean
Daniel Jones
John Walker
Joseph Wardlaw

John Moore
Stephen Anderson
James Holmes
Benjamin Durbrowe
James Edwards
Mekernis Good
William Mathews
Joseph Burton
James Mayson
William Moore
Julius Nichols
James Moore

PART OF THE LOWER
DISTRICT BETWEEN
BROAD AND SALUDA RIVERS

Thomas Gibson
James Pettey
Charles Pettey
Daniel Purkins
Jones Griffin
Horatio Griffen
Dorman Henson
Ethelder King
John Lark
Joseph King
David Brasel
Jacob Vanjant
John Wright
Philemon Waters
Abraham Thompson
Charles Thompson
William Hamilton
George Dawkins
William Dawkins
John Buchanan
George Roofe
John Griffin
Mana milliar
Michael Dickhart
Daniel Horsey
Robert Livert
Isaac Kelly
John Gorey
William Wadleton
John Robertson
Isaac Pemberton
William Pearson
Joseph Thompson
David Jenkins
George Gordon
John Turner
Isaac Grant

Jacob Brooks
George Pemberton
Isaac Cooke
Williamson Lasless
Avery Nowland
John Lindsay
William Curreton
John Lisles
George Suber
John Suber
Barnaby Mounts
John Johnson
James Shepheard
John Brown
John Steel
Charles King
Abel Anderson
Thomas Dawkins
Edward Waddleton
John Johnson junior
Thomas Gordon
Ephraim Cannon
Samuel Fickland
George Gray
George Gray junior
John Gallman
Peter Kerr
Samuel Kelly
Samuel Pearson

MIDDLE DIVISION
BETWEEN BROAD AND
SALUDY RIVERS

John Bays
Robert Mars
Thomas Yates
Major John Caldwell
John Evans
Hopkins Williams
John Porterfield
Arthur Duckham
William Richey
Ebeneser Sternes
James Wills
David Cunningham
George Carter
Nimrod Williams
Alexander Deal
Charles Pitts
Robert Level
John Philips
Thomas Geary
Henry Pitts

William Anderson
John Sims
William Finney
Samuel Henderson
Elijah Teague
Josiah Greor
John Abercrombie
John Caldwell Senior
John Cunningham
Thomas Norris
Thomas Largent
James Abernathey
John Newton
Caleb Gilbert
Isaac Davenport
William Burgess
James Castle
Robert Gillum
John Beard
Henry Steadman
Peter Edwards
John Donaho
Hans Hendrick
Hugh ONeal
Joseph Hays
Angus Campbell
James Pollard
James Dyson
James Griffin
William Johnson
James Burnside
James Henderson
Thomas Burden
Thomas Starks
Robert Mairs
Francis Shurer
Matthew Gillespy
Abraham Gray
Abner Casey
Thomas Garey
Thomas Wadlington
William Williams
William Wilson

SPARTAN DIVISION

James Massey
William Simpson
James Mackelvain
James Park
James Tillet
Col. John Thomas
Alex. Foster
Daniel Shaw

Daniel Jackson
Samuel Jackson
Thomas Jackson
William Patton
William Lee
James Gibbes
Hugh Means
John Thompson
Robert Faris
William Means
Robert Harris
Daniel Plumer
John Pinckston
Jeremiah Dutton
Giles Connel
Daniel Bush
George Goodwin
William Plumer
Riney Below
Barnet Coiler
William Gordon
Henry Clark
William Golightly
William Rodgers
William McClelan
John Ridingman
Joseph Buffington
Daniel Hagton
Elias Hollinsworth
William Farr
James Hammet
Patrick Robertson
William Wofford
Enoch Hollinsworth
Amuel Fincher
Col. William Wofford
Jonathan Parker
James Varnen
Col. Tho^S Fletchall
John Boggan
Thomas Ryan
Isaac Gregory
John Gregory
Thomas Blassingham
John Salter
James Hill
William Hill
John Taylor
James Hawkins
George Linam
John Johnston
James Anesworth
John Goodwin
Jonathan Cain

Thomas Smith
Walter Roberts
Hezekiah Gentry
Gavin Gordon
Samuel Otterson
Edward NcNeal
David Hudson
Richard Cruse
James Thomas
Daniel Thomas
John Mayfield
Turner Roundtree
Richardson Roundtree
George Potts
William Hughes
Edward Nixon
Daniel McKee
Jacob Cooper
William Tate
James Mayberry
John Grindall
Samuel LittleJohn
John Foster
Thomas Driper
Robert Coleman
James Steene
Daniel McClearing
John Elliott
Adam Potter
James Martin
David George
Nathan Grimes
Vardry McBee
Richard Hughes
Alexander McDougal
John Campbell
John Townsend
William Coleman
Robert Moore
Hugh Moore
Christopher Coleman
Nathaniel Jefferies
Curtis Caldwell
James Johnston
Zachariah Bulloch
John Anderson
John Hope
John Pritchard
Zachariah Gibbes
John Journey
John Nichols
John Cunningham
John Steen
Littleton Mapp

John Clark

BETWEEN TURKEY CREEK
AND SAVANNAH RIVER

Lacon Ryan
James Lemar
John Raneford
George Tillman
Lawrence Rambo
John Spencer
Robert Moseley
Richard Kirkland
Robert Stark
George Galphin
James Vasser
Francis Singuefield
Joseph Miller
John Carter
John Minten
Samuel Sakker
Thomas Jones
Thomas McGuinas
John Millar
Daniel Rodgers
Samuel Landoum
Philip Lemar
Hezekiah Walker
William Coventon junior
Robert Lemar
Archibald Offutt
John Murray
Moses Creie
James Baisdon
Valentine Lenn
David Bowers
John Bedingfield
John Dukes
Michael Mires
Lud Williams
Adam Hyle
Daniel Shaw
John Stuzengger
Henry Jones
Thomas Lemar (Belmount)
John Tobler
Little Berry Bortick
Thomas Lemar (Horse Creek)
Andrew Burney
Edward Rowell
David Zubly
Abraham Spears
John Ryan

Drury Minns
John Lucus
Archibald Coode
Lawrence Rambo
Michael Buckhalter
James Adams
Lewis Tillman
William Moseley
James Thomas
Herman Golman
Peter Day
John Clockler
Evan Morgan
George Mock Sen.
John Pussell
Benjamin Hatcher
James Joy
Jethro Roundtree
William Davis
John Clark
Rain Chaftair
James Carson
William Philips
James Butler
Thomas Cotton

LITTLE SALUDY

Solomon Pope
Thomas Green
David Nickleson
Thomas Appleton
William West Sen.
William Waring
Edward Couch
James Harrison
William Holston
Isaac Lewis
William Jones
Jacob Smith
Richard Williams
John Watson
Henry Heartell
John Mitchell
Wright Nickleson
Enoch Grigs
James Grigs
Joseph Conningham
Nathaniel Milton
Thomas Welst
Michael Deloch
Burded Eskeridge
Robert Allen
Elijah Paget

Michael Watson
Arthur Watson
John Sown
Henry Balton
Smallwood Smith
Joseph Hogans
Amos Richardson
Peter Foy
William West junior
Edward Blane
Thomas Delote Sen.
Frederick Sisson
Nathaniel Powell
John Saywer
Josiah Allen
Francis Jones

FOR THE UPPER PART OF THE
MIDDLE DIVISION BETWEEN
BROAD AND SALUDY RIVERS

William Bouland
Matthew Cunningham
Tundy Walker
Thomas Ducket
John Odle
Joseph Whitmore
William Barksdale
William Hendricks
John Whitmore
John Gray
John McCrae
George Downes
Reuben Flanigan
James Kirk
Thomas McKeary
Nathan Barksdale
Nehemiah Frank
Samuel Neighbours
John McHerds
James Gideon
Joseph Pearson
James Higgins
William McDaniel
Edward Gouot
William Bramblet
Holloway Poor
James Hall
Lewis Duvall
Andsworth Middleton
Joseph Adair
Thomas Grear
James Young

Joseph Wood
Cornelius Cargill
James Boyd
Hugh Young
Benjamin Lewis
John Mayson
John Ghent
John Dunlap
Isham East
Daniel Osborne
William Dendey
Thomas Ewing
Edward Musgrove
James Hancock
James Dunash
Coleman Brown
John Brown

John Patton
Cornelius McMahon
Nicholas Hill
James Abercrombie
William Ellison
Joseph Box
John Rodgers
William Berry
Charles Saxon
Robert McLeary
Andrew Rodgers
Richard Currell
Jonathan Downes
Robert Cunningham
Patrick Cunningham
Henry ONeil

"A LIST OF PETIT-JURYMEN AND JURY MEN IN CIVIL CAUSES"

PETIT-JURY LIST FOR NINETY-SIX DISTRICT

LONG CANES AND
PLACES ADJACENT

William Calhoun
Matthew Beraud
Peter Boragne
Peter Bayle
Peter Gibert
John Bert
John David
Nicholas Badjeaw
Jacob Langel
Peter Elie Balote
John Balote
Andrew Gibbooane
William Hutten
James Gray
James Millegan
Jacob Belard
Alexander Noble
John Williams
John Wilson
Alexander Hall
Peter Roger
Jeremiah Roger
Daniel Ramsey
James Noble
Samuel McElve
Alexander McBride
James McColloch
Arthur Reid
William Carson
Charles Williams
Charles Turney
Michael Devall
James Pettigrew Junr.
John Egar
George Crawford
Robert Boggs
John Brawford
James Davis
George Long
Joseph Able
Robert McAlpin
Alexr. McAlpin
John Sanderson
William Hanvey
William McDonald
Samuel Patton
David Grier
David Chester

Moses McCarter
Matthew Shank
John Young
Joseph Jones
Thomas Lee
John Anderson
John Craswell
James Thompson
Thomas Morris
John McGill
James Glasgow
Reuben Weed (Wood?)
John Bealy
Samuel Patterson
William Thompson
George McComb
James Bouner
James Keown
Andrew Reynolds
Patrick Dowing
John Dowing
Hugh Simpson
James Anderson
William Deal (Weaver)
John Simpson
William Boyd
Robert Melvil (Turkey Creek)
John Crawford
James Crawford Sen.
William Little Jun.
Daniel Carmichael
John Boggs
Hugh Esler
William Pratt
James Neil
Patrick John McMesterson
John Lindsay
Thomas Lissey
Robert Fraser
Adam Jordan
William Cannon
William Crawford (Rocky River)
James McGown
William McGown
William Shenkler
Samuel Lessly
John Price
Andrew Liddle
John Johnston
John Ewing Calhoun
Moses Brawford

Henry Johnston
Francis Johnston
Thomas Wilson
John Hunt
Thomas Langdon
Samuel Morrow
Aaron Steel
Thomas Holland
John Bole
John Pickens Jun.
Isaac Steel
Joseph Carmichael
Andrew Gillespie
Matthew Gillespie Jun.
Hugh McCay
James Liddle
James Carrithers
Thomas Shanklin
James Gillespie
John Miller
George Stephenson
James Stevenson
David Henderson
James Henderson
Matthew Robertson
William Luckie
John Luckie
Thomas Hamilton
Caleb Tiner
Samuel Lindsay
John Lindsay
John Dealwood
Joseph Turnbull
John Turnbull
Burrel Morris
Joseph Crawford
James Ponder
James Scott
John McKinley
William White
William Black
William Russel
Samuel Wilson
Nathaniel Wilson
Robert Black
Robert Boyd
Jameston Hatcher
William Baskins
John Varner
Thomas Strain
William Strain
Hugh Read
Robert Bond
Joseph Blackwood

James McCall
Robert Young
James Young
John Green Sen.
John Green Jun.
James Finley
Lewis Felaw
Hugh Graham
Israel Pickens
Samuel Black
John McGill
B. Smith
William Hall
Samuel Carson
James Galley
Alexander Ramsey
Thomas Ramsey
William McMaster
Patrick McMaster
John Posey
Harrison Posey
Edward Fletcher
Arthur Gray
Alexander Steel
Andrew Egar
Joseph Swearengain
John Harris (Bull-Town)
John Spratt
Joseph Martin
James Alexander
James Caldwell
William Hamilton
Matthew Thomson
William McKinley
Francis Carisle
Charles Parker
Joseph McCloeskay
Joseph Carson
John Jones
Thomas Turner
James Martin
Robert Martin
John Middleton
James Kerr
William Kerr
John Lawrence
James Long
George Pettigrew
Alexander McAlpin
Robert Anderson
William Harris
Moses Davis
Patrick Roach
Benjamin Green

Samuel Glasgow
James Hawthorn
John Campbell
Thomas Wells
Samuel Boggs
John Robinson
William Robinson
William Dorris
George Conn
Robert Erwin
Andrew Ross
James Morrow
David Wylly
Samuel Patton
William Hutchison
Isaac Mathews
Joseph Calhoun
William McClellan
William Moore
James Foster
William Hay
Robert Stewart
John Cappock
Joseph Cappock
John Cowan
Rivers Banks
Thomas Barksdale
James Cowan
James Cain
James Cain Jun.
James Carter
Robert Carter
John Martin
Samuel Winbush
Roger Martin
Edward Keating
James Gordon
Andrew Robertson
Hugh Porter
Arthur Morrow
Andrew Cochran
John Able
Allen Haggert
John Steadman
John Pickens (Son of Gabriel)
Andrew Jones
John Strain
Benjamin Lawrence
William McKeen
William Miles
Samuel Miles
Walter Harland
Andrew English
John Foster Jun.

John McFarland
William Crawford Senr.
Samuel Mann
Robert Yelden
James Sloan
Robert Ross
James Rockbridge
Ezekiel Evans
Henry Wylly
John White
Andrew White
Michael Wilson
Alex. McCrery
James Loosk
James Watt
Matthew Young
William McCarley
James Crawford Jun.
Henry McMurdy
Samuel Foster Sen.
Alexander White Sen.
John Cochran
Capt. Andrew Hamilton
Samuel Foster Jun.
James Foster Jun.
Thomas Weems
John McCord
John Turk
Jesse Campbell
John Cox
Matthew Donaldson
Robert Allen
William Spiars
William McElwee
Robert Norris
William Norris
William Hairston
Daniel McEntire
William Martin
Samuel McMartry
John Hairston
Andrew Pickens
Joseph Moore
John Moore
Thomas Edwards
James Huston
John Cozby Jun.
Samuel Brown
Alex. Henderson
John Moore (Smith)
Andrew Taylor
John Cunningham (Smith)
Willes Breaseal

William Lesley
John Griffin
William Gray
William Clark
Thomas Coffer
Elijah Baker
Gilbert McCrery
Jonathan Pickens
Joseph Bouchillon
Robert Messer
Elisha Baker
Alex. Foster
Enes Crawford
Robert Crawford
Archibald Hamilton
Samuel Gamble
John Gamble
Andrew Hamilton Jun.
Isaac Steel
Isaac Stewart
Alex. Clark
David McCleskey Jun.
Alexander Chevas
John Lesley
Samuel Watt
George Morrow
William Woods
Thomas Harris
Thomas Strain
David Presley
Benjamin Harrison
William McGaw
John McGaw
Thomas Crzer
William Cresley
Andrew McComb
Samuel Taylor
James McFerron Sen.
George Stringer
John Bell (Rockey River)
James Scott
George Whitfield
John Moore (Shoemaker)
Andrew Miller
Arthur Dickson
David Welsh
Matthew Carethers
Robert Carethers
Andrew Williamson
Samuel McClinton
Josiah Patterson
Joseph Pickens
William Wilson
John Norwood

Samuel Kerr
Joseph McCleskey
John Pickens Sen.
Benjamin Davis (Savannah River
John Barksdale
Alexander McCreary
Patrick Calhoun
Thomas Chaves
James Weems
Peter Tutten
Robert Wilson
William Little (Miller)
Archibald Murray

ABOVE NINETY-SIX
COURTHOUSE

Henry Logan
James Calhoun
John Wardlaw
Samuel Agnew
William Boman
James Brown Lee
Robert Peekins
James Seawright
Harman Culp
William Ross
Thomas Beaty
Thomas Watt
William Huggins
James Chaple
Joel Thacker
Alexander Irwin
William Moore
James Graham
William Robeson
James Heard
Robert Adair
James Stephens
Thomas Wales
Abraham Reed
Thomas Martain
Thomas Sanders
James Hathorn
James Forbes
John Calhoun
Samuel Thompson
John Logan
Nathan McCollister
Samuel Huston
Henry Purdy
John Edmiston

Isaac Mitchell
Ezekiel Smith
Robert Swanzey
William Hallems
James Kirkwood
James Richey
John Robeson
James Dunn
William Stewart
George Neel
Samuel Norwood
Robert Gibson
Reason Rutledge
Jeremiah Joyner
Richard Hodge
James Webb
Joshua Moore
Andrew Webb
John Rosemand
Samuel Rosemand
John Cobbs
John Johnson
George Reed
William Dickson
Adam Crain Jones
Alexander Branan
James Campbell
William McDowell
John Johnson
Joseph Parker
Victer Matthews
Jos. Matthews
Moses Edmison
Christopher Russel
Benjamin Edings
Hugh Wardlaw
John Maxwell
John Sample
Andrew Neel
Richard King
George Smith
Thomas Leach
John Buchanan
Nathaniel Bullock
James Mulheren
John Preter
Andrew Logan
John Irwin
Benjamin Mitchell
John Bowie
Samuel Hill
James Breden
John Murray
Adam McKee

William Canedy
Robert Alis
James Gray
John Russel
John Richey
John Moore
Robert Adair
Hugh Douglass
Robert Foister
John Beels
Richard Griffin
Francis Logan
John Brown Lee
Robert Stone
John Grinsley
William Benson
James Watt
Benjamin Hodge
Mark Ball
Henry Peacock
John Bailey
Armstrong Heard
Josiah Downing
William Boyd
William McMahon

NEAR NINETY-SIX
COURT HOUSE

Richard A. Rapley
Dennett Abney
John Bullock
Thomas Anderson
William Freeman
Thomas Ross
Richard Dean
John Bostick
Culbert Anderson
James Anderson
Thomas Mecrea
Samuel Ramsey
Archibald Todd
William Brown
Richard Moore
Matthew Mirthlan
John Hamilton
Thomas Reeling Smith
James Harkins
William Johnson
Hector Dickey
Isham Green
Frederick Glover

Elisha Brooks
Thomas Wilson
Robert Meriwather
William Merriweather
Roger McKinney
William Wilson
Gabriel Smithers
Robert Dickey
Andrew Colwell
William Holloday
John Akins
Hugh Akins
Caleb Holloway
Thomas Fanquhere
John Witsell
Matthew Wells
Obed Holloway
William Anderson
Joseph Drew
Field Perdue
James Wilson
William Neal
Joseph Closk
John Brown
David Hunter
Jacob Withrs
William Roberson
Adam Fraylick
Nathan Sims
William Bean
Daniel Jones
Robert Thompson
James Walker
John Walker
Joseph Wardlaw
William Walker
John Moore
Thomas Thornton
Henry Jevelah
John Gentry
Thomas Henderson
John Henderson
Shadrach Henderson
Jesse Harris
Stephen Anderson
James Homes
Azariah Lewis
Benjamin Durbrough
James Edwards
Mekernis Goode
William Mathews
Joseph Burton
William Moore
James Mayson

Julius Nickols
James Moore

BELOW NINETY-SIX
COURTHOUSE

John Walton
Samuel Abney
Paul Abney
William Chaney
Richard Tate
James Carson
George Dean
William Ellis
James Cook
Thomas Pinkett
William English
John Gorman
Josiah Stevens
Ebenetus Stevens
Garret Buckalve
Benjamin Smith
William Steward
Thomas Norrel
James Norrel
Christopher Gorman
Benjamin Moore
Charles Carson
Stokley Towles
Thomas Broadhead
John Harkins
Thomas Harkins
James Chaney Jun.
Michael Key
Henry Partman
Joseph Towles
Morris Gwin
John Halloway
Nathaniel Foskey
John Towles
Thomas Berry
Nathaniel Spraggins
Nathaniel Abney
John Berry
William Abney
Thomas Eastland
Francis Brown
Richard Allison
Richard Buckaleu
James Chaney
John Chaney
George Chaney
Bailey Chaney

Samuel Savage
John Ewards
Benjamin Cook

ABOUT CUFFEE TOWN
AND TURKEY CREEK

John Purves
John Scott
Benjamin Tutt
Richard Tutt
Hugh Middleton
Robert Wallace
William Perrin
James Wilson
James Harrison
John Adams
James Adams
Edward Morris
Arthur Killcras
William Cox
John Glantom
James Letcher
Thomas Butler
Robert Russel
Henry Key
George Blair
William Blair
Elisha Robertson
John Griffice
Thomas Harrison
Drury Pace
William Harvey
Thomas Harvey
James Harvey
Robert Garratt
Henry Ware
John Garratt
Edward Prince
Abraham Frets
Chambers Blakeley
Daniel Sulivan
Henry Dalton
Charles Williams
Joshua Grey
Nuby Man
Joseph Reed
Nicholas Gentry
Charles Blackwell
John Steward
Joseph Thomas
James Thomas
Isaac Edward Matthews

Samuel Scott
Thomas Dalton
Ebenezer Starns
Samuel Anderson
Philip Timberman
John James Tuffel
Patrick Gibson
Adam Boyer
David Blakney
Absolom McDonald
Sampson McClean
David McWill
Thomas Shaw
John Morrice
Thomas Gray
George Wise

THE LOWER PART OF NINETY-SIX
DISTRICT IN THE FORK OF
BROAD AND SALUDA RIVERS

Thomas Gibson
James Pettey
Charles Pettey
Thomas Miles
Moses Smith
John Jones
John Parmer
William Golle
Thomas Black
Daniel Purkins
Jones Griffin
David Purkins
Horatio Griffin
Dorman Henson
Etheldred King
John Lark
Joseph King
David Brazel
William McCartey
Jacob Vanjant
John Wright
Philemon Waters
Abraham Caridine
Peter Hawkins
William McConnel
Nehemiah Thomas
Hugh Johnson
John Barlow
Abraham Thompson
Charles Thompson
William Hamilton
George Dawkins

William Dawkins	John Robertson
Thomas Perry	Isaiah Pemberton
Thomas Felcher	Benjamin Vanhorn
Edward Colany	William Pearson
John Buchanan	John Elleman
Michael Elvin	Abner Ellerman
William Buchanan	Joseph Thompson
Jacob Hodges	David Jenkins
Thomas Wood	Marmaduke Coats
William Henry	Samuel Crompton
Daniel Gartman	John Coats
Philip Mith	Hugh Wiseman
George Roofe	Daniel Daugherty
Peter Deceskar	James Daugherty
Joseph Caldwell	David Ferguson
John Nox	Francis Wafer
John Griffin	John Godfrey
Alexander Johnson	Daniel Gorey
Alexander Beam	John Anderson
Henry Waker	George Gordon
Martin Sharp	John Wilkinson
Frederick Single	John Turner
Henry Mitts	William Gillum
James Nealy	Israel Gant
Jacob Lomanuk Sen.	William Stewart
John Johnson	Gabriel McCole
Joseph Smith	John Riley
George Montgomery	Daniel Clarey
Maximillian Haney	Chesley Davis
Thomas Risinger	Samuel Dunkin
Michael Dickhart	Joshua Stewart
Charles Coats	John Davis
Joseph Fish	James Douglas
Frederick Comer	David Humphrey
John Keller	George Anderson
Daniel Hossey	James Hall
English Stockman	James McConan
Joel Chandler	Hugh Creyton
Robert Liveret	Alexander Stewart
Joseph Hampton	Jacob Brooks
James Ford	John Copai
Andrew Crooks	James Wilson
William Tygert	John Perry
Daniel Hossey Jun.	William Aspenal
Charles Littleton	William Harris
Daniel Chandlor	Richard Right
James Chandlor	William Wright
Shadrach Chandlor	John Carmon
John Thomas	John Campbell
Isaac Kelley	Benjamin Atkins
Jacob Gilder	Francis Atkins
Stephen Rogers	Benjamin Inman
John Gorey	John Atkins
William Wadleton	George Pemberton

William Murray
Daniel Richardson
William Herbison
William Taylor
Isaac Cook
John Ridgall
Thomas Smith
John Duncan
Peter Ruble
Moses Emrey
John Coats
James Gulberath
Peter Black
John Gilbert
Shadrach Vessels
Williamson Lasles
James Lasles
William Green
Randol Robinson
William Walker
William Chandlor
John Clark
John Jay
George Arnold
Edward Kelley
Benjamin Hampton
Avry Nowland
Thomas Jones
John Spark
Isaac Cooke (Enoree)
Enos Elemon
Daniel Smith
Enoch Pearson
John Lindsay
George McCulloch
William Mayban
Nicholas Jones
Nathan Davis
William Cureton
John Liles
Samuel Nealy
George Suber
Adam Collins
Jacob Cromer
Jacob Lomanick
Cudgick Ruff
Barnabas Mounts
John Johnson
Isaac Morgan
James Shepard
John Brown
John Wadell
Peter Richardson
Tarina Riley

William Richardson
John Steel
Patrick Riley
Isaac Pamer
John Tarburt
Henry Anderson
Charles King
Abel Anderson
Isaac Lindley
John Bags
Matthew Hall
Thomas Dawkins
Roody Boozard
Edward Wadleton
John Johnson Jrn.
John Coale
David Glen
Joel Mabry
John Segler
John Stickman
Thomas Gordon
Benjamin Anderson
Thomas Hill
John Pearson
Ephraim Cannon
George Martin
Jeremiah Williams
Matthias Waker
Peter Fulker
James Daugherty
Nicholas Bansey
George Lightsey
Abraham Linsey
Peter Hays
Engle Stokman
William Meslemay
Samuel Frickland
William Wakard
Thomas Brooks
John Bartleson
John Cannon
Jacob Frederick
John Boozard
George Gray
Alexander Crosen
George Gray Junior
Peter Oats
Thomas Crosen
Jacob Boozard
John Linsey
Charles Wilson
William Reeder
Thomas Morgan
Abraham Anderson

William Herren
Daniel Johnson
John Gollman
John Chandler
George Mounts
James Murphey
Robert Wiseman
Thomas Pearson
Cornelius Cox
William Arington
Peter Karr
Stephen Elmore
Samuel Dennis
Samuel Kelley
Thomas Lewis
James Crossen
Samuel Steel
Samuel Pearson
John Pearson
John Volentine
Robert Evins
George McKeney
Robert Jones
William Hacheeson
James Daugherty
Dacker Jones

UPPER PART OF THE MIDDLE
DIVISION BETWEEN BROAD
AND SALUDY RIVERS

William Bouland
Matthew Cunningham
Tundy Walker
William Taylor
Crawford Lewis
William Huddleston
Thomas Ducket
James Adair
David Batey
John Odle
John Pruda
Joshua Rodgers
Joseph Whitmore
William Barksdale
William Hendricks
Basel Prator
Silas Garrot
Josiah Prator
James Kelly
James Kelly Jun.
John Whitmore

John Gray
James Mahon
James Duncan
Samuel Bishop
Eliphaz Reyley
Charles Puckett
John McCrae
William Baugh
John Jones
William Davis
James Adair
John Adair
George Downs
Brice Protor
John Garret
John Greor
Benjamin Adair
Ambrose Whittone
James McCord
John Duncan
David Jones
Charles James
William Adair
Andrew Owings
Reuben Flanigan
Robert Long
Joseph Greor
John Ramage
William Millwee
John Hunter Jun.
John Miller
John Mahone
Thomas Dendey
James Kirk
Thomas McKeany
Nathan Barksdale
Nehemiah Frank
George Martin
William Lacey
Samuel Neighbours
John McHerd
Benjamin Griffin
John Cox
Nicholas Brown
William Vaughn
Thomas Dean
James Gideon
John Lindsey
David Childers
Mordecai Moore
James Moore
James Allison
Joseph Pearson
Thomas Moore
John Waldrope
Ezekiel Lindsey

James Higgins
Newton Higgins
John McClintock
James McClintock
James McCrae
William McDaniel
John Boyd
Edward Garrot
John Gamble
William Bramblet
Arthur Breshar
Edward Pugh
Jacob Roberts
John Stone
Joseph Barton
Drury Smith
Spill C. Brown
Holloway Poor
John Hall
Joseph Patterson
James Hall
Lewis Duvall
John Edwards
Patrick Davis
Turner Gamble
Kitt Smith
Philemon Harvey
Thomas Blackly
Isaac Rodgers
John Ridgeway
Gibert Manarey
William Gray
Abner Bishop
Andsworth Middleton
Joseph Adair
Benjamin Saxon
James Adair
Andrew Anderson
Thomas Word
James Williams
Thomas Green
James Young
Joseph Wood
James Greor
John Nutt
George Capland
John Mudding
Cornelius Cargill
James Boyd
Robert Cooper
Samuel Fleming
Charles Parrot
Hugh Young
Jo^s Coker
Robert McNass

James McNeess
Robert Ross
William Bryson
Patrick Cunningham
Robert Sims
Hugh Wilson
Benjamin Lewis
John Mayson
John Ghent
James Tinsley
John Hunter
Josiah East
John Dunlap
Isham East
George Ware
Philip Tinsley
John Smith
William Harris
Thomas Ellison
Harten Deal
Thomas McDonald
James Lindley
Thomas McClurken
William Tweedey
Ratcliffe Joel
John Manley
Michael Waldrope
Daniel Osborne
Shadrach Martin
Alex. Hamilton
James Young (Little River)
Sherwood Allen
Samuel Powell
Manoah Tinsley
William Dendey
William Craddock
Samuel Dalrymple
John Blackley
James Blackley
John Owens
Thomas Cunningham
Alexander Fuisborn
William Brigs
Thomas Ewing
Edward Musgrove
Patrick McDavid
James Hannah
John George
Lazarus Benton
John Campbell
Aaron Lynch
John Millar
John McDavid
Lodwick Laird

Robert Templeton
James Duriah
Samuel Laird
David Templeton
John Jones
William Glen
James Cray
William Hannah
John Cunningham
James Cunningham
Richard Owings
Henry Crum
Samuel Dunlap
Richard Fowler Senior
Richard Fowler Junior
John Wallace
John Howard
Samuel Cobb
James Allison
Coleman Brown
John Brown
John Patton
Robert Goodwin
Benjamin Rainey
William McDaniel
William Gillet
Samuel Hanby
Samuel Simpson
Thomas Williamson
James McCain
Cornelius McMahon
James Williams
John Box
Jesse Jones
Nicholas Hill
James Abercrombie
William Martin
George Hollensworth
William Ellison
Joseph Box
Owen Read
John Rodgers
William Berry
Charles Saxon
Robert McCrery
Andrew Rodgers
Josiah Greor
Andrew Rodgers Junior
Richard Carroll
James Harvey
Jonathan Downes

LITTLE RIVER BETWEEN
BROAD & SALUDY

Peter Edwards
John Donaho
Hans Hendrick
Hugh ONeal
Richard North
Robert Young
John ONeal
Joseph Hays
Angus Campbell
James Pollard
James Dyson
James Griffin
Joseph White
Henry Hazell
John Smith
Robert Smith
William Burgess
Isaac Tinsley
Charters Nichols
William Furlow
William Finley
William Johnston
Thomas Davidson
John Meeks
James Burnside
James Henderson
William Lowery
George Gogins
Edmond Ellis
Thomas Burden
John Hunter
Joseph Kelly
Thomas Starks
Abraham Wright
William Campbell
William Nimmons
Jeremiah Dial
William Dial
Solomon Nichols
Robert Mairs
Francis Sherer
James Ray
James McMahon
James McCrackon
Matthew Gillespy
James Hughs
Ejeniah Verjen
George Hughes
Nathan Neighbours
Abraham Gray

William Woodall
Richard Marks
John Smith
Abner Casey
Thomas Garey
Thomas Duggins
Thomas Wadlington
James Wadlington
John Baptistere
Jeremiah Stark
Thomas Stark
Samuel Manau
William Beard
William Wilson
William Murray
Charles Crow
Frederick Jones
Daniel Simpson
Benjamin Burton
William Stone
James Johnston
John Johnston
Francis Davenport
Isaac Davenport
William Davenport
John Williams
Patrick Huggins
George Neely
John Satterwhite
Bartell Satterwhite
John Geary
Providence Williams
Thomas North
John Johnston
James Griffin
John Davis
Thomas Jones
Benjamin Neal
Matthew Love
James Puckett
John Dalrymple
Joseph Hettell
William Thompson
Ansell Bardin
Jacob Jones
Simeon Ellis
George Anderson
Robert Hood
James Burns
William Wilson
Joseph Young
Thomas Garrot
Henry Hendricks
William Verdiman
Richard Fowler
William Fowler
John Swindford

Daniel Blackburn
William Blackburn
Thomas Beard
William Neighbour
John Garrot
Isaac Evans
Joseph Campbell
William Sargent
Richard Brooks
Samuel Wharton
Gerard Smith
William Pitts
James Gogins
John Lucus
John Young
Joseph Smith
William Anderson
James Little
Charles Plunkett
Harry Pearson
John Nelly
Gibeon Jones
Francis Prine
William Stephens
John Newman
John ONeal
Henry ONeal
Robert Cunningham
Samuel Cannon
Daniel Williams
Allen Cox
Robert Plunket
John Wilson
Anthony Park
William Boyd
Vincent Roberts
Henry Roberts
John Roberts
John Bays
John Garrot
Robert Mars
Thomas Yates
John Caldwell
John Evans
Charles Edwards
Clement Handcock
Gilbert Turner
Hopkins Williams
Robert Carter
John Ryan
John Porterfield
Joseph Adkins
James Williams
Samuel Scott
John Carter
John Hughes
Enos Stimson

Thomas Carter	Josiah Greor
Arthur Durham	William ONeal
Robert Hinton	Moses Lindsay
William Ritchey	John Abercrombie
James Armstrong	Abel Bowlin
Samuel Withers	John Wells
Ebenezer Sterns	Thomas Boyce
William Parker	Clement Deal
Richard Lang	John Carter
John Mading	Benjamin Carter
Lock Madding	Joshua Reeda
Jacob Wright	Clem Davis
Theodosius Turk	James McGill
William Matthews	John Caldwell
James Wells	John Wilkison
David Cunningham	Isaac Williams
Peter Wood	John Cunningham
George Carter	John Douglass
Samuel Wharton	Robert Proctor
Stephen Hutchinson	Thomas Norris
Nimrod Williams	Thomas Largent
Daniel Williams	John Monk
Roger Murphy	William Lang
John Willard	Daniel Goggins
Andrew Cunningham	Barnard Barns
Alexander Deal	James Abernathey
James Bryson	Nathaniel Howard
Charles Pitts	John Richardson
Robert Levill	Henry Morgan
William Winchester	John Newton
Richard Griffin	Joshua Inman
John Phillips	Jehu Inman
John Phillips	Caleb Gilbert
Thomas Geary	Isaac Davenport
Henry Pitts	William Burgess
Joseph Campbell	Isaac Tikett
William Campbell	John Watts
William Goggins	Jonathan Taylor
William Anderson	James Lang
John Sims	David Lang
Henry Butler	James Castle
William Young	Robert Gillum
Edward Garrot	Robert Lang
Jesse Sparks	James Leffan
William Finney	Hugh Kelly
Thomas Clark	Robert Gillum
James Dalrymple	Clement Gore
James Stone	John Crumley
Samuel Henderson	James Stone
Hugh Boyd	John Beard
Herman Davis	William Dunlap
Matthias Cook	Peter Hughmane
Levy Anderson	Jacob Hughman
Elijah Teague	Henry Stedman
John Bowlin	James Kelly
John Owens	William Johnston
Michael Johnston	James Garner

David Rees
William Gilleland
William Turner
John Colvin
Bartholomew Flemingham
Charles ONeal
John Griffin
John Waldrope
John Gillum
Robert Speir
George Neely
William Lasley
George Adams
James Plunkett
John Abernathey
John Galloway
Solomon Wyatt
Philip Pheagins
Isaac Mitchell
Joseph Davenport
Joseph Wood
Samuel Proctor
John Lofton
Nathaniel Nickels
Anthony Golding
Christopher Neeley
James Cummins
John Hallum
Robert Neely
Joseph Johnston
James Waldrope
Thomas Gill
John Hunter
Joseph Carter
Abraham Hollingsworth
Benjamin Collier
Daniel Pitts
John Cole
James Jones
Joseph Hutchinson
James Williams
Thomas Johnston
William McTeer
William Lofton
John Griffin
David Turner
Jacob Bowman
Edward Turner
Absolom Turner
John Williams
Daniel McGin
Levi Pitts
Anthony Griffin
William Bagley
Jonathan Neal
Thomas Edgehill
Oliver Towles

Henry Pitts
William Burton

BETWEEN TURKEY CREEK
& SAVANNAH RIVER

Jonathan Gilbert
Edward Vann
William Morris
Lacon Ryan
James Lemar
Samuel Thomas
John Pounds
Jacob Summerall Sen.
Edward Furned
John Ransford
John Shaw
George Tilmon
Frederick Tilmon
John Vann
William Thomas
Laurence Rambo Jun.
John Spencer
John Doller
Robert Moseley
John Broughton
Richard Kirkland
Robert Stark
Richard Dukes
Thomas Young
George Galphin
James Scott
James Miller
George Boby
James Vasseks
Champness Taylor
John Sorugs
Francis Singuefield
Seth Howard
Barton Harris
Joseph Miller
Abraham Odom
John Curry
John Carter
Joshua B. Jones
John Minter
John Falk
John Henyard
Daniel McDaniel
Benjamin McKinney
LeRoy Hammond
Samuel Sakker
William Kirkland
James Barronton
William Humphreys

Vann Swearengain Junr.
Jacob Holley
William Robinson
Solomon Wood
Reuben Williams
John Cannada
Joel McClendon
Ezekiel McClendon
Reuben Taylor
John Allen
Ward Taylor
Thomas Good
William Good
William Homes
Levi Harris
Joseph Dupee
George Bussey
West Harris
Samuel Harris
John Davis
Hezekiah Odam
George Lunday
James Coursey
John Mefatrick
Timothy Rearden
John Evans
Thomas Boone
Obadiah Killcress
George Longmire
William Banks
William Coventon Senr.
Joseph Coventon
Ephraim Franklin
William Bennett
John Hammond
Charles Bussey
James Bruver
Edward Bussey
James Gray
Henry Ware
John Bennet
John Hancock
John Hill
John Day
Britton Dosson
William Murpley
Swan Rambo
Peter Guin
James Harris
Joseph Rees
Thomas Jones
Nathan Johnston
John Oliphant
Thomas Meguinas
Joseph Ronalds
Thomas Ray

John Miller
Newby Mann
Russel Bukim
Daniel Rogers
Samuel Landoum
Philip Lemar
Hezekiah Walker
Thomas Franklin
William Coventon Junr.
Robert Lemar
John Burks
Allen Henton
Archibald Offutt
John Murray
Moses Creie
James Baisdane
James White
Valentine Lynn
John Hicks
David Bowers
Jacob Shipes
John Bedingfield
John Dukes
Michael Mires
John Stare
Lud Williams
Gasper Nial
John Wise
Nathaniel Bacon
Adam Hyle
John Shentrobser
Nathaniel Howell
Daniel Shaw
John Stuzengger
Christopher Smothers
Henry Jones
Thomas Lemar (Belmount)
John Tobler
Littlebury Bostick
Thomas Lemar (Horse Creek)
Andrew Burney
Edward Rowell
David Zubly
Robert Hatcher
Abraham Spears
John Niblet
Daniel Bird
John Swearengain
John Salter
Jacob Odom
Philip Snipes
John Anderson
Benjamin Ryan
Benjamin Ryan Junr.
Edward Vann
John Ryan

Jacob Fudge
Nathan White
Isaac Foreman
Nicholas Dillard
Drury Mims
Matthew Divour
John Frazer
John Lucus
Joseph Doolittle
Archibald Cooda
Lawrence Rambo
Jeremiah Bentley
Samuel Marsh
John Mims
Thomas Roberts
Lott Waring
Angus McDaniel
Thomas Hagins
John Herndon
Jenkins Harris
John Cogburn
Christian Buckhatter
Thomas Jordan
Joseph Mark
Abraham Taylor
Michael Buckhalter
John Hog
Benjamin Moseley
John Conrad Gallman
Samuel Doolittle
Joseph Morris
John Mock
Richard Jones
Thomas Pierce
James Adams
Lewis Tilman
Frederick Tilman
John Block
Adam Sperdue
David Jester
William Moseley
Samuel Walker
John Wade
Benjamin Harry
Flud Mitchell
James Bouthe
James Thomas
Vann Swearingham Senr.
William Cogen
Harman Gallman
Thomas Sellars
Abraham Marshall
David Sigler
Matthew Devour
Peter Day
John Clockler

George Limbucker
Evan Morgan
Thomas Roberts
George Mock Senr.
John Pussell
John Roberts
Matthew Stocker
Thomas Buckham
John Morris
Benjamin Hatcher
James Foxe
Jethro Roundtree
Samuel Garner
Job Roundtree
William Davis
Joshua Groce
Thomas Evant
John Clark
Rain Chaffair
Bryan Green
Thomas Carter
Absolom Roberts
James Nipper
John Roderick
William Jones
William Hundon
James Ray
James Carson
Daniel Frazer
William Rhode
William Phillips
James Butler
Nicholas Baker
Thomas Cotton
Gosport Gallmon

LITTLE SALUDY

Solomon Pope
Lott Etheretheridge
John Argo
Edward Larimor
Thomas Green
Thomas Mosten Green
Alexander Frederick
Joseph Messer
Robert Davis
Andrew Nicholson
David Nicholson
Russel Wilson
Thomas Appleton
William West (Savannah)
Thomas Leopard
Andrew Lee

William Waring
John Pescott
Edward Couch
Lewis Watson
Michael McCartney
James Harrison
William Holston
Borris Whitel
Isaac Lewis
John Cotton
William Jones
Jacob Smith
William Clark
Richard Williams
William Barden
Howell Johnston
William Harron
Robert Melton
John Watson
Henry Heartel
Elijah Smith
Corneluis Rowe
John Mitchell
Wright Nicholson
Enoch Grigs
James Grigs
Joseph Cunningham
Jacob Fourtier
Nathaniel Melton
Thomas Welst
Michael Deloch
Burded Eskridge
John Watsman
Robert Allen
Zachariah Davis
Drivery Fortteman
William Lodge
Jesse Parten
William Norris
John Gilton
Elijah Paget
Isom Langley
Charles Partin
James Butler
Wichall Watson
Arthur Watson
John Sown
Henry Balton
Nathaniel Doby
John Dugles
John Dugles Junr.
Aaron Weaver
Smallwood Smith
Joseph Hogens
John Davis
Amos Richardson

Peter Foy
Lewis Clark
Thomas Banks
William West Junr.
Edward Blane
John Crowte
Thomas Delote Senr
Frederick Sisson
Nathaniel Powell
Silas Carter
John Saywer
John Lindley
Drury Fort Senr.
Josiah Allen
Francis Jones
John Boiole
Moses Fort
Thomas Kirkland
James Fridrick

SPARTAN DISTRICT

James Mayes
William Simpson
James Mekelvain
James Park
James Tillet
Col. John Thomas
Andrew Foster
Daniel Shaw
Samuel Thompson
Daniel Jackson
Samuel Jackson
Thomas Jackson
William Patton
William Lee
Joseph Breed
James Gibbes
John Shanes
Shanes Golightly
Moses Foster
William Ross
Jesse Conel
Hugh Means
John Thompson
Capt. Robert Faris
William Maens
Robert Harris
Edward Denny
Richard Ley
Joseph Davidson
Andrew Mayes
John Smith
Daniel Plumer
John Pinkston

Jeremiah Dutton
Giles Connel
Daniel Busk
William Simons
George Goodwin
William Plumer
Riny Below
Richard Powell
Barnet Coiler
Joseph Nisbett
William Gordon
Henry Clark
William Golightly
John Smith
Samuel Bird
Edward Bikett
John Davison
William Rodgers
Samuel Simpson
William McClelan
Philip Gibbes
John Ridingman
Joseph Buffington
Jeph Hollinsworth
Zachariah Istes
Daniel Hagton
David Coak
Charles James
Elias Hollensworth
William Tarr
James Hammett
Benjamin Mehanne
Handcock Smith
Patrick Robertson
William Wafford
Thomas Cocks
Henry Millhouse
John Hawkins
William Hawkins
Enoch Hollensworth
John Coak
Amuel Fincher
Col. William Wofford
Jonathan Parker
James Varnen
Charles Jones
John Hield
William Haild
Zachariah Stedam
Patrick Burk
Henry Travaler
George Harlin
Aaron Harlin
Col. Tho^S Fletchall
John Boggen
Thomas Ryan

Obidah Howard
Isaac Fraser
Thomas Springer
Hugh Nelson
Isaac Gregory
John Griggre
Thomas Blassingham
Benjamin Gregory
John Salter
James Hill
William Hardwick
Abner Mayes
William Hill
John Taylor
Robert Gregory
James Hawkins
William Savage
David Harris
George Linam
John Johnston
Thomas Melone
Thomas Tramel
John McPherson
Francis Possey
James Anesworth
John Goodwin
William Moore
James Martin
Jonathan Cain
William Browning
George Crossley
Evan Thomas
Richard Barrett
James Gray
Thomas Rhoden
Robert Rodgers
William Wood
Walter Homes
Thomas Smith
Avery Breed
William Bond
James Orr
James Jolley
Walter Roberts
Dudley Pruett
Jones Little
Hezekiah Gentry
Richard Anderson
Samuel Furlow
Gabriel Brown
George Little
John Little
James Benson
Gavan Gordon
William Rogers
Robert Wilson

Samuel Otterson
John Hughey
Jo^S Robinson (Gun Smith)
David Pruet
Edward McNeel
Gabriel Brown Junr.
Jacob Hammond
Michael Lee
David Hudson
Richard Crise
Jacob Powell
Jonathan Croak
Henry Long (B. Smith)
William Harmon
Benjamin Woodson
Joseph Little
William Teter
James Bogan
Joseph Bolson
Daniel Trammell
James Thomas
William Wright
Daniel Thomas
Shadrach Landtrys
Jonathan Postan
John White
Joseph Bates
Thomas Laton
James Palmer
Thomas Williams
Ellis Palmer
John Mayfield
George Earnest
John Kennedy
Joshua Laton
Edward Biddy
Philip Bryan
John Towns
Turner Roundtree
Richardson Roundtree
George Potts
William Hughes
Thomas Biddy
Jesse Vincent
John Palmer
Edward Nixon
Henry Penny
Daniel McKee
John Martin
Jesse Young
William Michel
Jacob Cooper
Thomas Green
John Hayes
Samuel McJunkin
Joseph McJunkin

Isaac Hawkins
William Tate
Jesse Tate
John Taggart
Thomas Cook
James Mayberry
Giles Dewberry
John Grindal
Joseph Collins
Moses Collins
Samuel Little John
John Scroggs
John Foster
Daniel McKissock
William Scison
Joshua Mickam
John Shipley
Charles Little John
Thomas King
Reuben Favours
Thomas Driper
Robert Coleman
William Grant
William Cain
Joel Farmer
Randel Hames
Christian Weedingman
John Bailey
John McMillen
Tobias Petteet
Peter Pettypooles
James Steen
John Portman
Daniel McClearing
John Elliott
David Hembre
Adam Potter
Lewis Aikin
Stephen Jones
James Fanning
William Steen
Elijah Wells
Charles Brandon
James Martin
David George
Nathan Grimes
Vardry McBee
Jacob Paulk
William Orr
Richard Hughes
William Sharp
Esquire Brown
Robert Smith
Joseph Jolley
William Morgan
Edward Insco

William Kennedy
Richard Addis
Alexander McDoogle
John Campbell
James Moorhead
John Townsend
James Parnell
John Pearson
Robert Bishop
James Campbell
Richd Brandon
John Brandon
Thomas Brandon
Adam McCord
William Clark
John Chandler
William Coleman
Richard Hawkins
William McRun
William Jolley
Abner Coleman
William Spears
Samuel Smith
John Jones
Charles Thomas
Peter Howard
Gabriel Patrick
Nicholas Curry
William Smith
Jacob Green
John Heany
Robert Moore
Hugh Moore
Patrick Moore
William Sanders
John Moorhead
William Welkin
Christopher Colleman
Nathaniel Jefferies
Robert Nelton
Hugh Warren
Henry Twitty
David Allen
Henry Clark
Curtis Caldwell
James Johnston
Adam Goudalock
James Philips
William Jones

Thos Wilfor (Wilton?)
Francis McLemarr
Peter Patterson
Thomas Dean
Zach^r Bullock
John Anderson
George Marchbanks
Lawrence Eastwood
John Hope
John Prichard
William Marchbanks
Hugh Queen
Nathl Robinson
Jonathan Gilky
John Johnston
William Saffold Senr.
James Fordren
Zacharias Gibbs
Joseph Buckfield
George Turner
Edmond Kennedy
William Barns
John Journey
Joseph Jolley
John Moseley
Richard Kelly
James Brown
John Liles
Isaac Parker
William Gillam
John Nuckols
Matthew Robinson
Peter Akin
Hugh Horton
Moses Qualls
George Bayley
John Thompson
Francis Lattimer
John Davison
John Cunningham
John Steen
Littleton Mapp
Joseph Guyton
John McWhortie
George McWhortie
Ely Cooke
John Wilson
Nathan Hawkins
John Clark

A LIST OF SPECIAL JURYMEN

William Anderson
James Moore
William Moore
John Bulloch
Robert Merrweather
Armstrong Heard
Joseph Wardlaw
Thomas Wilson
William Meriweather
John Moore
John Bostick
John Gentry
Samuel Ramsy
Matthew McMillan
James McMillan
Richard Moore
Benjamin Durbrough
Robert Dickey
Hector Dickey
Culbert Anderson
James Anderson
Thomas Fauguhere
Thomas Keeling Smith
James Harkins
Robert Thomson
William Wilson
William Robinson
Joseph Burton

William Freeman
James Wilson
John Wardlaw
James Homes
Isham Green
John Brown
William Johnson
William Bean
Henry Jeveley
James Edwards
Andrew Colwell
James Murray
Hugh Akins
John Eakins
Timothy McKinney
Roger McKinny
James Murphy
Stephen Anderson
McKernus Goode
John Wardlaw
John Moore (Rockey Creek)
Field Perdue
Hugh Douglass
William Holloday
William Haigwood
John Bell
Samuel Dwhitt

RATIFIED BY THE GENERAL ASSEMBLY
IN THE SENATE-HOUSE THE 20TH DAY OF FEBRUARY 1779
CH. PINCKNEY PRESID^T OF THE SENATE
JNO. MATHEWS SPEAKER OF THE HOUSE OF REPRESENTATIVES

AN ORDINANCE for appointing a new Jury List for the District of Ninety-Si:
and to empower and direct the Judges out of the same to draw a Grand an
petit Jury to serve at the next Court of General Sessions to be holden fo:
the said District next after the passing of this Ordinance, and for othe:
purposes therein mentioned.

(No. 2)

20th February 1779

Editor's Note: This notation follows:

leave out the names   1124
                       Cooper 1123

INDEX

AARON, Solomon 9, 23.
ABERCROMBIE, Jas. 82, 94; Jno. 9, 23, 79, 96.
ABERHART, Jno. 71.
ABERNATHEY, ABERNATHY, Jas. 79, 96; Jno. 97.
ABLE, Jno. 85; Jos. 83.
ABNEY, Dennet 77, 87; Nath. 77, 88, Paul 88; Saml. 88; Wm. 77, 88.
ABRAHAM, Emanuel 9, 23.
ADAIR, Benj. 92; Jas. 92 (2), 93; Jno. 92; Jos. 81, 93; Robt. 86, 87; Wm. 55, 92.
ADAMS, Alex. 54; David 8, 19, 61, 62; Fran. 56; Geo. 97; Godfrey 57; Jas. 57, 77, 81, 89, 99; Joel 53; Jno. 8, 19, 77, 89; Rich. 53, 61, 62; Robt. 58; Thos. 56; Wm. 56, 57, 61, 62; Wm. Jr. 61, 62; Willoughby 48.
ADAMSON, Alex. 9, 23; Jno. 44, 59.
ADARION, David 58.
ADDISON, Thos. 7, 17, 49; Wm. 51.
ADDIS, Rich. 103.
ADEY, Jas. 72.
ADKINS, Jos. 95; Saml. 46.
AIKISON, Shadrack 43.
AGGNEW, AGNEW, And. 61, 62, 65; Jno. 50; Saml. 86.
AIKEN, Lewis 102.
AIKENS, Robt. 42.
AIKINS, Jno. 41.
AINGER, Jos. 61, 63.
AKEMAN, Stephen 8, 20.
AKERIDGE, Jno. 70.
AKIN, Jas. 7; Peter 103; Thos. 18, 52.
AKINS, Hugh 88, 104; Jno. 88.
ALBERGOTTIE, Anthony 61, 62, 65.
ALCORN, ALLCORN, Jas. 57; Robt. 51.
ALDRIDGE, Wm. 51.
ALEXANDER, Alex. 3, 9, 23; Jas. 76, 84; Robt. 60.
ALFORD, Jas. 35.
ALIS, Robt. 87.
ALLEN, ALLIN, David 103, Jno. 49, 98; Josiah 81, 100, Robt. 81, 85, 100; Sherwood 93.
ALLISON, ALLESON, And. 45; Hugh 56; Jas. 38, 92, 94; Jno. 46; Jos. 42; Rich. 77, 88.
ALLRAN, ALRAN, Jno. 40, 41.
AILSTON, ALLSTONE, Fran. 29, 33; Jno. 29, 32, 38, 45; Jno. Jr. 29, 33; Jos. 29, 34; Peter 40, 41, Wm. 29, 33, Wm. Jr. 29, 33; Wm. Sr. 30, 33.
ALQUIER, Abraham 43.
AMAKER, Jac. 67, 69; Jno. 67, 69.
AMMON, Thom. 42.
AMMONET, Chas. 47.
ANCRUM, Geo. 66, 68; Geo. Jr. 9, 23; Wm. 3, 9, 23.
ANDERSON, Abel 78, 91, Abraham 91; Alex. 29, 32; And. 93; Benj. 91; Cornelius 55; Culbert 77, 87, 104; Geo. 90, 95; Henry 91; Hugh 22; Jacob 34; Jas. 3, 9, 23, 45, 83, 87, 104; Jno. 45, 58, 76, 80, 83, 90, 98, 103; Levy 96; Rich. 49, 101; Robt. 76, 84; Saml. 77, 89; Stephen 78, 88, 104; Thos. 77, 87; Timothy 56; Wm. 22, 35, 48, 52, 79, 88, 95, 96, 104.
ANDREW, ANDREWS, Jno. 40 (2); Saml. 60.
ANESWORTH, Jas. 79, 101.
ANSMENGER, ANSMINGER, Chrisr. 52, Peter 53.
ANTHONY, John 9, 23, 52.
APPLETON, Thos. 81, 99.
ARGO, Jno. 99.
ARINGTON, Wm. 92.
ARMOR, ARMOUR, And. 59, Jas. 57.
ARMSTRONG, James 45, 53, 57, 58 (3), 96; Jno. 20, 45, 53, 57; Saml. 50.
ARNET, Alex. 37; Jno. 37.
ARNOLD, Geo. 91.
ARRANT, Conrad 50.
ARTHUR, Geo. 6, 15; Nath. 15; Wm. 66, 72.
ASH, Jno. 21; Rich. Russell 61, 62; Robt. 59; Saml. 3, 9, 23.

ASHBY, Anthony 18; Thos. 7, 18.
ASKEW, Jas. 9, 23.
ASKINS, Hugh 35.
ASPENAL, Wm. 90.
ASTELEW, Jas. 70.
ATKINS, ATKIN, Benj. 90; Chas. 3, 9, 23; Fran. 90; Jas. 18; John 90.
ATKINSON, Fred. 47; Jas. 44; Jos. 3, 9, 23; Major 50.
ATMORE, Ralph 9, 23.
ATWELL, Ichabod 3, 9, 23.
AUGLAY, And. 64.
AUDEBERT, Jno. 64.
AUSTIN, Robt. 9, 23.
AUTING, Jno. 17.
AVANT, Jonathan 34; Joshua 30, 33.
AVERIT, Bright 51.
AXON, Wm. 16.
AXSON, Jacob 17; Wm. 9, 23.
AYERS, Thos. 40, 41.
BABB, Wm. 50.
BACKLEY, Garton 64.
BACON, Nath. 98.
BACOT, BACOOAT, Peter 3, 10, 23; Saml. 40, 41.
BADDELEY, Jno. 3, 9, 23.
BADGER, Jos. 10, 23.
BADJEAW, Nicholas 83.
BAGLEY, Wm. 97.
BAGNELL, Ebenezer 47.
BAILEY, BAYLE, BEALY, BAILY, BAYLEY, Fran. 10, 23; Geo. 103; Jno. 22, 83, 87, 102; Peter 83; Ralph 19.
BAIRD, David 51.
BAISDON, BAISDANE, Jas. 80, 98.
BAKER, Aaron 32, 38; Benj. 3, 10, 23; Danl. 51; Elijah 86; Elisha 86; Fran. 3; Jesse 17; Jno. 3, 10, 23, 49, 56; Nich. 99; Peter 49; Rich. Bohun 7, 17; Samp. 36; Wm. 34.
BALANTINE, Jas. 3, 10, 23.
BALDWIN, Thos. 3, 10, 23.
BALFOUR (SEE BELFOUR), Jno. 40.
BALL, Elias 9, 22; Elias Jr. 6, 16; Jos. 10, 23; Mark 87; Rich. 58.
BALLARD, Jesse 33.
BALLOW, Thos. 29, 32.
BALOTE, Jno. 83; Peter Elie 83.
BALTON, Henry 81, 100.
BANBURY, Wm. 3, 10, 23.
BANKS, Rivers 85; Thos. 100; Wm. 98.
BANSEY, Nich. 91.
BAPTISTERE, Jno. 95.
BARBA, Casper 68.
BARBER, Jas. 51; Jos. 51; Saml. 54.
BARDEN, BARDIN, Ancell 95; Jno. 48; Wm. 47,
BARE, Jacob 68; Jas. 37; Jno. 69.
BARFIELD, Joshua 35.
BARKER, Jacob 55; Jno. 67.
BARKSDALE, Geo. 6, 15, 61, 62, 65; Jno. 76, 86; Nathan 81, 92; Thos. 6, 15, 76, 85; Wm. 81, 92.
BARLAND, Wm. 42.
BARLOW, Jno. 89.
BARNARD, Noble 38.
BARNETT, BARNET, Elisha 9, 22, Humpy. 49; James 55; Jno. 9, 22; Saml. 57; Wm. 55.
BARNES, BARNS, Barnard 96; Isaac 22; Jno. 30, 36; Wm. 61 62, 103.
BARNWELL, Jno. Bernard 61, 62, 65; Jno. Jr. 61, 62; Jno.Sr.61,62; Nath. 65; Nath. Jr. 61, 62.
BAROK, Geo. 68.
BARR, Isaac 55; Thos. 56.
BARRELL, Jno. 67.
BARREN, Archd. 57; Jas. 58; Jno. 56; Thos. 57.
BARRETT, Rich. 101.
BARRON, BARRAN, Jas. 34; Wm. 43.
BARRONTON, Jas. 97.
BARROW, Wm. 46.

105

BARST, Geo. 66.
BARTLESON, Jno. 91.
BARTON, Jos. 93; Thos. 6, 15; Wm. 30, 36, 56.
BASKETFIELD, Jno. 22.
BASKINS, BASKENS, And. 47; Wm. 76, 84.
BATES, Isaac 35; Jos. 102.
BATHY, Wm. 30, 33.
BATOON, BATTOON, Isaac 8, 19.
BATT, Sampson 65.
BATTEY, BATTY, BATEY, David 8, 19, 92.
BATY, Saml. 20.
BAUCKNACHT, Geo. 72.
BAUGH, Wm. 92.
BAXTER, Chas. 43; Jas. 32, 38, Jno. 30, 32, 33; Jno. Jr. 38; Robt. 31, 38.
BAYER, Mich. 72.
BAYLE, SEE BAILEY.
BAYS, Jno. 78, 95.
BAZAQUIE, Jno. 64.
BEAL, BEALE, Jno. 3, 10, 23.
BEALY, SEE BAILEY.
BEAM, BEAMS, Alex. 90; Jas. 71.
BEAN, William 77, 88, 104.
BEARD, Adam 56; Hugh 50; Jas. 58; Jno. 79, 96; Jonas 66, 72; Robt. 3, 9, 23; Thos. 95; Wm. 55, 95.
BEARFEET, Wm. 34.
BEARFIELD, Chas. 38.
BEATY, BATEY, David 92, Saml. 8, Thos. 86.
BECKETT, Jas. 19.
BEDINGFIELD, Jno. 80, 98.
BEDON, Daniel 18.
BEE, Jos. 3, 9, 10, 21, 23; Mo. 73; Thos. 3, 10, 23, 72; Wm. 21.
BEEGLER, Henry 67; Martin 67.
BEEKMAN, Barnard 3, 9, 23; Saml. 3, 10, 23.
BEELER, BEILER, Jos. 10, 23.
BEELS, Jno. 87.
BEGUM, Jas. 52.
BEIGLEY, Thos. 72.
BELARD, Jacob 83.
BELFOUR, SEE BALFOUR, Jno. 41, 43.
BELIN, Peter 29, 32.
BELK, Jno. 56.
BELL, Ebenezer 58; Geo. 21, 54; Jas. 29, 32; Jas. Jr. 34; Jno. 86, 104; Jno. Jr. 51; Jno. Sr. 51; Jos. 18, 70; Rich. 53; Robt. 34; Saml. 21; Thos. 30, 33, 62; Valentine 53; Wm. 41, 59.
BELLAMY, Jno. 30, 33; Wm. 21.
BELLARD, Jesse 38.
BELLENGAIL, BELLINGALL, Robt. 8, 19.
BELLENGER, BELLINGER, Edmond 18, Edmond Jr. 8, 20; Jno. 8, 20.
BELLUNE, Jno. 34; Mich. 30, 33; Wm. 30, 33.
BELOW, Riney 79, 101.
BELTON, BELTAN, Abraham 46, 59; Jno. 44, Jonathan 59; Robt. 46; Sam 49.
BENBOW, Evan 48; Rich. 48.
BENBRIDGE, Henry 10, 23.
BENECAR, Jno. 66.
BENFIELD, Jno. 3, 9, 23.
BENNEA, John 68.
BENNETT, BENNET, Ed. 53; Hugh 45; Jas. 47; Jno. 22, 98; Mathew 45; Saml. Jr. 44; Thos. 10, 23; Wm. 15, 18, 48, 98.
BENNY, BENNIE, Wm. 10, 23.
BENOIST, Chas. 66, 72; Peter 16.
BENSON, Jas. 101; Jno. 43; Wm. 29, 32, 87.
BENTHAM, Jas. 3, 10, 23.
BENTON, Lazarus 93; Saml. 40, 41.
BENTLEY, Jeremiah 99.
BERAUD, Matthew 83.
BERKLEY, Jno. 21, Matthew 49.

BERRY, And. 35; Hugh 58; Jno. 77, 88; Rich. 69; Robt. 69; Thos. 77, 88; William 59, 82, 94.
BERT, Jno. 83.
BERWICK, Jno. 3, 10, 23.
BETTIE, Jas. 47, 60.
BETTIS, Fran. 49.
BEVERLEY, Benj. 42.
BIDDAL, Jno. 50.
BIDDY, Edward 102; Thos. 102.
BIERLY, Gaspar 50.
BIERS, SEE BYERS
BIGEM, HIGGEM, Jas. 38, 52.
BIGGER, Jos. 59; Matthew 59.
BIGLEY, Jacob 66, 72.
BIKETT, Edward 101.
BIRD, Daniel 98, Edward 34; Geo. 48; Saml. 101; Sutton 48.
BISHOP, Abner 93; Henry 54; Jno. 20, 58; Jos. 54; Nich^s 54; Robt 103; Saml. 92; Wm. 41.
BLACK, Jas. 61, 62, 65; Jno. 22; Jos. 57; Michael 9, 23; Peter 91; Robt 59, 84; Robt. Sr. 56, Saml. 84; Thos. 16. 58, 89; Wm. 84.
BLACKBURN, Daniel 95; Wm. 95.
BLACKENHORN, Henry 9, 23.
BLACKLEDGE, Zachariah 17.
BLACKLEY, BLACKLY, Jas. 31, 93, Jas. Jr. 31; Jno. 93; Thos. 93.
BLACKWELL, Chas. 89; Thos. 35.
BLACKWOOD, Jos. 84.
BLAIR, Geo. 89; Jas. 54; Robt 40, 41; Wm. 89.
BLAKE, Edward 3, 10, 23; John 22, 52; Rich. 22.
BLAKELEY, Chambers 89; Jas. 36; Jas. Jr. 37.
BLAKENEY, Jno. 40, 41.
BLAKNEY, David 89.
BLANCHARD, Benj. 52; Henry 44.
BLAND, Lancelot 61, 62.
BLANE, Edward 81, 100.
BLANKENHORN, Henry 23.
BLANTON, Jno. 53, 60.
BLASSINGHAM, Jas. 42; Thos. 79, 101; Wm. 40, 41.
BLENCO, Saml. 20.
BLESS, Henry 47.
BLOCK, Jno. 99.
BLOTT, Jno. 10, 23.
BLUNDELL, Nath. 3, 10, 23.
BLUNT, Thos. 34.
BOATWRIGHT, Jesse 34; Lewis 30, 33; Thos. 41.
BOBY, Geo. 97.
BOCQUET, Peter Jr. 3, 10, 23.
BOCHETTE, Lewis 29, 32.
BOCTER, David 57, Nath. 57.
BOGGAN, BOGGEN, BOGAN, Jas. 102, Jno. 79, 101.
BOGGS, BOGS, Jas. 59; Jno. 83; Robt 83; Saml. 85.
BOILLATE, BOILLATT, David 10, 23.
BOINEAU, Mich. 9, 22; Mich. Jr. 22.
BOIOLE, Jno. 100.
BOLDRIDGE, Jas. 66, 68.
BOLE, Jno. 84.
BOLLOUGH, Jas. 15; Jno. 15; Moses 19.
BOLSON, Jos. 102.
BOLTON, Allen 15.
BOLZIGER, Jno 67, 69, 73.
BOMAN, Wm. 86.
BONA, Lewis 62.
BOND, Abraham 34; Chas 34; Geo. Paddon 6, 15; Lewis 61; Moses 52; Robt. 84; Thos. 53; Wm. 46, 59, 101.

BONETE, Wm. 69.
BONHOIST, Wm. 15.
BONKOST, Jacob 22.
BONNEAU, Anthony 29, 32, 38; Josiah 3, 10, 23; Saml. 6, 16; Stephen 49.
BONNIOTT, BOUNIOTT, Jno. 10, 23.
BONSAL, BONSALL, BONSELL, Jno. 3, 10; Saml. 3; Wm. 19.
BONSAT, Jno. 23.
BOOKER, Jno. 65.
BOOKLESS, Henry 9, 23.
BOOMER, Jacob 3, 9, 23; Jno. 3, 9, 23.
BOON, BOONE, Capers 9, 22; Jno. 15; Saml. 52; Thos. 9, 98; Thos. Jr. 30, 36; Thos. Sr. 22; Wm. 7, 18, 37, 61, 62.
BOOZARD, SEE BUSSERD
BOOZER, Ulrick 71.
BORACNE, Peter 83.
BOSTICK, BORTICK, Jno. 87, 104; Little Berry 80, 98.
BOSTWICK, Jno. 47.
BOTNER, Lewis 51.
BOUCHETT, Peter 18.
BOUCHILLON, Jos. 86.
BOUGH, Leonard 71.
BOUGHMAN, Anthony 71.
BOULAND, Wm. 81, 92.
BOUMGARTNER, Conrad 69.
BOUNER, James 83.
BOUNETHEAU, Peter 3, 9, 23.
BOUNIOTT, SEE BONNIOTT
BOURDEAUX, Daniel 3, 9, 23; Jas. 48.
BOURQUIN, Jno. Lewis 62, 64.
BOURKE, Thos. 10, 23.
BOUTETON, BOUTITON, Peter 3, 9, 23.
BOUTHE, Jas. 99.
BOWEN, Jno. 3, 9, 23.
BOWERE, BOWER, David 80, 98; Patrick 61, 63; Philip 17, 21.
BOWIE, Jno 77, 87.
BOWLER, Jacob 10, 23; Jno. 8, 20; Wm. 8, 20.
BOWLIN, Abel 96; Jno. 96.
BOWMAN, Jacob 97, Jas. 47, Mathew 47, Robt. 47.
BOX, Jno. 94; Jos. 82, 94; Thos. 17.
BOYAKIN, Saml. 71.
BOYCE, Thos. 96.
BOYER, Adam 89.
BOYD, Andrew 56; David 52; Henry 16; Hugh 96; Jas. 82, 93; Jno. 45, 93, Robt. 84; Wm. 52, 54, 83, 87, 95.
BOYKIN, Burwell 44, 59; Saml. 44; Will 60; Wm. 44.
BRABANT, Daniel 61, 62.
BRACEY, Wm. 48.
BRADBURY, Francis 62, 64.
BRADEN, BREDEN, James 49, 87.
BRADFORD, Jno. 48; Nath. 47; Saml. 49; Thos. 48.
BRADLEY, Arthur 31, 37; Jas. 44; Jas. Jr. 31, 37; Jno. 34; Jos. 53; Mathew 48; Roger 48; Saml. 44; Thos. 48.
BRADWELL, Isaac 7, 16; Jno. 17; Nath. 7, 17; Nath. Jr. 17.
BRAILSFORD, Jno. 3, 8, 10, 21, 23; Jos. 62, 64; Robt. 3, 9, 23.
BRAMBLET, Wm. 81, 93.
BRANAN, Alex. 87.
BRANDON, Chas. 102; Jno. 103; Rich. 103; Thos 103.
BRANTON, Henry 16.
BRASWELL, Jos. 70.
BRATTON, Thos. 58, 59; Wm. 46.
BRAWFORD, Jno. 83; Moses 83.
BRAWN, Wm. 56.

BRAZEL, BRASEL, David 78, 89.
BREALER, Abraham 65.
BREASEAL, BRASEL, David 77, Willes 85; Willis 76.
BREDEN, SEE BRADEN.
BREED, Avery 101; Jos. 100.
BREESON, Jno. 58.
BREMAR, Francis 3, 9, 23.
BERKLEY, Mathew 49.
BRESHAR, Arthur 93.
BREWER, Jas. 98; Wm. 50.
BREZINA, Francis 71.
BRIAN, SEE BRYAN.
BRIANT, BRIENT - SEE BRYANT
BRICKEN, Jas. 10, 23.
BRICKET, Mathias 19.
BRIDGES, Jas. 56; Thos. 57; Wm. 19.
BRIDGWAY, Hope 48.
BRIERS, Lazarus 20.
BRIGGS, BRIGS, Federick 71, Wm. 93.
BRINDLEY, Frederick 16; Jno. Geo. 16.
BRINSON, Mathew Sr. 34.
BRISBANE, Jas. 62, 64; Wm. 62, 64.
BRISON, SEE BRYSON.
BRITTON, Fran. 30, 36; Henry 30, 33; Jos. 34; Philip 31, 36; Philip Jr. 31, 36; Stephen 38 Wm. 30, 33.
BROADHEAD, Thos. 88.
BROCK, Patrick 47.
BROCKINGTON, BROCKINTON, Jno. 30, 38, 40; Jno. Jr. 41; Rich. 30, 35.
BROOKER, Jno. 70.
BROOKS, Elisha 88; Jacob 78, 90; Rich. 29, 32, 38, 95; Thos. 61, 62, 91.
BROTHERS, Jno. 17.
BROUGHTON, Andrew Jr. 16; Edward 47; Jno. 97; Nath. 6, 16; Rich. 16; Thos. 16; Thos. Jr. 6, 16.
BROWER, Jermiah 18.
BROWN, _____ 53; Alex. 55; Bartled 71; Bartlett Jr. 70; Burrell 48; Casper 66, 68; Chas. 61 63; Christopher 33; Clement 40, 41; Coleman 82, 94; Esquire 102; Fran. 77, 88; Gabriel 101; Gabriel Jr. 102, Geo. 16, 29, 32; Henry 51; Hugh 67; Jas. 35, 44, 53, 55, 60, 103; Jas. Jr. 67; Jeremiah 42, 43; Jno. 46, 49, 53, 54, 78, 82, 88, 91, 94, 104; Jonathan 40, 41; Jos. 29, 32, 38, 54; Levi 43; Moses 31, 35; Nicholas 92; Rich. 45; Robt. 29, 32 48, 59, 62, 65; Saml. 30, 33, 42, 85; Spill C. 93; Stephen 29, 32; Thos. 42, 52; Wm. 38 48, 77, 87.
BROWNING, Wm. 101.
BRUCE, Alex. 10, 23; David 3, 10, 23; Donald 67, 69, 73.
BRUMMETT, Will 46.
BRUNER, BRUVER, Jas. 98; Jno. 17; Wm. 69.
BRUNES, Felix 17.
BRUNSON, BRUNSUN, Chas. 47; David Sr. 49; Isaac Jr. 48, Isaac Sr. 48; Jas. 48; Jos. 47; Mathew 48; Moses 48.
BRYAN, BRIAN, Jas. 3, 9, 23; Jno. 10; Jonathan 62,64; Philip 102.
BRYANT, BRIANT, BRIENT, Federick 70; Lewis L. 49; Wm. 70.
BRYSON, BRISON, Hugh 56; Jas. 96; Wm. 93.
BUCHE, Jno. 62, 64; Jno. Lewis 62, 64.
BUCHANAN, BUCHANNAN, Alex. 29, 32; Jas. 19; Jno. 29, 32, 78, 87, 90; Wm. 90.
BUCKALEU, Rich. 88.
BUCKALIE, Rich. 77.
BUCKALVE, Garret 88.
BUCKEND, Adam 69.

BUCKFIELD, Jos. 103.
BUCKHALTER, BUCKHATTER, Christian 99, Michael 81, 99.
BUCKHAM, Thos. 99.
BUCKHOLTS, Abra. 30, 33; Jac. 38; Peter 34.
BUCKLE, Thos. 3, 10, 23.
BUCKLER, Esekiel 22.
BUERGERT, Geo. 71.
BUFFINGTON, Jos. 79, 101.
BUFORD, Wm. 22.
BUGHTER, Jacob 72.
BUKIM, Russel 98.
BULL, Henry 67; Jno. 61, 62, 65; Stephen 61, 63; Wm. Jr. 6, 16.
BULLIN, Nathaniel 67.
BULLOCK, Jno. 77, 87, 104; Nath. 77, 87; Saml. 17; Zachariah 80, 103.
BURCH, Jos. 31, 38.
BURCHALL, Thos. 18.
BURCHMORE, Will. 47.
BURDELL, Jno. 66, 68.
BURDEN, Kensey 21; Thos. 79, 94.
BURGE, Rich. 50.
BURGER, David 10, 23.
BURGESS, Jac. 69; Jno. 45; Wm. 17, 79, 94, 96.
BURKERD, Jacob 72.
BURKMIRE, Chas. 10, 23.
BURKS, BURK, Jno. 98; Patrick 101.
BURLINE, Jos. 68.
BURNET, BURNETT, Rich. 49; Saml. 44.
BURNEY, Andrew 80, 98.
BURNHAM, Thos. 33, 38.
BURNS, Jas. 95; Laird 54; Saml. 56.
BURNSIDES, Alex. 49; Jas. 79, 94.
BURROWS, Arthur 31, 36; Geo. 31; Geo. Jr. 31, 36; Geo. Sr. 36; Jno. 31, 36; Rich. 34; Wm. 10, 23.
BURTON, Benj. 95; Jos. 78, 88, 104; Wm. 97.
BURY, John 10, 23.
BUSBY, Miles 50.
BUSH, Abra. 19 (2); Danl. 79; Isaac 67, 71; John 3, 9, 23, 70.
BUSK, Daniel 101.
BUSSERD, BOOZARD, Henry 69; Jacob 91; Jno. 91; Roddy 91.
BUSSEY, Chas. 98; Edward 98; Geo. 98.
BUTLER, Henry 96; Jas. 81, 99, 100; Jas. Henry 3, 9, 23, Major Pierce 62, 64; Pierce 10, 23; Saml. 10, 23; Thos. 17, 29, 33, 77, 89.
BUXTON, Jacob 67, 71.
BYERS, HIERS, David 59; Saml. 58; Wm. 44, 46, 58.
BYRD, Jno. 7, 17.
CABORNE, Robert 8, 20.
CADWORTH, Benjamin 24.
CAHOON, Geo. 10, 24.
CAHUSAE?, CAUHUSAC, Daneil 9, 22.
CAIN, Jas. 85; Jas. Jr. 85; Jno. 57; Jonathan 79, 101, Wm. 102.
CALDWELL, Andrew 77, Curtis 80, 103; Henry 10, 23; Jas. 76, 84; Jno. 66, 68, 95, 96; Major Jno. 78; Jno. Sr. 79; Jos. 90; Robt. 71, William 71.
CALHOUN, Jas. 86; Jno. 86; Jno. Ewing 76, 83; Jos. 76, 85; Patrick 76, 86; Wm. 76, 83.
CALLAHAN, CALLEHAN, Danl. 36; Jno. 3, 10, 24.
CALP, Jas. 58.
CALVERT, Jno. 3, 10, 24.
CAMBRIDGE, Tobias 10, 24.
CAMERON, Wm. 10, 24.
CAMP, Moses 57.
CAMPBELL, CAMPBLE, CAMPLE, Andrew 57; Angus 79, 94; Archibald 31, 37; Benj. 66, 68;
David 20, 35; Hugh 20; Jas. 57, 77, 87, 1(Jesse 76, 85; Jno. 54, 80, 85, 90, 93, 10; Jos. 95, 96; McCartan 3, 10, 24; Wm. 31, ; 94, 96.
CAMRON, Thomas 52.
CANMORE, James 51.
CANNADY, CANNADA, CANNEDY, CANEDY, Alex. 59; John 98; Soloman 69; Wm. 77, 87.
CANNAMER, Jacob 55.
CANNON, Daniel 3, 10, 24; Ephraim 78, 91; Jno. 70, 91; Robt. 70; Saml. 95; Wm. 76, 8
CANTSLER, John 57.
CANTEY, CANTY, Chas. 9, 22, 47; Jno. Jr. 44; Joseph 44.
CAPE, Brian or Bryan 3, 10, 24.
CAPERS, Chas. 61, 62; Gabriel 6, 15; Geo. Sinclare 15; Rich. 62; William 10, 24.
CAPLAND, George 93.
CAPPOCK, Jno. 85; Jos. 85.
CARGILL, CARGELL, Cornelius 82, 93; Magnus 40, 41, 43.
CARIDINE, Abraham 89.
CARISLE, Francis 84.
CARMICHAEL, Danl. 83; Jas. 69, 73; Jos. 84.
CARMON, John 90.
CARN, Robert 56.
CARR, Edmon 35; Edmond 30; Wm. 65.
CARRELL, CARELL, Jacob 52; Joseph 46.
CARROLL, Jno. 59; Rich. 94.
CARRITHERS, CARRETHERS, Jas. 84; Matthew 86; Robt. 86.
CARRON, Laurence 55.
CARSON, GARSAN, Chas. 88; Jas. 59, 81, 88, 99; Jno. 52, 54; Jos. 84; Saml. 84; Walter 58; Wm. 49, 76, 83.
CARTER, Benj. 52, 96; Geo. 21, 78, 96; Henery 52; Jacob 21, 54; Jacob Sr. 52; Jas. 48, 7(85; Jno. 80, 95, 96, 97; Jos. 97; Mathew Sr 48; Robt. 44, 76, 85, 95; Silas 100; Thos. 96, 99; Wm. 20, 41.
CARTHEDGE, John 43.
CARTWRIGHT, Jos. 10, 23.
CARY, Benj. 64; Jas. 44, 59; Nath. 44, 59.
CASEY, Abner 79, 95.
CASKEY, Jno. 55.
CASKIN, Jno. 19.
CASS, Jno. 47.
CASSELLS, Benj. 48; Henry 44; Henry Jr. 48; Jas. 30, 33; Wm. 48.
CASSITY, Thos. 44.
CASTLE, Jas. 79, 96.
CASTLELOW, CASTLELEW, Thos. 67, 71.
CASTON, Glass 56; Wm. 55.
CATER, Stephan 7, 16; Thos. 62, 65.
CATON, Jno. 17, Thos. 17.
CATTEL, Benj. 3, 10, 24; Robt. 7, 17; Wm. 3, 10, 24.
CAUHUSAC - SEE CAHUSEA
CAUSART, Archd. 55; Rich. 45.
CAVANEAU, CAVANA, James 8, 20.
CENTAR, Nathan 46.
CHADWICK, Jonathan 38.
CHAFTAIR, CHAFFAIR, Rain 81, 99.
CHALMERS, Gilbert 24.
CHAMBERLAIN, Hubart 20.
CHAMBERS, Gilbert 10; Jno. 3, 10, 23, 59; Jos. 8, 20.
CHANDLER, CHANDLOR, Daniel 90; Geo. 48; Jas. 90; Joel 90; Jno. 92, 103; Jos. 43; Saml. 48; Shadrach 90; Wm. 91.
CHANEY, Bailley 77, 88; Geo. 77, 88; Jas. 77, 88; Jas. Jr. 88; Jno. 77, 88; Wm. 88.
CHANNIN, Jeremiah 71.

CHAPMAN, Chas. 21; Dus 21; Jno. 50; Levi 37; Wm. 18.
CHAPLIN, Jno. 61, 62; Thos. 61, 62; Wm. 61, 62.
CHAPPEL, CHAPPLE, CHAPPELL, CHAPLE, Benj. 20; Henry 45; Jas. 22, 86.
CHARLTON, Thomas 44, 60.
CHARNAHOON, Jno. 58.
CHAUVET, Moses 10, 23.
CHAVAS, CHEVAS, CHAVES, Alex. 76, 86, Thos. 86.
CHERRY, CHERI, Geo. 42, 55; Joshua 51.
CHESNUT, CHESNUTT, Jno. 44, 60, 72; Saml. 55.
CHESTER, David 83.
CHIFFELLE, Philotheos 3, 10, 24.
CHINNERS, John 18.
CHILDERS, Creed 46, 59; David 92.
CHISHOLM, Jno. 44, 62, 65.
CHISOLME, Alex. 3, 10, 24; Wm. 21.
CHITTEH, Richard 20.
CHOVIN, Alex. 31, 37; Chas. 18.
CHRISTIE, James 21.
CIMBERT, John 58.
CLAMM, Geo. Wm. 70.
CLANDENOR, Thos. 59.
CLANTEN, CLANTON, David 50, Rich. 49.
CLAREY, CLARY, Daniel 90, Ethildred 41; Robt. 40, 41.
CLARK, CLARKE, Alex. 86; Alston 49; Bartley 32, 38; Henry 35 (2), 40, 41, 44, 79, 101, 103; Jas. 8, 19; Jno. 49, 80, 81, 91, 99, 103; Jonah 29, 33; Joseph 57 (2); Lewis 100; Malcolm 66, 68; Sampson 10, 23; Thos. 17, 96; Wm. 49, 54, 86, 100, 103.
CLARKSON, Levinus 3, 10, 23.
CLATTON, Jno 67, 69, 71.
CLEGG, Saml. 29, 33.
CLEMENTS, Jno. 3, 10, 23.
CLIME, Martin 3, 10, 24.
CLING, Geo. 20.
CLINTON, Jas. 57.
CLOCKLER, Jno. 81, 99.
CLOSK, Jos. 88.
CLOUD, Wm. 51.
CLYATT, Stephen 34.
COACHMAN, Benj. 6, 16; Benj. Jr. 7, 17; Jas. 29, 33; Wm. Pools 29, 32.
COAK, David 101; John 101.
COAKER, SEE COKER
COALE, John 91.
COATS, Chas. 90; Jno. 90, 91; Jos. 50; Marmaduke 90.
COBB, COBBS, Jno 77, 87; Saml. 94.
COHIA, Francis 10, 24, Michael 21.
COBURN, John 47.
COCKFIELD, Josiah 36.
COCKLERUS, Joboll 57.
COCKRILL, Moses 55.
COCKRAN, COCHRAN, Andrew 85; Jno. 20, 85; Robt. 3, 10, 24, 49; Thos 7, 17.
COCKS, Thos. 101.
COFFEE, Henry 56, Jno. 56.
COFFER, Thos. 86.
COGBURN, Jno. 99.
COGDELL, Jno. 29, 32, 38.
COGEN, Wm. 99.
COHEN, Isaac 10, 23; Jacob 10, 24; Moses 10, 23.
COIL, Patrick 18.
COILER, Barnet 79, 101.
COKER, COAKER, Jos. 93; Thos 10, 24, 42.
COLANY, Edward 90.
COLCOCK, Jno. 3, 10, 24.
COLCOTE, Henry 38.
COLDING, Blanchard 70, Saml. 70.

COLE, Jno. 97; Rich. 3, 10, 24; Wm. 31, 36.
COLEMAN, COLLEMAN, COLMAN, Abner 103; Christ. 80, 103; Frnac. 51; Jno. 38; Robt. 80, 102; Wm. 80, 103.
COLLAR, Benedink 69.
COLLIER, Benj. 97.
COLLINS, Adam 91; Chas. 66, 68; Hezik 57; Isaac 57; Jos. 57, 102; Joshua 55; Moses 70, 102; Robt. 18; Wm. 51 (2).
COLLINGS, Jno. 70.
COLLIS?, COLLIO?, Jacobus 33, 38.
COLVIN, Jno. 97.
COLWELL, Andrew 88, 104.
COMER, Frederick 90.
COMMANDER, Jas. 30, 35; Saml. 48.
COMMELANDER, John 72.
COMMINS, Andrew 70.
COMPTON, Thos. 48.
CONE, John 20.
CONN, Geo. 85, Thos. 40, 41.
CONNELL, CONNALL, CONEL, CONNEL, Giles 79, 101; Jesse 100; Simon 40, 41.
CONNOR, Thos. Jr. 42; Wm. 69.
CONSILL, Henry 41.
CONYERS, Jas. Jr. 48; Jas. Sr. 45.
COODE, CODDA, Aarhibald 81, 99.
COOK, COOKE, Abra. 41; Benj. 10, 23, 77, 89; Drury 55; Ely 103; Geo. 3, 10, 24, Isaac 78, 91 (2); Jas. 3, 10, 23, 45, 88; Jno. 16, 45, 52; Jno. Jr. 46; Jno. Sr. 44; Jos. 34, 68; Matthias 54; Thos. 46, 102; Wm. 6, 15, 42; Wilson 8, 19.
COON, COONE, Henry 67, Valentine 71.
COOPER, ____ 104; Hugh 55; Jacob 54, 80, 102; Jno. 58, 59; Nath. 56; Robt. 93; Thos. 9, 23, 31, 36; Wm. 31, 35.
COPAI, John 90.
COPELAND, Chas. 56; Isaac 21; Will 56.
COPPITHORN, Jno. 10, 24.
COPPLEY, Patrick 37.
CORAM, Henry 16; Jno. 10, 24; Thos. 10, 24.
CORBETT, Benchley 47; Thos. 3, 10, 23.
CORDES, Jas 16; Jno. 6, 16; Saml. 3, 6, 10, 16, 24; Thos. 22.
CORRAL, Dennis 51.
CORRY, Samuel 58.
COTHAN, COTHEN, Nath. 21, Thos. 42.
COTTINGHAM, Chas. 42; Jonathan 42.
COTTON, John 100; Thos. 71, 81, 99.
COUCH, Edward 81, 100.
COUNCIL, CONSILL, Henry 40, 41.
COUNTRYMAN, John 49.
COUPAR, Basil 62, 65.
COURSEY, James 98.
COURTONE, Jas. 3, 10, 24.
COUSINS, John 47.
COUTOURIER, Isaac 7, 16; Isaac Jr. 7, 16; John 9, 22; Peter 9, 22, 23; Philip 16.
COVENTON, Jos. 98; Wm. Jr. 80, 98; Wm. Sr. 98.
COVIN, John 54.
COWAN, Jas. 85; Jno. 76, 85.
COWARD, Benj. 10, 24, 50.
COWEN, COWIN, Hugh 19; Jacob 61, 62; Jno. 19, 61, 62; Matthew 57; Robt. 55, 58.
COX, Allen 95; Cornelius 92; Emanuel 40, 41; John 16, 34, 62 (2), 64 (2), 85, 92; Jos. 3, 10, 24; Joshua 19; Saml. 34 (2); Wm. 89.
COZBY, John Jr. 85.
CRADDOCK, Wm. 93.
CRADRICK, Jacob 53.
CRAIG, Alex. 42; Jas. 57; Robt. 53; Saml. 57.
CRASWELL, John 83.
CRAWFORD, Enes 86; Geo. 83; Jas. 35, 54, 55 (2);

Jas. Jr. 85; James Sr. 76, 83; Jno. 36, 83;
Jos. 84, Robt. 45, 86; Wm. 83; Wm. Sr. 85.
CRAY, James 94.
CREIE, Moses 80, 98.
CREIGHTON, Jno. 10, 24; Jos. 3, 10, 23; Wm.
 3, 10, 24.
CRESLEY, Wm. 86.
CRETTON, Hugh 90.
CRIBB, Jno. 35.
CRIM, Peter 53.
CROAK, Jonathan 102.
CROFT, Childermas 29, 32, Danl. 59; Geo. 29,
 32, 38; Henry 53; Jno. 34; Peter 6, 15;
 Ralph 59.
CROLE, John 19; Thos 20.
CROLL, John 8.
CROMER, Andrew 53; Jacob 91.
CROMPTON, Saml. 90.
CROMWELL, Oliver 31, 36.
CROOK, CROOKS, Andrew 90; Anthony 33, 38.
CROSBY, Jno. 51; Rich. 51; Thos. 54; Tim. 3,
 10, 24.
CROSEN, Alex. 91; Jas. 92; Thos. 91.
CROSSKEYS, CROSSKEYS, Jno. 8, 20; Wm. 7, 18.
CROSS, Edward 54; Saml. 10, 24.
CROSSLEY, Geo. 101.
CROUCH, Henry 3, 10, 24.
CROW, Chas. 95.
CROWTE, Jno. 100.
CRUM, David 66, 69; Henry 94.
CRUMLEY, Jno. 96.
CRUMTON, Henry 50.
CRUSE, CRISE, Abros 51; Rich. 80, 102.
CRZER, Thos. 86.
CUBBAGE, Philomon 48.
CUDWORTH, Benj. 10. 24.
CULLIATT, David 20, Jas. Lewis 19.
CULP, Augustion 51, Benj. 54; Harmon 86;
 Henry 54; Peter 46, Philip 21.
CUMMINS, Jas. 47, 97.
CUNNINGHAM, CONNINGHAM, Andrew 96; Arthur
 31, 37; David 78, 96; Humpy. 58; Jas. 94;
 Jno. 79, 80, 85, 94, 96, 103; Jos. 81, 100;
 Matthew 81, 92; Patrick 46, 82, 93; Robt.
 82, 95; Thos. 93; Wm. 10, 20.
CUNNINGTON, Wm. 23.
CURRELL, Rich. 82.
CURRETON, CURETON, Wm. 78, 91.
CURRY, Geo. 49; Jno. 97; Nicholas 103.
CURTIS, Jno. 21; Rich. Sr. 43; Thos. 67.
CUTHBERT, Isaac 62, 64; Jas. 61, 62, 65.
CUTTINO, Wm. 29, 32, 38.
DABBS, Jos. 40, 41.
DABEY, Jno. 45.
DABNEY, Jas. 53.
DACOSTA, Abra. 11, 24; Isaac 10, 24; Isaac Jr.
 11, 24.
DADDELEY, Jno. 23.
DALRYMPLE, Jas. 96; Jno. 95; Saml. 93.
DALTON, Danl. 8, 20; Darias 62, 64; Henry 77,
 89; Thos. 89.
DANCER, Peter 59.
DANDRIDGE, Jno. 17; Jos. 21.
DANIEL, DANIELS, Aaron 40, 41; Jas. 46; Josiah
 65; Robt. 3, 10; Thos. 65; William 49.
DANNES, John 58.
DANSBY, Isham 51.
DARBY, Jas. 3, 10, 24.
DARCIUS, John 24.
DARGAN, Timothy 48.
DARLING, Jos. 10, 24.
DARR, Valentine 15.
DARRELL, DARELL, Benj. 11, 24; Ed. 3, 11, 24;

Joseph 3, 10, 24.
DART, Benj. 3, 10, 24; Jno. 3, 10, 24; Jno.
 Sandford 15.
DAUGHERTY, Daniel 90; Jas. 90, 91, 92.
DAUHADY, Gervis 54.
DAVENPORT, Fran. 95; Isaac 79, 95, 96; Jos.
 97; Wm. 95.
DAVID, Jno. 83, Joshua 42.
DAVIDSON, DAVISON, Hugh 55; Jno. 101, 103;
 Jos. 100; Robt. 30, 36; Thos. 94; Wm. 30, 36
DAVIS, Arch. 56; Benj. 30 (2), 33 (2), 40, 41,
 76, 86; Chesley 90; Clem 96; Fran. 34;
 Herman 96; Henry Jr. 30, 33, Henry Sr. 30,
 33; Isaac 70; Jas. 34, 44, 59, 83; John 3,
 11, 47, 50, 54, 58, 61, 63, 90, 95, 98,100;
 Moses 76, 84, Nathan 65, 91; Patrick 93;
 Robt. 99; Saml. 22; Thos. 41, 53; Wm. 30,
 33, 48, 55, 57, 61, 63, 81, 92, 99;
 Zachariah 100.

DAWKINS, Geo. 78, 89; Thos. 78, 91; Wm. 78,90.
DAWSEY, Fowler 34; Wm. 30, 33.
DAWSON, Christian 11, 24; Jno. 3, 11, 24.
DAY, Jno. 33, 98; Peter 81, 99.
DEAL, DILL, Alex. 78, 96; Clement 96; Harten
 93; Jno. 7, 18; Jos. 3, 10, 24; Wm. 83.
DEALWOOD, Jno. 84.
DEAN, Geo. 88; Rich. 87; Thos. 42, 92, 103.
DEARINGTON, Jno. 7, 18; Rich. 18; Robt. 44;
 Thos. 7, 18.
DEAS, Jno. 3, 11, 24, 48.
DEHAY, Jno. 36.
DELASHMET, Jno. 55.
DELESSLINE, Isaac 67.
DELEBARE, Jno. 61, 63.
DELKA, Jno. 3, 11, 24.
DeLOACH, DeLOCH, DELOTE, Jesse 65; Michael
 81, 100; Thos. Sr. 81, 100.
DEMSOILL, Zachary 49.
DENER, Peter 11, 24.
DENDY, DENDEY, Thos. 92; Wm. 82, 93.
DENKINS, DINKINS, Joshua 45, 60; Wm. 48.
DENLY, Robt. 23; Wm. 52.
DENNIS, Rich. 44; Saml. 92.
DENNY, DENNEY, Ed. 100, William 3, 11, 24.
DENTON, Saml. 57.
DENZLER, Henry 67; Jacob 67, 76; John 68;
 John Henry 68; John Ulrick 67.
DERAMES, DERAMS, John 68, 73.
DERR, Michael 17.
DeSAUSSURE, Danl. 61, 63; Henry 62, 64;
 Lewis 62.
DESBERRY, John 19.
DESCHAMP, Jos. 22; Peter 22.
DEVAL, DEVALL, DUVAL, DUVALL, Jno. 3, 11, 24
 Lewis 81, 93; Michael 76, 83; Stephen 10,
DEVANT, Chas. 63; Isaac 61, 62; Jas. 62; Jno
 61, 62.
DEVEAUX, Andrew 61, 62, 65; Jacob 61, 62;
 Wm. 61, 63 (2).
DEVOUR, DIVOUR, Matthew 99 (2).
DEW, Abraham 34.
DEWAR, Robt 10, 24, Stephen 11.
DEWBERRY, Giles 102.
DEWEES, Cornelius 3, 10, 24; Philip 11, 24.
DEWITT, Chas. 42; Jas. 17, Jno. 42, 43; Wm.
 17, 38, 40, 41, 43.
DIAL, Jeremiah 94; Wm. 94.
DIAS, Thos. 33, 38.
DICK, Jno. 31, 36; Robt. 31, 36.
DICKEY, Ed. 45; Geo. 37; Hector 87, 104; Jas
 56; Jno. 48, 58; Robt. 59, 77, 88, 104;
 Stewart 44.

DICKHART, Michael 78, 90.
DICKSON, Arthur 76, 86; David 56, 66, 68;
  Jno. 37, 49; Mathew 57, 58; Mich. 46; Wm. 87.
DILL, SEE DEAL.
DILLARD, Nicholas 99.
DINGLE, Robt. 44 (2).
DINKINS, SEE DENKINS.
DISSAKER, DECESKAR, Jacob 53; Peter 90.
DISTO, Anthony 67.
DIXON, DIXSON, Robt. 49; Wm. 31; Wm. Jr. 31,
  36; Wm. Sr. 37.
DOAN, Saml. 51.
DOBEIN, DOBBEIN, DOBBINS, Jno. 31, 36, 49;
  Jno. Jr. 31, 37; Jos. 8, 19; Wm. 57.
DOBBS, DABBS, Joseph 40, 41.
DOBY, Nath. 100.
DOETREY, Josiah 42.
DOHARTY, DORHARTY, Jas. 61, 62; Jno. 45.
DOKINS, Geo. 72.
DOLLARD, Patrick 21.
DOLLER, Jno. 97.
DOMINI, Andrew 52.
DONAHO, Jno. 79, 94.
DONALDSON, Jas. 3, 10, 24; Jno. 41; Matthew 85.
DONNAVAN, Jas. 10 (2), 24 (2).
DOOLITTLE, Jos. 99; Saml. 99.
DOOZ, Jno. 22.
DORSIUS, DORCIUS, Jno. 3, 10, 24.
DORES, Benj. 11, 24.
DORRELL, Jno. 15; Jonathan 15.
DORRIS, Wm. 85.
DORSE, Isaac 7; Daniel 7.
DORTCH, Thos. 52.
DORTREY, Josiah 42.
DOSSON, Britton 98.
DOUGHTY, Thos. 3, 10, 24; Wm. 3, 10, 24.
DOUGLASS, DOUGLAS, DUGLES, Geo. 55; Hugh 87,
  104; Jas. 90; Jno. 96, 100; Jno. Jr. 100;
  Joshua 42, 43; Nath. 42, 43; Will 46.
DOUXSAINT, Paul 3, 11.
DOVER, Jno. 57.
DOWD, Caleb 53.
DOWDELL, Robt. 59.
DOWING, Jno. 83; Patrick 83.
DOWNES, DOWNS, Arthur 3, 10, 24; Geo. 81, 92;
  Jno. 41, 43; Jonathan 82, 94; Wm. 3, 10, 24, 47.
DOWNING, Jno. 58, 76; Josiah 87.
DOYLE, Thos. 43.
DOZIER, DOZER, Jas. 40, 41; Jno. 30, 33.
DRAKE, Edward 42, John 9, 22.
DRAKEFORD, Jno. 50.
DRAXLER, Geo. 7, 17.
DRAYER, Godfied 66, 72.
DRAYTON, Jno. 3, 11; Wm. Henry 3, 11, 24.
DREW, Jos. 88.
DRIFFLE, Jno. 19.
DRIPER, Thos. 80, 102.
DROSE, Daniel 7, 17, Isaac 7, 16.
DUBBERT, Ferk. 52.
DUBOSE, DUBOIS, Andrew Sr. 43; Daniel 40, 41;
  David 22; Elias 40, 41; Isaac 9, 22, 40, 41;
  Jos. 43; Peter Sr. 43; Saml. 66, 68.
DUCK, Michael 69.
DUCKET, Thos. 81, 92.
DUCKHAM, Arthur 78.
DUEITT, Wm. 32.
DUET, Jos. 35.
DUFF, Jas. 58.
DUGGINS, Thos. 95.
DUKE, DUKES, Benj. 31, 37; Jno. 50, 80, 98;
  Rich. 97; Robt. 53.
DUNASH, James 82.
DUNBAR, Archbd. 72.

DUNCAN, DUNKIN, Geo. 10, 24; Jas. 10, 11, 21
  92; Jno. 57, 91, 92; Patrick 57; Saml. 90.
DUNLAP, Geo. 56; Jas. 56; Jno. 55, 82, 93;
  Robt. 56; Saml. 8, 20, 29, 55, 94; Wm. 56,
DUNN, Alex. 30, 33; Jas. 87; Sylvester 44.
DUNNAM, Ebenezer Jr. 30, 33; Ebenezer Sr. 30
  33; Jno. 29, 32.
DUNNING, Jas. 10, 24, Wm. 8, 21.
DUPONT, Chas. 62, 64; Cornelius 62, 64;
  Gideon 61, 63.
DUPRE, DUPEE, Jos. 98, Saml. 22.
DUPUIS, Jas 65.
DURAND, Jas. 31; Levi 9, 22.
DURANT, Geo. 30, 33; Henry 30, 33, Jas. 36;
  Jno. 31, 37, Thomas 34.
DURBROUGH, DUREROWE, Benj. 78, 88, 104.
DURHAM, Arthur 96.
DURIAH, James 94.
DURIN, Geo. 49.
DURNER, Jos. 70.
DUROCK, Jno. 59.
DUTARGUE, Jno. 3, 10, 24.
DUTTON, Jeremiah 79, 101.
DUVALL, SEE DEVALL.
DUYLMIRE, Albert 21.
DWHITT, Saml. 104.
DWIGHT, Nath. 30, 33; Saml. 30, 33.
DYE, Elisha 51.
DYSON, James 79, 94.
EADY, Jas. Sr. 36; Saml. 36.
EAGER, EGAR, Arch. 84, Hugh 57; Jno. 83.
EAGLE, Arch. 70.
EAKINGS, EAKINS, Alex. 58; Jno. 104.
EARNEST, Geo. 102.
EARKLE, Michael 72.
EAST, Isham 82, 93; Jos. 52; Josiah 93.
EASTLAKE, Saml. 20.
EASTLAND, Thos. 77, 88.
EASTON, Wm. 11, 24.
EASTWOOD, Lawrence 103.
EATON, Jeremiah 19; Saml. 19; Wm. 19.
EBERLEY, Jno. 11, 24.
ECKLES, Wm. 6, 16.
EDDINGS, Benj. 8, 19; Jos. 19; Jos. Jr. 21.
EDEN, Jas. 15; Jno. 15; Joshua 11, 24.
EDINS, EDINGS, Benj. 77, 84.
EDGEHILL, Thos. 97.
EDMANSON, Thos. 16.
EDMISON, Moses 87.
EDMISTON, Jno. 86.
EDWARD, EDWARDS, Abel 40, 41, 43; Chas. 95;
  Jas. 3, 11, 24, 78, 88, 104; Jno. 3, 11, 24
  41, 77, 93; Jno. Jr. 61, 63; Joshua 40, 41;
  Peter 79, 94; Thos. 71, 76, 85; Wm. 3, 11,
  24, 42, 43, 48, 53.
EGAN, Edmund 3, 11, 24; Jno. 22; Thos. 22.
EGAR, SEE EAGER.
EHNEI, Geo. 11, 24.
EILANDS, Absalon 70.
ELEMON, ELLEMAN, ELLERMAN, Abner 90; Enow 91;
  John 90.
ELFE, Thos. 66, 68.
ELIZER, Stephen 72.
ELKS, Jas. 29, 33.
ELLERBEE, Jno. 49; Thos. Jr. 40, 41; Thos. Sr.
  43; Wm. 40, 41.
ELLIOTT, Barnard 3, 11, 24; Benjam 14, Benj.
  3, 15, 24, Benj. Jr. 29, 32; Chas. 3, 11;
  Jno. 50, 80, 102; Robt. 51; Saml. Jr. 33;
  Thos. 7, 18.
ELLIS, Edmund 61, 63, 94; Jno. 51, 57, 63;
  Nathan 48; Rich. 15, 24; Simeon 95; Thos. 16
  William 88.

111

ELLISON, Jno. 51; Robt. 45; Thos. 93; Wm. 82,94.
ELMORE, Stephen 92.
ELVIN, Michael 90.
EMBRY, Wm. 46.
EMREY, Moses 91.
ENGLISH, Andrew 85; Jno. 44; Joshua 45, 60; Robt. 44, 59; Thos. 47, 60; Wm. 88.
ENLOS, Benj. 56; Isaac 56.
ERVIN, Hugh 30; John 32, 38.
ERWIN, Hugh 36, Robt. 48, 85.
ESKERIDGE, ECKRIDGE, Bweded 81, 100.
ESLER, Hugh 83.
ETHERETHERIDGE, Lott 99.
EVANS, Chas. Jr. 40, 41; Chas. Sr. 41; Danl. 19; Elias 15; Enock Sr. 42, 43; Ezekiel 85; Geo. 7, 17, 44; Isaac 95; Jacob Jr. 48; Jacob Sr. 48; Jas. 15; John 41, 49, 78, 95, 98; Josiah 42, 49; Ludwell 52; Nathan 30, 33; Rich. 52; Rowland 66, 68; Thos. 43; Thos. Jr. 42, 43; Thos. Sr. 40, 41, 43; Wm. 19.
EVANT, Thos. 99.
EVELEIGH, Nicholas 3, 15, 24; Thos. 3, 11, 24.
EVERETT, EVERIT, Benj. 46; Wm. 70.
EVERHART, Philip 63.
EVINS, Robt. 92.
EVIT, Jesse 68.
EUSTACE, Thos. 11, 24.
EWARD, Jno. 89.
EWING, Thos. 82, 93.
EZARD, Jno. 7, 17.
FAHAN, Jno. 21.
FABRE, Jno. 11.
FAIL, FELL, Thos. 4, 11, 24, 43.
FAIR, Jas. 70; Wm. 4, 11, 24.
FALK, Jno. 97.
FALLOWS, Jas. 64.
FANNING, Abram 59; Jas. 102; Jno. 59.
FANGUHERE, FAUGUHERE, Thos. 88, 104.
FARDO, Jno. Geo. 11, 24.
FARQUAND, Paul 66, 68.
FARICE, David 51; Wm. 51.
PARIS, Capt. Robt. 100; Robt. 79.
FARMER, Joel 102.
FARR, (ALSO SEE TARR) John 9, 21; Nath. 21; Thos. 3, 11, 21, 24; Thos. Jr. 9; Wm. 79.
FARRASTEAU, Anthony 11, 24.
FARY, Wm. 69.
FAULKNER, Wm. 47.
FAVOURS, Reuben 102.
FEARIS, FEARRIS, Jno. 58; Robt. 59; Wm. 63.
FEARS, Jas. 58.
FEAVOR, Theophilus 57.
FELCHER, Thos 90.
FELDER, Frederick 69, 73; Henry Jr. 69; Henry Sr. 67, 73; Jacob 73; Jno. 69; Saml. 69, 73.
FELL, SEE FAIL.
FELLAW, FELAW, Lewis 84; Mathias 51.
FENDEN, Jno. 63.
FENWICK, FENWICKE, Edward 7, 18; Jno. 62, 65.
FERGUSON, Aaron 46; Adam 54; Benj. 46; David 90; Edw. 64; Henry 67, 71; Jas. 54 (2), 55, 59; Jno. 55; Jos. 46; Moses 58; Paul 55; Robt. 56, 57; Thos. 4, 11, 24; Wm. 49, 52, 61, 63.
FICKLAND, FRICKLAND, Samuel 78, 91.
FICKLING, Geo. 8, 19; Geo. Jr. 19; James Jr. 19; Jeremiah 19; Jos. 8, 19; Jos. Jr. 19.
FIELDER, Jacob 68.
FIELDS, Jno. 46; Jno. Cato 20.
FINCHER, Anmel 79, 101.
FINDLEY, Christian 16; Jas. 84; Wm. 20, 94.
FINKLEY, Chas. 38.
FINLAYSON, Mungo 11, 24.

FINNEY, Wm. 79, 96.
FISH, Jos. 90.
FISHER, Chas. 46; Jas. 4, 11, 24; Jno. 3, 4, 11 (2), 24 (2); Wm. 49.
FITZGERALD, Gabl. 44.
FITZPATRICK, Jared 66, 68; Patrick 20.
FITZSIMONS, FITZSIMMONS, Christopher 5, 11.
FLAGG, Geo. 4, 11, 24.
FLANIGAN, Reuben 81, 92.
FLAVOR, Theophilus 57.
FLECONING, Robt. 58.
FLEESON, Geo. 33, 38.
FLEDGER, Chas. 30, 33.
FLEMING, Alex. 58; Elijah 58; Jas. 31, 38, 50; Jno. 48, 54; Saml. 93.
FLEMINGHAM, Bartholomew 97.
FLETCHALL, Col. Thos. 79, 101.
FLETCHER, Edward 84; Henry 8, 21; Saml. 20; Wm. 32, 38.
FLEY, Saml. 4, 11, 24.
FLINN, FLENN, Chas. 19, Florence 19.
FLINT, Wm. 16.
FLORIN, Lucas 4, 11, 24.
FLOWERS, David 33, 38; Henry 35; Rich. Woodard 61, 63.
FLOYD, Chas. 63; Matthew 57; Wm. 48.
FLUDD, FLOOD, Wm. 66, 68.
FLURRY, Zachariah 21.
FOGARTIE, Jas. 11; Jos. 7, 17.
FOISSIN, Elias 29, 32.
FOISTER, Robt. 87.
FOLLMER, Jno. 72.
FONIRING, Jno. 46.
FONTIUS, Sebastian 66, 70.
FORBES, Jas. 86.
FORGES, Jno. 86.
FORD, Daniel 53; Geo. 8, 21, 29, 32; Geo. Jr. 70; Isaac 8, 19; Jas. 90; Jas. Jr. 30, 33; Jessy 50; Stephen Jr. 29, 32 (2), Stephen Sr 29, 32; Thos. 54, 70.
FORIREN, Jas. 103.
FOREMAN, FORMAN, Geo. Jr. 71; Isaac 99, Jacob
FORSHAW, David 20; Edward 8, 20.
FORSYTH, Jas. 65.
FORT, Drury Sr. 100; Elias 44; Moses 42, 100.
FORTTEMAN, Drivery 100.
FORTUNE, Mark 47.
FOSKEY, FOSHEY, FOSHY, Brian 4; Bryan 11, 24; Nath. 88.
FOSTER, Andrew 46, 59, 100; Alex. 79, 86; Henry 45; Isaac 38; Jas. 85; Jas. Jr. 85; Jno. 47, 56, 80, 102; Jno. Jr. 76, 85; Moses 100; Saml. Jr. 85; Saml. Sr. 85.
FOUNTAIN, Fran. 21.
FOURTIER, Jacob 100.
FOUST, Buritt 53, Gasper 53; Jno. 52, 53; Wm. 53.
FOWLER, Rich. 95; Rich. Jr. 94; Rich. Sr. 94; Wm. 95.
FOX, FOXE, Jas 99; Wm. 53.
FOXWORTH, Job 34; Jos. 34.
FOY, Peter 81, 100.
FRAMPTON, Jno. 61, 63.
FRANK, Nehemiah 81, 92.
FRANKLIN, FRANKLYN, Ephraim 98; Jno. 53; Jos. 53; Thos. 54, 98.
FRAYLICK, Adam 88.
FRAZER, FRASER, Alex. 4, 11, 24; Danl. 99; Isaac 101; Jas. 61, 63, 65; Jno. 18, 42, 99, Jos. 15; Robt. 76, 83; Wm. 50.
FREDERICK, FRIDRICK, Alex. 99; Andrees 70; Andrias 66; Jacob 91; Jas. 100.
FREE, Jacob 49.

FREEMAN, Jas. 22; Jno. 19; Wm. 87, 104.
FREIR, Jno. 18, Solomon 18.
FRETS, Abraham 89.
FREY, Geo. 18.
FRIDAY, David 71.
FRICK, Jacob 11, 24.
FRIERSON, Aaron 45; Geo. 47; James Jr. 44; James Sr. 44; Jno. 31, 36; Philip 66, 68; Robt. 31, 36; Thos. 31, 37; Wm. 31, 37; Wm. Jr. 37.
FRINK, Jabesh 30, 33; Saml. 30, 33, Thos. 30,33
FRIPP, Jno. 61, 63; Paul 63; Wm. 61, 63; Wm. Jr. 61, 63.
FROGG, Robt. 11, 24.
FROUCHET, Chas. 64.
FRUIT, Elijah 42.
FRUWICKS, FRUWEEKS, Geo. 40, 41.
FRYDIG, Jacob 66, 72.
FRYER, Jacob 35.
FUDGE, Jacob 99.
FUISBORN, Alex. 93.
FULFORD, Wm. 22.
FULKER, Peter 91.
FULLER, Benj. 7, 18; Jos. 42; Nath. 7, 18; Thos. 7, 18.
FULLERTON, Jno. 7, 17.
FULLWOOD, Wm. 45.
FULMER, Jno. 16.
FULTON, Jno. 55; Paul 48; Saml. 55; Thos. 47, 60.
FUNDERBURG, SEE TUNDERBURG
FURLOW, Saml. 101, Wm. 94.
FURMAN, Josiah 47, Wood 44.
FURNED, Edward 97.
FURNISS, Wm. 42, 43.
FUTHEY, FUTHY, Fran. 36; Henry 31, 36; Jno. 30, 36.
FYFE, Jno. 11.
GABBY, Jos. 57; Robt. 59.
GABLE, Michael 68.
GABORIEL, Jno. 11, 25.
GADSDEN, Christopher 4, 11.
GAGAS, Danl. 54.
GAILLARD, GAILLIARD, Chas. 9, 22; David 9, 23; Jno. 9, 23; Theodore 4, 9, 22; Theodore Jr. 11, 25.
GALE, Josiah Sr. 47.
GALLASPIE, Fran. 42.
GALLAWAY, GALLOWAY, Absolam 43; Jas. 43; Jno. 97.
GALLEY, James 84.
GALLMAN, GALLMON, GOLLMAN, GOLMAN, Gosport 99; Harman 99; Herman 81; Jacob 71; John 71, 78, 92; John Conrad 99.
GALPIN, GALPHIN, Geo. 80, 97.
GAMBLE, GAMBALL, GAMBELL, Hugh 48; Jno. 44, 86, 93; Robt. 38; Saml. 50, 86; Turner 93; Wm. 31, 37 (2).
GANAWAY, Maranadick 71.
GANEY, Thos. 34.
GANT, Isreal 90.
GANTTER, Geo. 60.
GARDEN, Col. Benj. 62, 64; Jno. 7, 18.
GARINER, Edward 61, 63, 65; Robt. 49; Stephen 43; Will 46.
GAREY, GEARY, Jno. 95; Thos. 78. 79, 95, 96.
GARISH, Andrew 68.
GARNETT, Jos. 65; Thos. 65.
GARNER, Jas. 96; Jno. 42; Melcher 9, 21; Philip 21; Saml. 99; Wm. 8, 21.
GARNISON, David 58.
GARREL, GARRELL, Benj. 34; Jas. 30, 33.
GARRET, GARRATT, GARRETT, GARROT, Ed. 93,96;

Jno. 77, 89, 92, 95 (2); Robt. 77, 89; Silas 92; Thos. 52, 95.
GARTMAN, Barth^W 72, Danl. 90; Jno. 72.
GARVAN, GARVIN, Edw. 62, 64; Jno. 59; Thos. 59.
GASTON, Hugh 52; Jno. 52, 54; Jos. 55; Robt. 55; Wm. 53.
GATER, Thos. 46.
GAULTIER, Joseph 11, 25.
GAUZE, Benj. 30, 33; Chas. 30, 33.
GAY, Saml. 59; Theodore 65.
GAYTON, GUYTON, Jos. 57, 103.
GEAR, Jno. 41.
GEARY, SEE GAREY.
GEE, Chas. 29, 32, 38; Jno. 53.
GEEGLEMAN, Jacob 67.
GEIGER, GIGER, Abraham 72; Harman 66, 72; Jacob 66, 72; Jno. 46, 72; Jno. Jacob 71; Wm. 66, 72.
GENDRAT, Abraham 65; Henry 62, 65.
GENTRY, Hezekiah 80, 101; Jno. 88, 104; Nicholas 89.
GEORGE, David 80, 102; Jno. 93; Rich. 42.
GEROUD, David 62, 64.
GERVAIS, Jno. Lewis 4, 11, 25.
GHENT, Jno. 82, 93.
GIBBES, GIBBS, Jas. 79, 100; Jno. Walter 11, 24; Philip 101; Wm. 4, 11, 18, 25; Zachareah 80; Zacharias 103.
GIBBONS, Thos. 64.
GIBBOOANE, Andrew 83.
GIBSON, Ebenezer 37; Fenneous 48; Gauvin 57; Geo. 57; Jas. 44, 59; Jno. 37; Jno. Jas. 48; Jos. 50 (2); Luke 53; Patrick 77, 89; Robt. 29, 32, 87; Roger 51, 60; Thos. 78, 89; Wm. 8, 20, 35.
GIDEON, Jas. 81, 92.
GIGNILLIATT, Benj. 8, 20, 62, 64; Gabriel 7, 16; Jas. 62, 65.
GILBERT, GIBERT, Caleb 79, 96; Jno. 64, 91; Jonathan 97; Peter 83; Seth 11, 25.
GILES, Abraham 30, 33; Hugh 32, 38; Jno. 4, 11, 25; Othneil 11, 25.
GILDER, Jacob 90.
GILKY, Jonathan 103.
GILL, Geo. 52; Jas. 52; Jno. 52, 54; Jno. Jr. 52; Philip 71; Robt. 46; Thos. 97.
GILLAM, GILHAM, GILLUM, Ezekl. 58; Jno. 97; Robt. 79, 96 (2); Thos. 57; Wm. 44, 90, 103.
GILLAND, Claudius 25.
GILLAUDEAU, Jas. 11, 25.
GILLEAUD, Claudius 11 (SEE GILLAND)
GILLELAND, William 97.
GILLESPIE, GILLESPY, And. 84; Jas. 84; Matthew 79, 94; Mathew Jr. 84.
GILLET, Wm. 94.
GILLON, Alex. 4, 11, 24; Chas. 46.
GILMAN, Henry 22.
GILTON, Jno. 100.
GIOHAM, Phillip 7
GIRARDEAU, Peter 8, 20.
GISSENDANER, Henry 68, 73.
GIVENS, Chas. 61, 63; Danl. 53; Jno. 61, 63; Wm. 59.
GIVHAM, Philip 7, 17.
GLAINEY, Rich. 50; Saml. 50.
GLANTOM, Jno. 89.
GLASGOW, Ezekiel 47; Jas. 83; Saml. 85.
GLASS, Jos. Alex. 37.
GLAZE, Jno. 7, 17.
GLEGG, Jno. 33, 38.
GLEN, GLENN, Danl. 16; David 55, 91; Jno. 16; Wm. 56, 94; Wm. Jr. 7, 17.
GLENCROST, Jos. 64.

GLOVER, Frederick 77, 87; Jno. 58; Jos. 4;
  Jos. Jr. 8, 20; Robt. 58; Wm. 58.
GODBOLT, GODBOLD, Jas. 34; Jno. 35; Thos. 35.
GODDARD, Fran. 30, 33.
GODFREY, Anthony 64; Jno. 18, 20, 55, 90;
  Wm. 8, 20, 29, 32.
GOFF, Jno. 3, 38.
GOGINS, GOGGINS, Danl. 96; Geo. 94; Jas. 95;
  Wm. 96.
GOING, Jno. 51; Michael 35.
GOLDEN, Jno. 48.
GOLDIE, Jno. 7, 18.
GOLDING, Anthony 97.
GOLIGHTLY, Shanes 100; Wm. 79, 101.
GOLLE, Wm. 89.
GOLSON, Lewis 67.
GOOD, GOODE, Henry 59; Mekernis 78, 88, 104;
  Thos. 98; Wm. 98.
GOODEN, GOODING, Jno. 53; Rich. 42.
GOODWIN, GODWIN, Fran. 46, 71; Geo. 79, 101;
  Jno. 79, 101; Robt. 46, 94; Wm. 52, 66, 72.
GORDON, Alex. 40, 41; David 58; Gavin, Gavan
  80, 101; Geo. 78, 90; Jas. 29, 32, 38, 48,
  76, 85; Jno. 48, 56, 58; Moses 44; Roger
  31, 36; Saml. 57; Thos. 78, 91; Wm. 32,
  38, 79, 101.
GORE, Clement 96; James 54.
GOREY, Danl. 90; Jno. 78, 90.
GORMAN, Christopher 88; Jno. 88.
GORRELL, Robt. 55.
GOTEAR, GOLTIER, GOTARE, GOTTIER, Fran. 4,
  11, 25; Jno. 35; Jno. Jas. 30, 35.
GOUDALOCK, Adam 103.
GOUGH, Rich. 16.
GOUOT, Edward 81.
GOURDINE, Isaac 16.
GOURLEY, Jno. 11, 25; Jos. 32, 38.
GOWDY, Wm. 11, 25.
GRANGER, Micajah 50.
GRAHAM, David 29, 33; Geo. 30, 33; Hugh 84;
  Jas. 86; Jno. 34; Jno. Jr. 35; Jno. Sr. 30,
  33; Jos. 35; Wm. 4, 11, 25, 35, 61, 63.
GRANT, Isaac 78, Jno. 4, 11 (2), 24, 25, 67,
  71; Wm. 102.
GRATTON, Daniel 11, 24.
GRAVES, Jas. 11, 24.
GRAW, Wm. 36.
GRAY, GREY, Abraham 79, 94; Arthur 84; Geo.
  78, 91; Geo. Jr. 78, 91; Jas. 63, 64, 83,
  87, 98, 101; Jno. 61, 63, 81, 92; Jno. Jr.
  63; Joshua 89; Robt. 40, 41; Solomon 21;
  Thos. 89; Wm. 86, 93.
GRAYSON, Jno. 63.
GREAVES, Jno. 34; Jno. Jr. 50; Jos. 30, 33.
GREGG, GREGGS, Clemard 33; Jas. 32, 38; Jno.
  32, 38; Jos. 36.
GREEN, Benj. 84; Bryan 99; Danl. 70; Danl.
  Jno. 61, 63, 65; Fran. 30, 36; Geo. 37;
  Isham 77, 87, 104; Jacob 103; Jno. 29, 33,
  37; Jno. Jr. 84; Jno. Sr. 84; Moses 47;
  Nath. 61, 63; Rich. 30, 33, 34, 36; Thos.
  81, 93, 99, 102; Thos. Mosten 99; Wm. 91;
  Wm. Jr. 38.
GREENLAND, Geo. 4, 11, 25; Jos. 7, 16; Thos.
  22; Wm. 22.
GREENWOOD, Wm. 11, 24.
GREGORY, GRIGGRE, Benj. 101; Howell 53;
  Isaac 79, 101; Jno. 79, 101; Robt. 101.
GRESHAM, Philip 54.
GRICE, Thos. 34.
GRIER, GREAR, GREER, GREOR, David 83; Geo.
  55; Jas. 29, 32, 51, 93; Jno. 29, 32, 56,
  92; Jos. 29, 32, 92; Josiah 79, 94, 96;
  Saml. 29, 32; Thos. 81.
GRIFFIN, Absolom 53; Anthony 97; Benj. 92;
  Horatio 78, 89; Jas. 79, 94, 95; Jno. 78,
  86, 90, 97 (2); Jonas 49; Jones 78, 89;
  Joshua 23; Rich. 87, 96; Sampson 70.
GRIFFITH, GRIFFICE, David 49, Jno. 66, 68,
  77, 89; Jos. 43; Mathew 42; Peter 70;
  Saml. 69; Thos. 70.
GRIGG, Jno. 50.
GRIGS, Enoch 81, 100; Jas. 81 100.
GRIMBALL, Jno. Sr. 62, 65.
GRIME, GRIM, Lowrinds 71; Wm. 70.
GRIMES, David 55; Hugh 35; Jno. 35; Nathan
  80, 102; Nelson 31, 35; Nelson Jr. 35;
  Wm. 36, 46.
GRIMKE, Frederick 4, 11; Jno. Paul 4, 11, 25.
GRINDALL, GRINDAL, Jno. 30, 102.
GRINEAU, Peter 64.
GRINSLEY, Jno. 87.
GRIVE, Jno. 63.
GROCE, GROSS, Jas. 11, 24; Joshua 99.
GROANING, GROUNING, Jno. 11, 25.
GROSSMAN, Lewis 17.
GROTT, Fran. 11, 24.
GRUBB, Nicholas 53.
GRUBER, Christian 11, 25, Christopher 4;
  Saml. 11, 25.
GUERARD, Benj. 61, 63; Danl. 61, 63; Rich.
  61, 63.
GUERIN, Alex. 67; Matharin, Jr. 18, Nath. Jr.
  18; Vincent 18.
GUERRY, Jas. 9, 22; Jno. 9, 22; Peter 9, 22;
  Peter Jr. 22.
GUESS, Wm. 31, 37.
GUIGNARD, Jno. G. 44.
GUIN, Peter 98.
GUINA, GUINES, Jno. 4, 11, 25.
GULBERATH, Jas. 91.
GUTHERRE, Fran. 57.
GUTTERY, Wm. 56.
GUYTON, SEE GAYTON.
GWIN, Morris 88.
HABERT, Thos. 50.
HACHEESON, Wm. 92.
HAGGERT, allen 85.
HAGLER, Peter 67.
HAGINS, Thos. 99.
HAGTON, Danl. 79, 101.
HAIG, Geo. 22; Jno. Jas. 66, 72.
HAIGWOOD, Wm. 104.
HAIL, HALES, Benj. 49; Robt. 66, 68; Wm. 4,
  11, 25.
HAILD, Wm. 101.
HAINSWORTH, Henry 44.
HAIRGROVE, Saml. Jr. 34, Saml. Sr. 34.
HAIRSTON, Jno. 85; Wm. 85.
HALDEWANGER, Jacob 72.
HALES, SEE HAIL.
HALEY, Geo. 67.
HALL, Alex. 83; Andrew 7, 17; Danl. 18;
  Elisha 17; Geo. Abbott 4, 11, 25; Jas. 81,
  90, 93; Jno. 59, 63, 93; Matthew 91; Thos.
  4, 12, 25; Wm. 56, 84.
HALLEMS, HALLUM, Jno. 97; Wm. 77, 87.
HALLIS, Moses 50.
HAM, Rich. 12, 25; Thos. 4, 12, 25.
HAMBLETON, David 58; Jno. 30, 33, 52; Robt.
  44, 48; Wm. 19.
HAMES, Randel 102.
HAMILTON, HAMELTON (SEE MAMILTON), Alex. 16,
  93; Andrew Jr. 86; Capt. Andrew 76, 85;
  Archibald 76, 86, Jas. 8, 20; Jno. 30, 36,
  87; Paul 19; Saml. 51; Thos. 76, 84;

114

William 8, 31, 36, 51 (3), 78, 84, 89.
HAMLIN, Geo. 6, 15; Thos. 6, 15; Wm. 18.
HAMMET, Jas. 79, 101; Thos. 11, 25.
HAMMOND, Jacob 102; Jno. 98; LeRoy 76, 97.
HAMPHILL, Alex. 56.
HAMPTON, Benj. 91; Jno. 11, 25, 67, 71; Jos. 90; Wm. 47.
HAMSON, Jas. 49.
HANBY, Saml. 94.
HANCOCK, HANDCOCK, Clement 95; Jas. 82; John 98.
HANDLEN, Benj. 30, 35; Thos. 31, 36; Wm. 30, 35.
HANEY, HEANY, Jno. 103; Maximillian 90.
HANKINS, Dennis 30, 33.
HANKINSON, Robt. 67, 71.
HANLEY, Barney 57.
HANNAGAN, Barnabas 42.
HANNAH, Jas. 46, 93; Wm. 94; Wm. Sr. 58.
HANNAHAN, Jno. 19; Thos. 19; Wm. 19.
HANNER, Robt. 36; Wm. 37.
HANSCOMB, Thos. 7, 18.
HANVEY, Wm. 76, 83.
HARBESON, Jas. 52.
HARDAGE, Hazel 55.
HARDEN, Wm. 62, 64.
HARDICK, Wm. 42.
HARDING, Henry 53.
HARDREDGE, Jos. 50.
HARDWICK, Wm. 101.
HARDY, Jno. 43.
HARE, Edward 11, 25.
HARGROVE, Wm. 59.
HARKINS, Danl. 50; Jas. 77, 87, 104; Jno. 88; Robt. 45; Thos. 88.
HARLAND, Walter 85.
HARLESTON, Isaac 4,12; Jno. 6,16; Jno. Jr. 4,11.
HARLEY, James 7, 17; Jos. 67, 71.
HARLIN, Aaron 101; Geo. 101.
HARLOCK, Jasper 19.
HARLONG, Jacob 69.
HARLOW, Wm. 53.
HARMAN, HARMON, Jacob 71; Jno. 20; Wm. 102.
HARNER, Christian 68.
HARPER, Danl. 45; Donald 11, 25; James 44; Solomon 21; Thomas 11, 25.
HARRELL, Jas. Jos. 36; Lewis 38.
HARRELSON, Benj. 35.
HARRIS, Barton 97; Chas. 11, 25; David 101; Geo. 54; Jas. 98; Jenkins 99; Jesse 88; Jno. 84; Levi 98; Robt. 79, 100; Saml. 98; Thos. 4, 12, 19, 25, 29, 33, 86; West 98; Wm. 76, 84, 90, 93.
HARRISON, Benj. 76, 86; Ephraim 45; Jas. 38, 45, 77, 81, 89, 100; Jno. 45; Thos. 20, 43, 56, 89.
HARRY HARREY, Benj. 99; Jas. 17; Thos. 41, 43.
HARSHAM, Daniel 58.
HART, HORT, Jas. 45; Joshua 4, 12, 25; Philip 4, 12, Wm. 4, 11, 12.
HARTHER, Hargrove 52.
HARTLEY, Jno. Newton 11, 25.
HARTMAN, Jno. 15.
HARTSTONE, Joachim 62, 64.
HARVEY, Jas. 89, 94; Philemon 93; Thos. 4, 12, 25, 89; Wm. 4, 89.
HARVIN, Jno. 48.
HARWIN, Rich. 44.
HARZOG, Barn 69; Geo. 69; Tobias 69.
HASE, Dennis 71.
HASELL, Andrew 7, 17; Thos. 29, 32, 38.
HASFORD, Saml. 34.
HATCHER, Benj. 81, 99; Isham 43; Jameston 84; Robt. 98.

HATFIELD, Jno. 4, 11, 25; Saml. 48.
HATLEY, Robt. 50.
HATTER, Jno. 15.
HAUGENBOUGH, Jacob 71.
HAWKINS, Isaac 102; Jas. 79, 101; Jno. 101; Nathan 103; Peter 89; Philip 11; Rich. 103; Wm. 101.
HAWTHORN, HATHORNE, Jas. 85, 86.
HAY, David 45; Howel 45; Wm. 25.
HAYNE, HAYNES, Abraham 21; Isaac 8, 20.
HAYS, Jas. 42, 46; Jno. 102; Jos. 79, 94; Peter 91.
HAZARD, HAZZARD, Wm. 61, 63.
HAZELL, Henry 94.
HAZELTON, Saml. 38.
HAZLE, Wm. 64.
HEAD, Sir Edmond 11.
HEANY, Jno. 103.
HEARD, Armstrong 87, 104; Edward 51; Jas. 86.
HEARNE, Jno. 7, 18.
HEARSMAN, Godfrey 71.
HEARTELL, HEARTEL, Henry 81, 100.
HEATH, Jno. 42.
HEATHLEY, Wm. 36.
HEATLEY, HEATLY, Chas. 66, 68; Wm. Jr. 66, 68; Wm. Sr. 66, 68.
HEICKLER, Jacob 68.
HELMS, Jas. 51.
HEMBRE, David 102.
HEMELL, Jas. 58.
HEMPHILL, Jas. 54.
HENCOCK, Geo. 45.
HENDERSON, Alex. 85; David 84; Fran. 54; Jas. 79, 84, 94; Jno. 88; Nath. 46; Robt. 45; Saml. 79, 96; Shadrach 88; Thos. 88; Wm. 54.
HENDRICK, HENDRICKS, Benj. 42; Hans 79, 94; Henry 95; Wm. 81, 92.
HENDLEN, Thos. 29, 32, 38.
HENNING, Jos. 29, 32, 38; Thos. 29, 32, 38.
HENNZAR, Geo. 21.
HENRY, HENERY, Alex. 57; Jas. 56; Jno. 34; Philip 18; Wm. 57, 90.
HENRICK, HENRICKS, Fran. 11, 25.
HENSLER, Herman 45.
HENSON, Dorman 78, 89.
HENYARD, Jno. 97.
HERRISON, Wm. 91.
HERIG, Frederick 71.
HERRIOT, HERRIOT, Geo. 29, 32, 38; Robt. 29, 32, 38; Wm. 29, 32, 38.
HERISPERGER, Jno. 67, 69.
HERNDON, Jno. 99.
HERREN, HARROW, Wm. 92, 100.
HERRING, David 34; Wm. 30, 33; Wm. E. 48.
HESKETT, Jno. 17.
HESSY, HESSEY, Geo. 68; 73.
HETTELL, Jos. 95.
HEUSTES, HEUSTEES, Jno. 40 (2)
HEWES, Patrick 7, 16.
HEWSON, Wm. 38.
HEYWARD, Jno. 64; Thos. Jr. 4, 12, 25; Thos. Sr. 62, 64.
HEXT, HEST, Philip 61, 64; Thos. 19, 22; Wm. 4, 11, 25.
HIBBEN, Andrew 6, 15.
HICKLIN, Arthur 49; Wm. 55.
HICKMAN, Geo. 43; Joshua 38; Saml. 43; Wm. 43, 49.
HICKS, Benj. Jr. 40, 42; Benj. Sr. 40, 41; Geo. 40, 41; Jas. 40, 41; Jno. 98; Robt. 46; Thos. 19, 40, 41; Wm. 42.
HICKSON, Jno. 48; Thos. 42.
HIELD, Jno. 101.

115

HIGGINS, Jas. 81, 93; Newton 93; Thos. 12.
HIGHET, Ezekiel 35.
HILL, Geo. 66, 72; Green 71; Jas. 79, 101; Jno. 98; Nicholas 82, 94; Robt. 45; Saml. 87; Theophilus 50; Thos. 51, 69, 91; Wm. 46, 51, 66, 70, 79, 101.
HILLHOUSE, Wm. 58.
HINCKLEY, Wm. 4, 11, 25.
HINDS, Patrick 4, 12, 25.
HINSON, Phillip 50.
HINTON, HENTON, Allen 98, Robt. 96.
HIPP, Geo. 61, 63; Jno. 72.
HIRONS, Simon 45.
HODGE, HODGES, Benj. 87; Geo. 59; Isham 42; Jacob 90; John Jr. 42; Jno. Sr. 40, 41; Jonathan 53; Rich. 42, 87; Wm. 42.
HOFF, John 17.
HOFFMAN, Geo. 68; Jno. 68.
HOG, HOGG, Jno. 57, 99.
HOGANS, HOGENS, Jos. 81, 100.
HOLDEN, Mathew 43.
HOLDER, Jno. 34.
HOLLAND, Thos. 84.
HOLLANSHEAD, Jas. 72.
HOLLBECK, HORLBECK, Jno. 4, 11, 25; Peter 7, 16.
HOLLBROOK, Jacob 65.
HOLLIDAY, HALLIDAY, HOLLODAY, Wm. 4, 11, 12, 25, 88, 104.
HOLLINSWORTH, HOLLENSWORTH, HOLLINGSWORTH, Abra. 97; Elias 79, 101; Enoch 79, 101; Geo. 94; Jeph 101.
HOLLIS, Edward 53.
HOLLON, Jno. 35.
HOLLOWAY, HOLLAWAY, Caleb 88; Jas. 48; Jno. 40, 41, 42, 88; Mark, Obed 77, 88.
HOLLY, HOLLEY, Jacob 98; Thos. 70.
HOLMAN, Andrew 72; Conrad 66, 68; Jno. 7, 18.
HOLMES, HOMES, Daniel 7, 18; Isaac 3; Jas. 43, 78, 88, 104; Joel 4, 11, 25; Jno. 7, 18; Walter 101; Wm. 7, 18, 98.
HOLSEY, Geo. 51.
HOLSINGER, Jno. 52.
HOLSTON, Wm. 81, 100.
HOOBER, Jos. 68, 73.
HOOD, Jno. 49; Robt. 95; Wm. 55 (2).
HOOK, HOOKE, Jno. 69, 73.
HOOVER, Jacob 68; Wiley 68.
HOPE, John 44, 56, 80, 103.
HOPKINS, Jno. 16; Saml. 4, 11, 25; Wm. 4, 11, 25.
HOPTON, Wm. 4, 12.
HORLBECK, SEE HOLLBECK.
HORN, Ephraim 43, Henry 53, Peter 11, 25.
HORRY, Danl. 4, 12; Elias Jr. 4, 11, 25; Hugh 29, 32; Peter 29, 32; Thomas 4.
HORSEY, HOSSEY, Danl. 78, 90; Danl. Jr. 90.
HORT, SEE HART.
HORTON, Daniel 49; Hugh 103; Jno. 49; Wm. 50.
HOTHO, Chas. 69; Jacob 69.
HOUSE, HOUZE, Christian 71; Jno. 45; Thos. 44, 52.
HOUSLITER, Michael 68.
HOWARD, HAWARD, HOWERT, Hill 48; Jno. 70, 71, 94; Nath. 96; Obidah 101; Peter 49, 103; Robt. 4, 11, 25; Seth 97.
HOWE, David 59; Jno. 4, 11, 25, 59; Jos. 46; Wm. 59.
HOWELL, Arthur 53; Jno. 4, 12, 25; Malachi 45; Mathew 52; Nath. 98; Patineau 52; Robt. Jr. 53; Wm. 45; Wm. P. 53.
HOWLEN, Edward 35.
HOY, Jas. 53.
HUDDLESTON, Wm. 92.

HUDSON, HUTSON, David 80, 102; Jno. 38; Lodurick 47; Rich. 4, 11; Rush 49; Thos. 38, 62, 64; Wm. 21.
HUEY, HUGHEY, Jas. 54; Jno. 102.
HUFSTITLER, Jacob 57.
HUGER, Benj. 4, 12; Fran. 12, 25; Isaac 4, 12, 25; John 4, 11, 25.
HUGGINS, Jno. 45; Jos. 9, 22, Mark 29, 32, 38; Mark Jr. 34; Patrick 95; Wm. 86.
HUGHBANKS, Jno. 43.
HUGHES, HUGHS, Caleb 17; Geo. 94; Henry 22, 30, 38; Jas. 94; Jno. 20, 42, 43, 95; Jonathan 17; Meredith 30, 36; Rice 52; Rich. 80, 102; Thos. 46, 61, 63, 70; Wm. 80, 102.
HUGHEY, Jno. 102.
HUGHMAN, Jacob 96; Peter 96.
HUMBART, Melchoir 64.
HUMPHRIS, HUMPHREY, HUMPHREYS, HUMPHRIES, David 53, 90; Ralph 66, 72; Thos. 18; Wm. 97.
HUNDON, Wm. 99.
HUNGERBEALER, Jacob 67 (2).
HUNT, Jno. 84.
HUNTER, Dalzel 11, 25; David 77, 88; Geo. 64; Henry 45 (2); Jno. 55, 93, 94, 97; Jno. Jr. 92; Narra 45; Robt. 22.
HUR, HURR, Jacob 70; Jos. 35.
HURTER, Nich^S 69.
HURGER, Jacob Sr. 67.
HURST, Robt. 16.
HURTS, Michael 54.
HUSBAND, Jno. 42.
HUSSAR, Felix 19.
HUSTON, Jas. 85; Jno. 55; Saml. 86; Thos. 55.
HUTCHINS, HUTCHINGS, Hillman 21; Jno. 47, 60; Jos. 4, 12, 25; Wm. 11, 25.
HUTCHINSON, HUTCHISON, Jas. 95; Jno. 50; Jno. Elias 8, 20; Jos. 97; Mathias 4, 11, Rice 52; Rich. 80, 103; Stephen 96; Thos. 4, 8, 11, 17, 20, 25; Thos. Jr. 8, 20, Wm. 76, 85.
HUTSON, SEE HUDSON.
HUTTON, HUTTEN, Wm. 76, 83.
HUXFORD, Harlock 38.
HYLE, Adam 80, 98.
HYRNE, Henry 8, 20.
IMBODEN, Peter 69.
IMFINGER, Jno. 69.
IMRIE, Jno. 12, 25.
INABNIT, Christian 69; Jno. 69; Saml. 70, 73.
INGLEMAN, Jacob 50.
INGLIS, Alex. 4, 12, 25.
INGLISH, John 15.
INGRAM, Alex. 47; Jas. 47.
INKLES, Jacob 18.
INMAN, Benj. 90; Jehu 96; Joshua 96.
INSCO, Edward 102.
IRBEY, Chas. 40, 41; Edmond 42, 43.
IRISH, Geo. Sr. 67.
IRNST, (SEE JRNST) John 12.
IRONS, Simon 17.
IRVEY, Thos. 12.
IRVIN, Jas. 56; Wm. 58.
IRWIN, Alex. 86; Jno. 87.
ISENHOOD, Abraham 66, 70.
ISTES, Zachariah 101.
IZARD, EZARD, Jno. 7, 17; Ralp 12.
JACKSON, Benj. 42; Danl. 79, 100; Henry 43; Isaac, Jr. 47; Isaac, Sr. 48; Jno. 21, 40, 41; Saml. 79, 100; Stephen 43; Thos. 79, 100.
JAMAYON, Jas. 59.
JAMES, Alex. 12; Chas. 92, 101, Gavin 38; Jno. 30, 36; Jno. Jr. 35, 44; Jno. Sr. 44; Saml. 30, 35; Thos. 40, 41, 43, 56; Wm. 38, 42.
JAMISON, JAMIESON, David 38; Jas. 42.

JAUDON, Elias 61, 63; Jas. 18; Jno. 9, 22;
 Paul 30, 36; Saml. 36.
JAY, Jno. 91.
JEFFER, Jno. 12, 25.
JEFFORDS, Danl 6, 15; Jno. 6, 15; Jno. Jr. 4.
JEFFREYS, JEFFERIES, Nath. 80, 103; Rich. 52;
 Thos. 52.
JEMSTER, Saml. 54.
JENKINS, Benj. 8, 19; Benj. Jr. 19; Danl. 8,
 19; David 78, 90; Franc. 54; Jas. 16; Jno.
 61, 63; Jos. 8, 19, 34, 61, 63; Saml. 34;
 Thos. 30, 33; Thos. W. 44, 47; Wm. 70.
JENNERET, Jacob 9, 22.
JENNINGS, Gideon 70; Jas. 12; John Sr. 67,
 69, 73; Phillip 67, 73; Phillip Jr. 70.
JERMAIN, Edward 9, 22.
JERVEY, Thos. 25.
JERVIS, Jno. 21.
JESMAN, Philip 17.
JESTER, David 99.
JETER, Jno 63; Wm. 54.
JEVELAH, JEVELEY, Henry 88, 104.
JOEL, Ratcliffe 93, Thos. 7, 18.
JOHN, Jonathan 42.
JOHNSON, Alex. 90; Danl. 92, Hugh 89; Jacob 42;
 Jas. 30; Jno. 78, 87 (2), 90, 91; Jno. Jr. 78,
 91; Jos. 67, 71; Patrick 20; Robt. 57; Wm. 4,
 12, 25, 79, 87, 104.
JOHNSTON, And. 9, 21; Barnard 47; Chas 4, 12,
 25; Fran. 76, 84; Gilbert 30, 33; Henry 84;
 Howell 100; Jas. 30 (2), 33 (2), 56, 80, 95,
 103; Jno. 61, 63, 65, 76, 79, 83, 95 (2),
 101, 103; Jos. 97; Mich. 96; Nathan 65, 98;
 Patrick 19; Robt. 7, 18; Thos. 97; Wm. 47,
 94, 96.
JOHNSTONE, Thos. 36.
JOINER, Jos. 53.
JOLLY, JOLLEY, Archibold 36; Jas. 101; Jos.
 30, 36, 102, 103; Jos. Jr. 35; Wm. 103.
JONES, Adam Crain 77, 87; Andrew 85; Chas. 101;
 Dacker 92; Danl. 77, 88; David 92; Edmond 70;
 Edward 40, 41; Evan 70; Fran. 22, 81, 100;
 Frederick 95; Gibeon 95; Henry 80, 98; Jacob
 53, 95; Jas. 42, 97; Jesse 94; Jno. 34, 36,
 53 (2), 65, 84, 89, 92, 94, 103; Jonathan 54;
 Jos. 12, 25, 83; Joshua 43; Joshua B. 97;
 Moses 57, Nicholas 91; Rich. 99; Ralph 51;
 Robt. 92; Saml. 12 (2), 18, 25 (2); Stephen
 102; Thos. 4, 12, 25, 59, 80, 91, 95, 98;
 Wm. 34, 51 53, 54, 70, 81, 99, 100, 103.
JOOR, Geo. 29, 32; Jno. 7, 17; Jos. 17.
JORDAN, Adam 34, 83; Christopher 20; Jno. 43,
 56; Robt. 20, 34; Thos. 99; Wm. 34.
JOSEPH, Irael 12, 25.
JOURNEY, John 80, 103.
JOY, Benj. 15; Jas. 81; Rich. 22; Thos. 15.
JOYNER, SEE JOINER, Jas. 61, 63; Jeremiah 77,
 87; Jno. Jr. 61, 63; Jno. Sr. 61, 63
JRNST, SEE IRNST, John 25.
JUDY, Henry 69.
JULIAN, Jacob 57.
JUNE, Jno. 37; Peter 31, 37.
KALLER, Jacob 68.
KALTEISEN, Michael 4, 12, 25.
KANN, Andrew 9; Jos. 9.
KARNER, Jacob 69.
KARR, Henry 56; Jacob 67; Peter 92; Philip 69.
KARWON, Thos 7, 17.
KAUFMAN, KOFFMAN, David 12, 25.
KATSER, Christian 66, 72.
KEABER, Henry 71.
KEAL, David 62, 64; Geo. 64.
KEAN, KEEN, Geo. 12, 25; Jno. 61, 63, 65; Wm. 4.

KEASON, Canan 51.
KEATING, Edward 76, 85; Jno. 62, 64; Rich. 64.
KECKERLEY, Geo. 16.
KEER, Jno. 54.
KEELOCK, Isaac 58.
KEIGLER, KAIGLER, And. 72; And. Jr. 71.
KEITH, Benj. 32, 38; Jas. 4, 12, 25, 32, 38.
KELL, Jno. 52.
KELLER, Danl. 67; Jno. 67, 90, Mich. 12, 25.
KELLOUGH, Jno. 58; Robt. 59.
KELLSALL, Jno. Bellinger 65.
KELLY, KELLEY, Danl. 66, 68; Edw. 91; Gersham
 66, 68; Hugh 96; Isaac 78, 90; Jas. 92, 96;
 Jas. Jr. 92; Jno. 59; Jos. 94; Rich. 103;
 Saml. 78, 92; Thos. 17; Wm. 58.
KEMMEL, KIMMEL, Jos. 4, 12, 25.
KEMP, Thos. 46.
KEMPSTER, Benj. 16.
KENLINE, Christopher 66, 68.
KENNEDAY, KENNEDY, Edm. 103; Felix 55; Jno.
 51, 56, 102, Thos. 43; Wm. 103.
KENNEG, Geo. 20.
KENNERLY, Jno. 46; Jos. 72; Saml 66, 72;
 Thos. 66.
KENNINGTON, Edw. 49
KENVILY, Jas. 72.
KEOWN, James 83.
KERKNER, Jno. 12, 25.
KERN, Lewis 67.
KERR, Jas. 84; Malc. 47; Peter 78; Robt. 58;
 Saml. 76, 86; Wm. 84.
KERSHAW, Eli (Ely) 40, 41, 44, 60; Jos. 44, 60;
 Wm. 44, 60.
KETTLES, Jno. 65; Peter 65.
KEY, Henry 77, 89; Michael 88.
KEYLER, Henry 18.
KICKER, Andrew 71.
KICKELEY, Conrad 16.
KILLCRAS, KILLCRESS, Arth. 89, Obadiah 98.
KILLINGSWORTH, Jacob 51.
KILPATRICK, Jas. 58; Thos. 58.
KILSAW, Robt. 52.
KIMBALL, Benj. 47; Chas. 47; Fredk. 49.
KIMBROUGH, Jno. 40, 41.
KIMMEL, SEE KEMMEL
KINCAID, Jno. 59; Wm. 56.
KINEWINDER, Geo. 66 -SEE STINWINDER
KING, Chas. 78, 91; Ethelder 78; Etheldred 89;
 Fredk. 68; Geo. 41, 49; Geo. Sr. 66, 68;
 Hartwell 52; Henry 49, Jas. 4, 12, 25; Jno.
 45; Jos. 78, 89, Nathl. 52; Rich. 77, 87;
 Robt. 49; Thos. 31, 37; 102, Wm. 18.
KINSLER, John 71.
KINSLEY, Zephaniah 4, 12, 25.
KIRBY, Wm. 35.
KIRCH,   bd 71.
KIRK, Gideon 64; Jas. 81, 92; Wm. 64.
KIRKINDALL, Peter 46.
KIRKLAND, Fran. 51; Jos. 45; Rich. 70, 80, 97;
 Thos. 100; Wm. 45, 97.
KIRKPATRICK, Fran. 54; Jas. 54.
KIRKWOOD, Jas. 87.
KLEKLEY, Jno. 71.
KNIGHT, Jas. 42; Moses Jr. 48; Zachariah 65.
KNOBLE, KNODLE, Fredk. 69, 71.
KNOWLES, Jacob 51.
KNOX (SEE NOX), And. 45; Jas. 46; Jno. 36;
 Robt. 12, 25; Saml. 31, 37; Wm. 34.
KOFFMAN, SEE KAUFMAN
KOGER, Joseph 8, 19.
KOLB, Abel 40, 41, 43; Benj. 42.
KOPSTATS, Jno. 68, 73.
KOUBENSACK, Michael 16.

117

KRITER, Conrad, 69.
KUYKENDALL, Simon 56.
LABRUCE, Joseph 29, 33; Thomas 29, 33.
LACEY, LACY, Edward 54; Reuben, 53;
    Saml. 15; Wm. 92.
LAIBSON, Abraham 7, 18; Robt. 8, 21;
    Thomas 8, 18, 20; Wm. 9, 21.
LAHIFF, John, 12, 25.
LAIRD, Lodwick 93; Robt. 52; Saml. 94.
LALY, John 46.
LAMBERT, John 8, 21.
LAMBRIGHT, John 20.
LAMPRIER, Clement 6, 15.
LAND, John 54.
LANDOUM, Samuel 80, 98.
LANDTRYS, Shadrach, 102.
LANE, James 31, 36; Peter, 38.
LANG, David 96; James 96; Richard 96;
    Robt. 96; Wm. 42, 44, 59, 96.
LANGDON, Thomas 76, 84.
LANGEL, Jacob 83.
LANGFORD, Nicholas 12, 27.
LANGLEY, Isom 100.
LANNEAU, Bazil, Bazille, 4, 12, 25;
    John 4, 12, 25.
LANSDALE, Thomas, 37.
LARESEY, John, 70.
LARGENT, Thomas, 79, 96.
LARIMOR, Edward, 99.
LARK, John 78, 89; Robert, 67, 71.
LAROACH, James 8, 19.
LARRY, Robert 12, 25.
LASLESS, LASLES, James 91; Williamson,
    78, 91.
LATHAM, Moses, 57; Richard, 12, 25;
    Thomas, 4, 12, 25.
LATIMORE, LATIMER, LATTIMER, Francis 103;
    John 56; Robert, 58; Samuel, 34.
LATON, Joshua 102; Thomas, 102.
LAUGHLIN, William, 56.
LAUGHTON, Winburn, 19.
LAURENCE, LAWRENCE, Benj. 85; Henry 4;
    John 84; Wm. 12.
LAURENS, Henry 12, 26.
LAW, John 48; Wm. 31, 37.
LAWTON, Joseph 62, 65.
LAYFIELD, George, 12, 26.
LAZARUS, Markes, 12.
LEACH, LEECH, David 59; Thomas 77, 87.
LEARNY, William 57.
LEARY, Edward 59.
LEDENHAM, Wm. 51.
LEE, Andrew, 99; Anthony, 47; Edw. 58;
    James Brown 86; John 34, 46; Jno. Brown,
    87; Joseph 56; Maurice 7, 17; Michael,
    102; Robt. 49, 67, 71; Stephen 3, 10,
    24; Thomas, 76, 83; William 4, 12, 16,
    26, 79, 100.
LEEPER, Robert 46.
LEESON, Joseph 4, 12, 25.
LEFFANE, James 96.
LEGARE, LAGARE, Daniel 4, 12; Daniel Jr.
    26; Isaac 15; Joseph 9, 22; Nathan 6,
    15; Samuel 4, 12, 25; Soloman 4, 12, 25;
    Thomas 4, 12, 25; Thos.Jr. 4, 12, 25.
LEGER, John 37.
LEGGE, Edward 18; Edward Jr. 20.
LEGRAND, Isaac 9, 22.
LEICHTENSTENKENGSTIGER, Melchoir, 64.
LEIGNER, John, 53.
LEITCH, Andrew, 8, 21.
LEMAR, James, 80, 97; Philip 80, 98;
    Robert, 80, 98; Thomas, 80 (2), 98 (2).
LEMOCKS, John, 19.
LEMON, David, 37; James, 55.

LENNOX, Enoch 52; James 4, 12, 25; William
    4, 12, 25.
LENORE, Isaac, 47; Thomas, 46, 59.
LEOMAS, Thomas 70.
LEONARD, Davice, 51; John, 51.
LEOPARD, Thomas, 99.
LEPEAR, Paul, 29, 32.
LE POOLE, Peter, 12, 25.
LEQUEX, LEQUEUX, Peter, 31, 37.
LESESNE, Daniel, 29, 32; Isaac, 7, 17;
    Peter, 29, 32, 38.
LESLEY, LESSLY, LASLEY, James, 57; John,
    76, 86; Samuel, 83; William, 86, 97.
LESTER, William, 30, 35.
LETCHER, James, 77, 89.
LEVEL, LEVILL, Robert, 78, 96.
LEVISTON, John, 47.
LEWIS, Adam, 22; Azariah, 88; Benj. 82, 93;
    Crawford, 92; George, 52; Isaac, 81, 100;
    Jacob 53; James 57; Jeremiah 49; John 51;
    Robt. 48; Thomas, 17, 50, 92; Wm. 9, 22,
    54, 65; William Henry, 29, 33.
LEY, Richard, 100.
LEYTON, Patrick, 49.
LIBBIE, Nathaniel, 63.
LIBEBRAND, Christopher, 71.
LIBECAP, Matthew, 66, 72.
LIBHARD, Casper, 72.
LIBINDER, Barnard, 17.
LIDLE, Andrew, 76, 83; James, 76, 84.
LIDE, Robert, 40, 41; Thomas, 40 (2),
    William, 40 (2).
LIEBENHENTZ, Henry, 21.
LIGHTNER, Geo. 50; Michael, 66, 72.
LIGHTSEY, George, 91.
LIGHTWOOD, Edward 4, 12, 25; John 62, 64.
LIKES, George, 71.
LILEBRIDGE, Hampton, 21.
LILES, LISLES, Amenus 55; John 78, 91, 103
LIMBUCKER, George, 99.
LINAM, George, 79, 101.
LINDER, Jacob, 17; John Jr. 64; John Sr. 64.
LINLEY, Isaac, 91; James 93; John 100.
LINDOWER, LINDOUR, Henry, 4, 12, 28.
LINDSAY, LINDSEY, LINSEY, Abraham, 91;
    Ezekiel 92; James 31, 35; John 78, 83,
    84, 91 (2), 92; Moses, 96; Robert, 4,
    12, 25; Samuel, 84; William 37.
LINGETON, Richard, 33.
LINN, see LYNN.
LINNING, Charles, 12, 25; John, 7, 18.
LISSEY, Thomas, 83.
LISTER, Andrew, 50.
LISTON, Thomas, 12, 25.
LITMAN, Zerobabel, 34.
LITTLE, Aaron 66, 68; Geo. 101; Jas. 95;
    John, 101; Jones 101; Jos. 102; Robt. 20;
    Samuel 44; Wm. 44, 86; Wm. Jr. 83.
LITTLEJOHN, Charles, 102; Samuel, 80, 102.
LITTLETON, Charles, 90.
LIVERT, LIVERET, Robert, 78, 90.
LIVINGSTON, Geo. 8, 21; Henry 19; John 21;
    Robt. 53; Thos. 34; Wm. 4, 12, 25.
LIZARD, LYZARD, John, 69, 73.
LLOYD, LOYD, Benja. 49; Jos. 45, 61, 63.
LOCKHART, Aaron, 54; John 56, Robert, 56.
LOCKWOOD, Joshua, 4, 12, 25.
LODGE, William, 100.
LOFTON, John, 97; William, 97.
LOGAN, Andrew, 87; Francis, 87; Henry, 86;
    John, 8, 19, 86; Joseph, 22; William, 4,
    12, 25, 97.
LOGDRIDGE, Robert, 57.
LOMANICK, LOMANUK, Jacob Sr. 90; Jacob, 91.
LONER, Michael, 55.

LONG, Felix 4, 12, 25; Geo. 83; Henry, 102;
  Jas. 84; Robt. 92; Thos. 72; Wm. 4, 12, 25.
LONGMIRE, George, 98.
LOOCOCK, Aaron, 4, 12, 25; Wm. 4, 12, 25.
LOOSK, James, 76, 85.
LORD, Andrew, 4, 12, 26; Benjamin, 4, 12,
  26; Joseph, 55; Thomas, 41.
LOVE, Alex. 46; Andrew, 58; Benj. 52; Isaac,
  45; James, 47, 59; John, 53; Matthew, 95;
  Robert, 51, 53; William, 56.
LOWERY, LOWERRY, LOWRY, John, 49; Robert,
  45, 57; William, 19, 55, 94.
LOWNDES, Rawlins, 12, 25, 73.
LOWTHER, Edward, 41.
LUCAS, Harrison, 35; John, 42, 43, 81, 95,
  99; Joshua, 42.
LUCKIE, John, 84; William, 76, 84.
LUDLAM, Isaac, 30, 33.
LUICH, John, 12, 25.
LUKE, Daniel, 42.
LUNDAY, LUNDY, Daniel, 42; George, 98;
  Simon, 42.
LUPTAN, William, 29, 32, 38.
LUSHINGTON, Richard, 4, 12, 25.
LUSK, Robert, 58; Samuel, 58.
LYBERT, LYBURT, Henry, 4, 12, 25.
LYLE, LYELL, James, 8, 20; Robert, 53.
LYNCH, Aaron 93; Jas. 12, 25; Thos. 4, 12.
LYNES, Samuel, 16.
LYNN, LENN, LINN, John, 51; Vallentine, 8,
  21, 80, 98; William, 56.
LYON, John, 4, 12, 25, 54.
McALPIN, Alexander 76, 83, 84; Robt. 83.
McBEE, Vardry, 80, 102.
McBETH, MACBETH, Alexander, 5, 13, 26.
McBRIDE, Alexander, 83; Archd. 43.
McCAA, William, 51.
McCAIN, Andrew, 54; James, 94.
McCALL, Charles, 40, 41; James, 5, 13, 26,
  84; John, 5, 12, 13, 26 (2), 40, 41;
  John Jr. 12, 26; Thomas, 32, 38.
McCALLY, John, 54.
McCAMMON, William, 51.
McCANTS, Alexander, 36; John 38; Nathaniel,
  35; Thomas, 30, 35.
McCARLEY, William, 85.
McCARTER, Abraham, 56; Moses, 83.
McCARTNEY, Michael, 100.
McCARTY, McCARTEY, Cornelius, 61, 63;
  Michl. 52; William, 89.
McCAULEY, McCAULLEY, Jas. 47; Jno. 31, 37.
McCAUTRY, Robert, 31; William, 31.
McCAXS, John, 54.
McCAY, Hugh, 76, 84.
McCELLEN, Hugh, 58.
McCLANAHAN, McCLENEHAN, James, 12, 26;
  John, 51; Samuel, 55.
McCLEAN, John, 58; Sampson, 89.
McCLEARING, Daniel, 80, 102.
McCLELLAN, McCLELLEN, McLELAN, Robert, 58;
  William, 79, 85, 101.
McCLENDON, McLENDON, Bryan, 53; Dennis, 48;
  Ezekiel, 98; Joel, 98; Lewis, 48.
McCLENNAN, Archd. 22.
McCLESKEY, McCLOESKAY, David Jr. 86;
  Joseph, 84, 86.
McCLINTICK, McCLINTOCK, James, 93; John 93;
  Timothy, 54.
McCLINTON, Samuel, 86,
McCLOCKLAN, McCLOCKLAN, Robert 13, 26.
McCLUER, McCLUIR, James, 52; John, 52;
  Samuel, 47.
McCLURG, Jas. 48.

McCLURKEN, Thomas, 93.
McCOLE, McCOOLE, Adam, 52; Gabriel, 90;
  Joseph, 52.
McCOLLESTER, McCOLLISTER, Nathan, 86;
  William, 55.
McCOLPIN, John, 54.
McCOMB, Andrw. 86; George, 83.
McCOMMON, James, 54.
McCONAN, James, 90.
McCONICO, Wm. 44.
McCONNELL, McCONNEL, George, 37; James 37;
  Robt. 31, 37; Thos. 37; Wm. 31, 36, 89.
McCORD, Adam, 103; James, 92; John, 85.
McCORKEL, McCORKALL, Archibald 56;
  Samuel, 12, 26.
McCORMICK, James, 48.
McCORTH, Abraham, 58.
McCOTTRY, Robert, 36; William, 36.
McCOWN, John, 55; Moses, 54.
McCOY, Wm. 45.
McCRACKEN, McCRACKIN, McCRACKON, Alexr. 37;
  James 94; Robert 34.
McCRARY, McCREARY, McCRERY, Alex. 85, 86;
  Gilbert 86; Robert 50, 94.
McCREA, McCRAE, MECREA, Alex. 37; Alex. Jr.
  31, 37; Alex. Sr. 31; James, 93; John,
  37, 81, 92; Thomas, 36, 87.
McCREADY, McREADY, Edward, 13, 26.
McCREW, John, 36.
McCULLEIGN, William, 57.
McCULLOUGH, McCOLLOUGH, McCOLOUGH,
  McCULLOUCH, McCULLOCH, George 64, 91;
  Hance, 21; Hugh, 31, 36; James, 36, 48,
  49, 83; John, 37; Nathl. 36; Thomas, 58;
  William, 20, 34.
McCURDY, Robert, 57.
McCUTCHEN, James Jr. 35.
McDANIEL, Angus, 99; Daniel, 97; Hugh, 46;
  John, 55; William, 81, 93, 94.
McDAVID, John, 93; Patrick, 93.
McDILL, Nathl. 53.
McDONALD, Absolem, 89; Adam 31, 37; Arch.
  31, 37; James 36, 44; John 31, 37; Middle-
  ton 49, Peter 22, Thos. 93; William, 31,
  37, 46, 83.
McDOUGAL, McDOOGAL, Alexander, 80, 103.
McDOW, James, 57; William, 57.
McDOWELL, McDOWALL, Archd. 29, 32; Enoch 43;
  John, 36; Wm. 36, 40, 41, 58, 87.
McELFEE, Robert, 56.
McELVEEN, McKELVEEN, Adam 49; John 31, 37.
McELVE, Samuel, 83.
McELVERIN, Daniel, 56.
McELWEE, William, 85.
McENTIRE, Daniel, 85.
McFADDEN, John, 45, 54; William, 54.
McFARLAN, McFARLAND, McFARLEN, John 8, 21,
  85; Mordacai, 68.
McFERRON, James Sr. 86.
McGARAH, Wm. 49.
McGARTH, Michael, 58.
McGAW, John, 86; William, 76, 86.
McGILL, James 96; John 83, 84; Roger 30, 36;
  Saml. 31; Saml Jr. 37. (SEE MAGILL)
McGILLIVERY, McGILLEVIRY, McGILVEREY,
  Robert, 19; William, 13, 26.
McGIN, Daniel, 97.
McGINNEY, Daniel, 30, 35.
McCLOMORY, John, 51.
McGOWEN, McGOWN, James, 62, 64, 83; Wm. 83.
McGRAW, David 50; Edward, 50; Wm. 50.
McGREGOR, McGREGER, Alexander, 29, 32;
  Daniel, 9, 22.

McGRIFF, Patrick, 53.
McGUINAS, Thomas, 80, 98.
McHAFFY, Robt. 49.
McHERD, McHERDS, John, 81, 92.
McINTOSH, MACKINTOSH, Alex. 40, 41; Lachlan, 20.
McJUNKIN, Joseph, 102; Samuel, 102.
McKAY, John, 48; Jos. 44; Samuel, 48.
McKEALY, James, 58.
McKEARY, Thomas, 81.
McKEE, Adam, 77, 87; Alex. 49; Allen 61, 63; Daniel, 80, 102; Wm. 50.
McKEEN, William, 85.
McKELVEEN, see McELVEEN
McKELVIAN, William 35.
McKEMMY, McKIMMY, William 5, 13, 26.
McKENZIE, Robert, 19.
McKEWN, McKEWEN, Hugh, 50; James, 8, 21.
McKINLEY, John, 84; William, 76, 84.
McKINNEY, McKINNIE, McKENNY, McKEANY, McKENEY, Benj. 97; Geo. 92; John 51, 53, 55; Joseph 57; Roger 88, 104; Samuel 51; Thomas 92; Timothy 104; Wm. 46.
McKINS, Elisha 51.
McKISSOCK, Daniel 102.
McKNIGHT, Alexr. 31, 36; John 36; Wm. 37.
McKOWN, Alexander 51.
McLAUGHLIN, William, 8, 21.
McLEARY, Robert, 82.
McLEMARR, Francis, 103
McLEMORE, Joel, 45.
McMAHON, Cornelius 82, 94; Jas. 94; Wm. 87.
McMANUS, Thomas 43.
McMARTY, Samuel, 85.
McMASTER, Patrick 84; William 84.
McMEEN, Joseph 56; Thomas 55.
McMESTERSON, Patrick John 83.
McMICKLE, George 69.
McMORRIS, McMILLEN, James, 104; John 102; Matthew 104.
McMORRIS, Wm. 50.
McMULDROUGH, Hugh 42; Jno. 40, 41; Jno. Jr. 42.
McMULLIN, John 50.
McMURDY, Henry, 85.
McMURRAY, Samuel, 57.
McNABB, Andrew 58; James 59; John 58.
McNALLY, Henry, 12.
McNAMUS, James 49.
McNARNEY, George, 19.
McNASS, Robert, 93.
McNEAL, McNEEL, Edward, 80, 102.
McNEESS, James, 93.
McNELLIDGE, Alexander, 15.
McNETT, Mackey, 41, 43.
McNKNIGHT, John, 59.
McPHERSON, Elias 36; Isaac 8, 21; Job 62, 64; John 62, 64, 101; Ulysses 62, 64.
McQUATERS, Alexander, 50.
McQUEEN, Alex. 5, 13; John 5, 13.
McQUIN, Daniel, 35.
McQUISTON, David, 52; James, 52.
McREADY, see McCREADY
McREE, John 31; William 36.
McRIGHT, Quinton, 53.
McRUN, William, 103.
McTIER, McTEER, John 62, 64; Wm. 97.
McVERVEY, William, 56.
McWALTER, Heugh, 16.
McWATERS, James, 58.
McWEE, William, 56.
McWHORTER, McWHORTIE, Alex. 59; George, 103; John, 103.

MacWILLIAMS, John, 66, 68.
McWILL, David, 89.
MABRY, Ephraim, 55; Joel, 91.
MACBETH, see McBETH
MACK, Philip, 17.
MACKAY, Elisha, 48.
MACKEE, Joseph, 31.
MACKELVAIN, MEKELVAIN, James 79, 100.
MACKELWAIN, Andw. 55.
MACKEY, Charles, 49; John, 45.
MACKIE, James, 12, 26.
MACKINTOSH, see McINTOSH.
MACKLEMURRY, Patrick, 67, 71.
MADDING, MADING, John, 96; Lock, 96.
MADDOX, Wm. 49.
MAGILL, John 29, 33.
MAGUS, Thomas 35.
MAHAM, Hezekiah, 9, 22.
MAHON, James, 92.
MAHONE, John, 92.
MAHONY, MAHONNEY, Dennis, 8, 20.
MAINE, MAYNE, James, 17; Walter, 12, 26.
MAIRS, Robert, 79, 94.
MALONE, Lewis, 42. See MELONE
MALTBY, William, 64.
HAMILTON, John 77. See HAMILTON
MANAREY, Gibert, 93.
MANAU, Samuel, 95.
MANDERSON, George 42; John 40, 41, 43.
MANLEY, John 93.
MANN, MAN, James, 53; Newby, Nuby, 89, 98; Samuel, 85.
MANNER, Samuel, 65.
MANNON, Moses, 35; Thomas, 57.
MANSFIELD, Richard, 34.
MANSON, Daniel, 6, 15.
MAPLES, Thomas, 44.
MAPP, Littleton, 80, 103.
MARCHBANKS, George, 103; William, 103.
MARGEW, see MARQUE
MARION, Benj. 7, 17; Benj. Jr. 16; Francis, 16; James 16; Job 16; Jos. 7, 16; Paul 16.
MARK, MARKS, John 68; Jos. 99, Richard 95.
MARKELL, John 23.
MARKLEY, MARTLEY, MERKLEY, Abra. 5, 13, 26.
MARL, Benjamin 57.
MARLOW, Robert 65; Wm. 50.
MARPOLE, Thomas, 15.
MARQUE, MARGEW, Henry 13, 26.
MARS, Robert, 78, 95.
MARSDEN, William, 37.
MARSH, John, 42; Samuel, 99.
MARSHALL, Abraham 99; Alex. 4, 12, 26; James 49; John 45, 53.
MARTIN, MARTAIN, Benj. 43; David 51, 60; George 91, 92; Hawkins 21; James 52, 55, 80, 84, 101, 102; John 50, 60, 76, 85, 102; John Christopher, 16; Joseph 45, 84; Lachlan 12, 26; Moses 35; Robt. 50, 51, 52, 84; Roger 85; Shadrach 93; Thomas 86; William 44, 85, 94.
MARTINANGET, Francis 61, 63; Philip 62, 64.
MASON, MAYSON, Charles 40, 41, 43; James 78, 88, John 82, 93; Joseph 41; Wm. 12.
MASSER, James 50.
MASSEY, James 79; William 12, 45.
MATHENSHED, Chris. 49.
MATHEWS, MATTHEWS, MATHEWES, Benj. 4, 7, 18; Edmond 66, 68; George 7, 18; Isaac 31, 37, 85; Isaac Edward 89; James 42; John 4, 12, 13, 16, 26, 31, 37, 104; John Raven 4, 12, 26; Jos. 87; Moses 50; Thos. 42; Victor, 87; Wm. 7, 18, 31, 37, 78, 88, 96.

MAUL, David, 12, 26.
MAVERICK, Samuel 12, 26.
MAXEY, Joseph 19; Robert 19.
MAXWELL, John, 87; William 8, 19.
MAY, John 35, 44, 52.
MAYBAN, William 91.
MAYBANK, Joseph 6, 15.
MAYBERRY, James 80, 102.
MAYES, Abner 101; Andrew 100; James 100.
MAYFIELD, John 80, 102.
MAZYCK, Alexander 6, 16; Benjamin 6, 16; Isaac 4, 13, 26; Stephen 5, 13, 16; Stephen Jr. 6, 16.
MEADOWS, Jason 43.
MEANS, MAENS, Hugh 79, 100; Wm. 79, 100.
MECREA see McCREA.
MEDILE, Thomas 51.
MEEKS, John 94.
MEFATRICK, John 98.
MEGEE, James 38.
MEGUINAS see McGUINAS
MEHANNE, Benjamin 101.
MELCHEROFF, John 71.
MELICKAMP, Thomas 21.
MELL, Thomas 18; William 21.
MELLARD, William 17.
MELLETT, Peter 44.
MELONE, Thomas 101.
MELTON, MILTON, Nathaniel 81, 100; Robt. 100.
MELVIL, Robert 76, 83.
MENTZ, MENZ, Casper 69, 73.
MENTZING, Philip 13, 26.
MERCER, Richard 5, 13, 26.
MERRIWEATHER, MERIWATHER, MERRWEATHER, Robt. 77, 88, 104; Wm. 77, 88, 104.
MESLEMAY, William 91.
MESSEL, Joseph 50.
MESSER, Joseph 99, Robert 76, 86.
METZ, Christopher 69.
MEWHANNY, William 5, 13.
MEYER, MYER, Frederick, 69; Philip 5, 13, 26.
MEYERS, MYERS, MYRES, Adrian 62, 64; Daniel, 32, 38; George 40, 41; Jacob 45, 67; John, 66, 67, 68; John Adam 17; Wm. 45.
MICHAEL, John 13, 26.
MICHAU, MICHAW, Daniel 31, 36; Isaac 31, 36; Paul 31, 36; William 31, 37.
MICHEL, William 102.
MICHAM, Joshua 102.
MICKIE, Joseph 37.
MICKLER, Joseph 66, 68; Nicholas 66, 72.
MIDDLETON, Andsworth 81, 93; Arthur 5, 13, 26; Henry 13; Hugh 77, 89; John 76, 84; Martyn 33; Rich. 47; Thomas 4, 12; William 30, 33.
MIGGET, William 61, 63.
MIGHTLER, Peter 72.
MIKELL, MICKLE, MICKELL, Ephraim 19; John, 40, 41, 43; Joseph 46, 61, 63.
MILES, MYLES, Allen 8, 21; Aquilla 62, 65; Edward 70; Francis 53; James 54; Jeremiah 8, 20; John 8, 20, 52; Josiah 20; Lewis 9, 22; Robt. 21; Saml. 85; Thos. 89; Wm. 85.
MILEY, Henry 53.
MILIAR, Mana 78.
MILLEGAN James 83.
MILLER, MILLAR, Abra. 69; Andrew 51, 86; Charles 55; David 20, 49; Emanuel 69, 73; Jacob 63; James 20, 97; John 46, 50, 68, 76, 80, 84, 92, 93, 98; John Jr. 69; John Sr. 69; Jos. 80, 97; Martin 4, 12, 26; Moses 31, 37; Samuel 12, 26; Thomas 20; William 4, 12.

MILLHOUS, MILLHOUSE, Henry 101; John 44.
MILLING, MILLIN, David 4, 12, 26; Robert 54; William 54.
MILLS, MILL, John 55; Wm 5, 8, 13, 20, 26; 45; Wm. Henry 40, 41, 43.
MILLWEE, William 92.
MILNER, John 15; Solomon 18.
MILTON See MELTON
MIMS, MINNS, Drury 81, 99; John 99.
MINERS, Jacob 16.
MINGLEDORF, George 64.
MINICK, Adam 13.
MINIGH, Barthw. 72.
MINIS, James 17.
MINOT, John 12.
MINTER, John 97.
MINTON, MINTEN, Jesse 47; John 80; Wm. 57.
MIOT, MIOTT, John 12, 26.
MIRES, MICHAEL 80, 98.
MIRTHLAN, Matthew 77, 87.
MITCHELL, Anthony 7, 16; Benj. 77, 87; Edw. 29, 33; Ephraim 4, 13; Flud 99; Isaac 77, 87, 97; John 9, 21, 40, 41, 43, 48, 81, 100; Nimrod 53; Thomas 29, 32, 38.
MITH, Philip 90.
MITTER, Henry 52.
MITIS, Henry 90.
MIXON, Frans. 35; John 48; Michael 34, 43; Samuel 43; William 35, 48.
MOAKE, Jacob 71.
MOBLEY, Benjamin 51; Clemen 51; Edward 55; Eliazer 46; Samuel 51.
MOCK, George Sr. 81, 99; John 99.
MOFFETT, John 57.
MOLHOLLAND, Henry 22.
MOLLERY, Joseph 37.
MOLLETT, John 20.
MONK, John 66, 68, 96.
MONT (MOUT?) George 64.
MONTGOMERY, MONGOMERY, Geroge 90, Henry 44; Hugh 31, 37; James 48; John 56; Nathaniel, 31, 36; Robt. 56; Wm. 44, 56.
MOODY, Charles 35.
MOON, James 64; Patrick 5, 13, 26.
MOORE, Benj. 88; David 57; Horatio 34; Hugh, 80, 103; Isham 44; Jacob 34; James 54, 56, 59, 62, 67, 71, 78, 88, 92, 104; John 7, 17, 36, 47, 59, 62, 64, 78, 85 (2), 86, 87, 88, 104 (2); Joseph 85; Joshua 77, 87; Mordecai 92; Patrick 103; Richard 77, 87, 104; Robt. 80, 103; Thos. 52, 92; Wm. 30, 33, 36, 48, 78, 85, 86, 88, 101, 104.
MOORER, MURER, Jacob 73, John 73; Peter Jr. 69; Peter Sr. 66, 70.
MOORHEAD, Charles 56; James 103; John 103.
MOORLDOON, James 58.
MORGAN, Chrispen 55; Evan 81, 99; Henry 96; Isaac 91; Lewis 65; Nathaniel 4, 12, 19, 26; Thomas 91; Wm. 7, 17, 55, 102.
MORGANDOLLAR, John 6, 16.
MORRAL, Daniel 30, 33; John 29, 33.
MORRIS, MORRICE, Burrel 84; Edward 89; George 12, 26; James 70; John 52, 89, 99; Joseph 99; Mark 5, 13, 26; Robt. 46, 58, 59; Thomas 59, 83; William 97.
MORROW, Arthur 85; George 86; James 85; John 52; Samuel 84; Thomas 68.
MORTON, Hugh 54; John 52; Thomas 54.
MOSELEY, Benjamin 99; John 103; Robert, 80, 97; William 81, 99.
MOSES, Barnard 13, 26; Jacob 12, 26; Myer, 13, 26; Philip 13, 26; Robert 48.
MOSS, George 63.

MOTTE, Charles 4, 12, 26; Christopher 21;
  Isaac 5. 13; Jacob 5, 13; Stephen 48.
MOTTELY, John 53.
MOULTRIE, MOULTREY, Alex. 12, 26; John 54;
  Thos. 5, 13; Wm. 4, 12; Wm. Jr. 6, 16.
MOUNTS, Barnabus 91; Barnaby 78; Geo. 92.
MOURDAH, John 18.
MOUZON, MOUSON, Henry 37; Peter 9, 22.
MUCKELHANY, James 54.
MUCKENFUSS, MUCKINFUSS, George 17;
  Michael 5, 13, 26.
MUCKLEDUFF, Adam 34; Thomas 34.
MUDDING, John 93.
MUIRSET, MUERSET, Peter 5, 13, 26.
MULHEREN, James 87.
MULLENAX, John 56.
MUNCREEF, Richard 5, 13, 26; Robt. 4, 12, 26.
MUNNERLING, James 35.
MURFF, John 66, 72.
MURPHY, MURPHEY, James 58, 92, 104; John 49,
  59; Malachi 30, 33, 47, 59; Roger 96;
  William 70.
MURPLEY, William 98.
MURRAY, MURRY, Archibald 69, 76, 86; Isaac,
  34; James 8, 19, 104; John 80, 87, 98;
  Thomas 67; William 91, 95.
MURRELL, John 6, 15; Paul 6, 15; Peter 15;
  Robt. Jr. 6, 15; William 37.
MUSE, Daniel 53; Thomas 51, 53.
MUSGROVE, Edward 82, 93.
MYERS, See MEYERS.
NANCE, Peter 54.
NANN, Frederick 13, 26.
NARRIMER, Edwd. 47.
NAVILL, Isaac 42.
NEAL, NEIL, NEEL, NEELL, NEALE, Andrew
  87; Benj. 95; David 57; Geo. 87; Hugh 59;
  Jas. 83; Jonathan 97; Thos 46, 47; Wm. 88.
NEALY, NEELEY, NEELY, NEILY, NELLY, Chris.
  97; George, 95, 97; Hugh 58; James 51, 90;
  John 95; Matthew 58; Robert 58, 97; Saml.
  91; Wm. 51, 58.
NEATZ, Aberhart 52.
NEDHAMMER, George 13, 26.
NEEBLING, Jacob 68.
NEIGHBOURS, NEIGHBOR, Nathan 94; Samuel 81,
  92; William 95.
NEILSON, Isaac 31; James 5, 13, 26; Jared,
  44; William 59.
NEIZAR, Philip 13, 26.
NELAND, John 49; William 49.
NELLONS, Gilbert 47.
NELSON, Cornelius, 36; Hugh 101; Isaac 36;
  John 49; Robt. 51; Samuel Sr. 45; Samuel
  47; William 56.
NELTON, Robert 103.
NESMITH, Samuel 31, 35, 36.
NETTLE, NETTLES, George Jr. 36; Jesse 47;
  Robert 43; Zachariah 42.
NEUFVILLE, Edw. Jr. 13, 26; John 5, 13, 26.
NEWELL, Peter 38; Wm. 48.
NEWHALL, Thomas 33, 38.
NEWMAN, John 48, 67, 71, 95; Thomas 48;
  William 31, 37, 50.
NEWTON, Constantine 34; John 79, 96.
NEYLE, Sampson 5, 13.
NIAL, Casper 98.
NIBLET, John 98.
NICHOLS, NICOLL, NICKELS, Charters 94;
  Henry 8, 21; James 8, 21; John 80; Julius
  78, 88; Nathaniel 97; Soloman 94; Wm.
  13, 26.

NICHOLSON, NICKELSON, NICKASON, Andrew 99;
  David 81, 99; James 43; Wright 53, 81, 100.
NIMMONS, William 94.
NIPPER, James 99.
NISBETT, Joseph 101; Wm. 13, 26, 56.
NIX, Charles 51.
NIXON, Edward 55, 80, 102; John 51.
NOAK, John 17.
NOBLE, Alexander 76, 83; James 76, 83.
NODDINGS, George 5, 13, 26.
NOOK, Wm. 57.
NORMAN, Peter 22; Richard 16.
NORRELL, James 88; Thomas 88.
NORRIS, James 42; Robert 76, 85; Thomas 79,
  96; Wm. 49, 85, 100.
NORTH, Edward 5, 13, 26; John 13, 20;
  Richard 94; Thomas 35, 95.
NORTON, William 61, 63.
NOWLAND, Avery 78, 91.
NORWOOD, John 86; Samuel 77, 87; Theophelus
  43.
NOTT, Epaphras 33, 38.
NOX, John 90. See KNOX.
NUCKOLS, John 103.
NUGENT, Matthew 36.
NULEY, Richard 50.
NUNEMAKER, Benedict 72.
NUTT, Andrew 49; John 93; Wm. 50.
OATS, Edward 5, 13, 26; Peter 91.
ODAM, ODOM, Abraham 97; Hezekiah 98; Isaac
  70; Jacob 98; Michael 70; Moses 70; Owen
  70; Richard 70.
ODLE, John 81, 92.
OFFUTT, Archibald 80, 98.
OGELVIE, OGLEVIE, Geo. 44, 60.
OGELSBIE, OGELSBY, Elijah 70; Richard 70.
OGIER, OGEIR, Lewis 5, 13, 26.
OGLE, Robert 61, 63.
OGLETHORPE, Thomas 60.
OHAIR, OHARE, James 13, 26.
OLIPHANT, James 13, 26; John 98.
OLIVER, James 16; John 66, 68; Thomas 13.
ONEAL, ONEALE, ONEIL, Charles 97; Henry 82,
  95; Hugh 79, 94; John 41, 43, 94, 95;
  William 96.
ONSILD, Henry 16.
OPRY, Hugh 35.
OQUIN, Daniel 50.
ORR, James 101; William 31, 36, 102.
OSBORN, OSBORNE, Danl. 82, 93; Thos. 9, 21.
OSTA, Thomas 47.
OSWALD, Joseph 20, 61, 63; Michael 71;
  William 8, 19.
OTH, OTT, Casper 67, 69; Jacob Jr. 69; Jacob
  Sr. 73; John 73; Peter 69; Ulrick 68, 73.
OTTERSON, Samuel 80, 102.
OULEM, John 55.
OWEN, OWENS, Benja. 50; David 35; Edw. 35;
  James 36, 50; John 5, 13, 26, 93, 96; Jos.
  50; Philip 31, 36; Saml. 17; Walter 35.
OWINGS, Andrew 92; Richard 94.
PACE, Drury 77, 89; Nath. 44.
PACKROW, John 33, 38.
PADDEY, Peter 35.
PADDOM, Darby 34.
PAGAN, Alex. 52.
PAGE, Henry 50; Thomas 62, 64.
PAGET, Elijah 81, 100.
PAISLEY, John 47; Robt. 31, 36; Thos. 31, 36.
PALL, Archibald 50.
PALMER, Charles 62, 65; Ellis 102; James 102;
  Job 13, 26; John 9, 22, 102; John Jr. 9,

22; Joseph 9, 22, 66, 68; Peter 22.
PALMERIN, PALMERINE, Peter 64; Samuel 18.
PAMER, Isaac 91.
PANNEL, William 51.
PARISH, Gideon 35.
PARK, Anthony 95; Jacob 68; James 79, 100; William 67.
PARKER, Charles 84; Eliasha Jr. 42; Elisha Sr. 42; Gabriel 52; Isaac 103; John 5, 13, 35; Jonathan 79, 101; Joseph 87; Stephen 42; William 5, 13, 26, 34, 96.
PARKINS, John 49.
PARKINSON, John 67, 71; Nicholas 16.
PARLIN, Robert 43.
PARMENTER, Isaac 61, 63; John 64; Philip, 61, 63; Samuel 63.
PARMER, John 89.
PARNELL, James 103.
PARNERTON, Joseph 19.
PARROIK, John 47.
PARROT, Charles 93.
PARSONS, James 5, 13; Joseph 41.
PARTER, Frederick 67.
PARTIN, PARTEN, Charles 100; Jesse 100.
PARTMAN, Henry 88.
PATE, Charles 35.
PATRICK, Gabriel 103; Henry 66, 72; John 70; Robert 58; William 57.
PATTERSON, PATERSON, Andrew 37, 53; James 69, 73, 76; John 58; Joseph 93; Josiah 86; Mathew 53, 64; Peter 103; Samuel 83; Thomas 55; William 5, 13, 26.
PATTON, PATTEN, PATEN, Jas. 46; John 46, 57, 82, 94; Matthew 52; Michael 51;Robt. 46; Saml. 83, 85; Thos. 59; Wm. 79, 100.
PAUET, David 51.
PAULK, Jacob 102.
PAULLING, William 30, 35.
PAVELL, James 57.
PAWLEY, Anthony 29, 33; George 40, 41; Percival Jr. 29, 33; Percival Sr. 29, 33.
PAXTON, Samuel 36.
PAYNE, George 59; Geo. Sr. 46; John 44, 59; Joseph Sr. 46, 59.
PEA, George 49.
PEACE, Isaac 5, 13, 26.
PEACH, William 49.
PEACOCK, Abraham 70; Henry 87.
PEAK, Stephen 34.
PEARCE, PIERCE, Abraham 13; Francis 18; James 52; Josiah 40, 41; Thos. 42, 99.
PEARSON, Aaron 42; Enoch 91; Harry 95; John 45, 91, 92, 103; Jos. 81, 92; Joshua 33, 38; Moses 42; Philip 46; Samuel 78, 92; Thomas 92; Wm. 44, 78, 90.
PEAY, Nicholas 51.
PECK, Conrad 67; Peter 67.
PEEKINS, Robert 86.
PEGUES, Claudius Jr. 40, 41; Claudius Sr. 40, 41; William 40, 41.
PELOT, James 65; Samuel 65.
PEMBERTON, Geo. 78, 90; Isaac 78; Isaiah 90.
PEMBLE, Thomas 60.
PENCE, Hugh 58.
PENDAR, John Arnold 56.
PENDARVIS, Richard 62, 64; Thosas 17; Thomas Jr. 17.
PENDERGRASS, Darby 5, 13, 26.
PENDLETON, Henry 5, 13.
PENNY, Henry 102; Samuel 55.
PEPPER, Park 65.
PERDRIAU, PERDRIEAU, Andrew 17; Samuel 5, 13, 26.

PERDUE, Field 77, 88, 104.
PERKINS, PURKINS, Daniel 78, 89; David 32, 38, 43, 89; James 43; Joshua 35.
PERRICLARE, Michael 63.
PERRIMAN, Benjamin 20.
PERRIN, William 77, 89.
PERRY, Benj. 45; Edw. 8, 21; Francis 21; James 45; John 48, 90; Richard 8, 21; Silas 48; Thomas 90.
PESCOTT, John 100.
PESNEGAR, Martin 13, 26.
PESNER, Joseph 68.
PETER, PETERS, Christopher 9, 21; John 49, 57; Michael 21.
PETERSON, PETTERSON, Peter 56; Robert 57.
PETTETT, Tobias 102.
PETTICREW, PETTIEREW, Robert 31, 35.
PETTIGREW, Geo. 76, 84; James Jr. 83.
PETTY, PETTEY, Abner 49; Charles 78, 89; James 78, 89; Luke 49.
PETTYPOOL, PETTYPOOLES, Abraham 48; Ephraim 49; Peter 102.
PEYRE, John 9, 22; Samuel 9, 22.
PHEAGINS, Philip 97.
PHEPOE, Thomas 5, 13.
PHILHOUR, George 16.
PHILIPS, PHILLIPS, Benj. 58; Jas. 103; John 13, 26, 35, 43, 50 (2), 78, 96 (2); William 81, 99.
PHILP, Robert 5, 13, 26, 62, 64.
PHILPOT, Thomas 67, 71.
PICKENS, Andrew 76, 85; Gabriel 85; Isreal, 84; John 85; John Jr. 76, 84; John Sr.86; Jonathan 86; Joseph 76, 86; Saml. 70.
PIDGEON, Benja. 50, 60; Isaac 47.
PIERR, John 57.
PIGOT, PIGOTT, PIGGOTT, John Sr. 40, 41; Micajah, 50.
PINCKNEY, PICKNEY, Charles 5, 13, 104; Charles Cotesworth 5, 13; Hopson 7, 17; Thomas 5, 13.
PINCKSTON, John 79, 100.
PINKERTON, James 57.
PINKETT, Thomas 88.
PISLER, Frederick 67.
PITTS, Charles, 78, 96; Daniel 97; Henry, 78, 96, 97; Levi 97; William 95.
PLATT, Geo. 49; Randall 47.
PLAYER, Thomas 15; William 15, 45.
PLEDGER, John 40, 41; Joseph 40, 41; Philip 40, 41; Thomas 67.
PLOTTS, Chas. 64; Christian 70; Jacob 64.
PLOWDEN, Edward 31, 37; William 31, 37.
PLUMER, Daniel 79, 100; Wm. 79, 101.
PLUNKET, Charles 95; James 97; Robt. 95.
POAUG, John 5, 13, 26.
POLK, Daniel 43.
POLLARD, James 79, 94.
POLLOCK, Hugh 13, 26.
PONDER, James 76, 84.
POOLE, Philip 71.
POOR, Holloway 81, 93.
POOSER, George 6, 16; Henry 7, 17.
POPE, Barnaby 50; Lewis 50; Solomon 81, 99; Thomas 53.
PORCHER, Isaac 9, 22; Paul Jr. 62, 65; Paul Sr. 62, 65; Peter 9, 22; Phillip 5, 13; Samuel 62, 65.
PORT, Benjamin 30, 33.
PORTBOUS, Robert 61, 63.
PORTER, Benj. 29, 32, 38; Hugh 85; John 54; Samuel 54; William 34, 35, 38.
PORTERFIELD, John 78, 95.

PORTMAN, John 102.
POSEY, POSSEY, Francis 101; Harrison 76, 84; John 76, 84.
POSTAN, Jonathan 102.
POSTELL, Andrew 61, 64; Francis 17; James 44; Jas. Jr. 8, 20; John 29, 32, 44, 48.
POTTER, Adam 80, 102; Miles 47.
POTTS, George 80, 102; John 32, 38, 50; Thomas 32, 38.
POU, John 67, 70, 73; Philip 70; Wm. 67, 70.
POUNDS, John 97.
POUNEY, POUNCY, Anthony 40, 41.
POWE, Thomas 40, 41, 43.
POWELL, Geo. 5, 13, 26, 55; Geo. Gabriel 5, 13; Jacob 102; John 70; Jos. 61, 63; Nathaniel 81, 100; Richard 101; Robt. Wm. 5, 13, 26; Saml. 93; Thomas 67.
POWERS, John 35; Paul 53.
POYAS, John Ernest 5, 13, 26.
PRATOR, Basel 92; Josiah 92.
PRATT, William 76, 83.
PRENTWOOD, Augustine 47.
PRESLEY, PRESSLEY, David 76, 86; Wm. 31, 37.
PRESTWOOD, William 42.
PRETER, John 87.
PRETHRO, PRETHRA, Evan 42, 43.
PRICE, PRISE, Daniel Sr. 46; Hopkin 5, 13, 26; John 46, 59, 83; Richard 56; Samuel 5, 13, 26, 30, 33; Wm. 5, 13, 26.
PRIESTWOOD, Augustine 60.
PRINCE, Edward 89; Nicholas 34.
PRINE, Francis 95.
PRING, William 22.
PRINT, William 13, 26.
PRIOLEAU, Hext 5, 13, 26; John 62, 64; Philip 13, 26; Saml. 13; Saml. Jr., 5, 13, 26.
PRIOR, Luke 34; Seth 64; Thomas 18.
PRITCHARD, PRICHARD, John 80, 103; Paul 5, 13.
PROCTOR, Richd. 61, 63; Robt. 96; Saml. 97.
PROTOR, Brice 92.
PROW, Peter 13, 26.
PRUDA, John 92.
PRUETT, PRUET, David 102; Dudley 101.
PUCKETT, Charles 92; James 95.
PUGH, Edward 93; Willoughby 64.
PUNCH, Nicholas 35.
PURDY, Henry 86.
PURKET, Ephraim 70.
PURSLEY, James 59.
PURTZ, Frederick 69.
PURVIS, PURVES, Alex. 44; John 77, 89.
PUSSELL, John 81, 99.
PYATT, John 30, 33.
PYE, Peter 38.
QUALLS, Moses 103.
QUANT, Zebukun 50.
QUASH, Robert 7, 17.
QUATLIBAUM, John 72.
QUEEN, Hugh 103.
QUELCH, Andrew 6, 15.
QUINLEY, Dennis 49.
RABB, Robert 50.
RADCLIFFE, RATCLIFF, James 45; Richard 45; Samuel 48; Thomas Jr. 5, 13, 26.
RAFIELD, John 47.
RAGINS, Wm. 47.
RAIGLER, Andrew 66.
RAINEY, Benjamin 94.
RAINS, John 34, 39.
RALPH, John 13, 26.
RAMADGE, RAMAGE, Charles 13, 28; John 92.

RAMBERT, REMBERT, Ebijah 46; Isaac Jr. 31, 37; Isaac Sr. 31, 37; James 44; John 34, 53; Peter 34; Peter Jr. 34.
RAMBO, Lawrence, 80, 81, 99; Laurance Jr. 97; Swan 98.
RAMSEY, RAMSAY, RAMSY, RAMCY, Alex. 76, 84; ¨unl. 83; Geo. 36; James 57; Robt. 56; Saml. 77, 87, 104; Thos. 72, 84.
RANSFORD, RANSFORD, John 80, 97.
RAPER, Robert 5, 13.
RAPHEL, John 37.
RAPLEY, Richard A. 77, 87.
RASBROW, Alex. 50.
RATCHFORD, William 59.
RATLIVE, Saul, 51.
RAVENEL, Daniel 6, 16; Henry 6, 16; Henry Jr. 7, 16; James 6, 16.
RAVER, Mickel 71.
RAWLINS, Rhoddom, 29, 33.
RAWLINSON, Wm. 52.
RAY, RAE, James 94, 99; Jno. 30, 33; Nichl. 22; Robt. 5, 13, 26; Thos. 98; Wm. 49.
RAYFORD, Isaac 45; Mathew 55; Philip 50.
RAYMOND, David 62, 64.
RAZOR, Michael 20.
REACE, Henry 69.
READHEMER, John 16.
REANY, Samuel 59.
REAPSON, REAPSOM, Hans 52; Peat 53.
REARDEN, Timothy 98.
REEDA, REEDER, Joshua 96; Wm. 91.
REES, David 97; Hugh 48; John 48; Joseph 98; William 48.
REEVES, Henry 5, 13; John 51; Moses 51; Timothy 51; Timothy Jr. 45; Wm. 45.
REID, READ, REED, Abra. 86; Andw. 5, 13, 26; Arthur, 83; Geo. 77, 87; Hugh 76, 84; Jacob 5, 13; John 55; Jos. 89; Murry 49; Owen 94; Robt. 64; Wm. 5, 13, 26, 66, 68.
REILEY, Charles 13, 26; Robt. 47. See RILEY, REYLEY.
REMINGTON, Jacob 13, 26.
RENERSON, George 69.
RENNELLS, Richard 32, 38.
RENNOLDS, William 19.
RENSLER, Chrisr. 53.
RENTFROW, Enoch 43.
REST, John 68.
REYLEY, Elipahy 92; Miles 64. See RILEY
REYNALDS, REYNOLDS, Andrew 83; Benj. 61, 63; David Jr. 44; James Jr. 63; John 63, 71; Robert 40, 41.
RHEME, Joseph 20.
RHODEN, Thomas 101.
RHODES, RHODE, ROAD, ROADS, Danl. 37; Godfried 68; John 63; Joshua 49; Nathl. 47; William 36, 99.
RICE, Micajah 53.
RICH, Chris. 22; Meredith 63; Wm. 61, 63.
RICHARD, RICHARDS, RITCHARD, James Lyton, 66, 72; John 72; Robert 63.
RICHARDSON, Amos 81, 100; Danl. 91; Edw. 44; John 13, 26, 50, 96; Peter 91; Rich. 44; Rich. Jr. 44; Thos. 50; Wm. 44, 91.
RICHBOUGH, Clauds. 44; Henry 44; James 44; John 47; William 47.
RICHBOURG, Rene 9, 22.
RICHEY, RITCHEY, Jas. 87; Jno. 87; Wm. 78, 96.
RICHMAN, Jacob 71.
RICKENBAKER, RISHENBAKER, Henry 67, 69, 73.
RICKETT, Jacob 68.
RIDGEWAY, John 93.

RIDINGMAN, John 79, 101.
RIDLESPARGER, Christian 7, 17.
RIGELL, RIGILL, REGELL, RIDGALL, John 91;
   Richd. 35, 47; William 47.
RIGGS, RIGG, Jno. 43, 59; Saml. 17; Wm. 17.
RIGHT, Richard 90.
RIGHTON, RIGHTEN, McCully 5, 13, 26.
RILEY, John 90; Miles 67, 71; Patrick 91;
   Saml. 20; Tarina 91. See REYLEY, REILEY.
RIMLEY, Martin 13, 26.
RIOCH, Alexander 34, 39.
RIPLEY, John George 6, 16.
RISINGER, Thomas 90.
RISKPARRET, John 56.
RISSEL, Frederick 69.
RITTER, Jesse, 17.
RIVERS, Francis 21; Geo. 18; James 22;
   John 7, 18; Jos. 18; Malory 7, 18; Robt.
   18, 21; Saml. 18; Thos. 5, 13, 26.
RIVES, Robert 45.
RIXPOPER, Isaac 50.
ROACH, ROUCH, Ebenezer 7; Patrick 84; Peter
   40, 41. See ROCHE
ROATH, Christian 17.
ROBERTS, ROBERT, Absolem 99; Chas. 14, 27;
   Elias 65; Geo. 65; Henry 95; Jacob 93;
   John 61, 63, 70, 95, 99; Josiah 44; Moses
   34; Owen 5, 13; Peter 22; Robt. 65; Roger
   48; Thos. 8, 19, 48, 99 (2); Vincent 95;
   Walter 80, 101; William 34, 45.
ROBERTSON, Andrew 76, 85; Ed. 21; Elisha
   89; James 29, 32, 38, 54; John 13, 26,
   49 (2), 50, 56, 78, 90; Matthew 84;
   Patrick 79, 101; Peter 51; Wm. 34, 77.
ROBESON, ROBERSON, ROBISON, Anthony 69;
   John 87; William 73, 86, 88.
ROBINSON, Alex. 50; David 49; Drury 56;
   Elisha 77; Geo. 67, 71; John 48, 50, 67,
   69, 85; Jos. 54, 102; Matthew 103; Nathl.
   103; Nicholas 47; Patrick 57; Randol 91;
   Saml. 59; Wm. 59, 67, 71, 76, 85, 98, 104.
ROCHE, ROCKE, Ebenezer 18; Francis 66, 68;
   James 13, 26. See ROACH
ROCHEL, James 49.
ROCKBRIDGE, James 85.
ROCKFORD, James 16.
ROCUHEN, William 52.
RODENS, Thomas 54.
RODERICK, John 99.
ROGER (KOGER?) Joseph 19.
ROGER, ROGERS, RODGERS, Andw. 82, 94; Andw.
   Jr. 94; Benj. 40 (2), Chrisr. 5, 13, 24;
   Clayton 54; Danl. 80, 98; David 47; Isaac
   93; James 55; Jeremiah 83; John 29, 32,
   35, 44, 82, 94; Joshua 92; Matthew 59;
   Peter 83; Richd. 71; Robt. 101; Stephen
   90; Thos. 35; Wm. 79, 101 (2).
ROMNEY, Andrew 71.
RONALDS, Joseph 98.
RONE, Casper 53.
ROOFE, George 78, 90.
ROPER, William 5, 13, 26.
ROSE, Alex. 14, 27; Francis 18; John 5, 13,
   26, 61, 63, 65; Robt. 8, 19; Thos. 7, 18.
ROSEBOROUGH, Alex. 54.
ROSEMAN, ROSEMAND, John 77, 87; Samuel 87.
ROSS, Andw. 85; Arthur Brown 50, 60; Francis
   46; Geo. 44; Hugh 55; James 58 (2), 64;
   John 46; Peter 13, 26; Robt. 85; 93; Thos.
   87; Wm. 58, 62, 65, 86, 100.
ROSTIG, Andrew 69.
ROTH, Peter 69, 73; William 69.
ROTHMAKLER, Job 29, 32, 38.

ROULAIN, Abraham 18.
ROUNDTREE, Jethro 81, 99; Joab 70; Job 99;
   Richardson 80, 102; Turner 80, 102.
ROUT, George 5, 13, 26.
ROWAN, Samuel 53.
ROWAND, Robert 5, 13, 26.
ROWE, ROW, ROE, Christopher 67, 69, 73;
   Cornelius 100; Henry 68, 73; James 34, 47;
   John 54; Saml. 73; Thos. 40, 41.
ROWELL, Edward 80, 98.
ROYALL, William 7, 18.
RUBERRY, John 13, 26.
RUHLE, Peter 98.
RUFF, Cudgick 91.
RUMNEY, Joseph 20.
RUMPH, David Jr. 17; David 17; Jacob Jr. 69;
   Jacob Sr. 67, 69, 73.
RUSH, Abraham 49; Fredk. 49; James 57.
RUSHING, Mathew 41.
RUSSELL, RUSSEL, Alex. 13, 26; Chrisr. 87;
   Geo. 18; James 43, 50; John 5, 13, 26,
   46, 87; Jos. 17; Matthew 56; Michael 43;
   Nathaniel 5, 13, 26; Robt. 89; Saml. 60;
   Wm. 5, 14, 27, 76, 84.
RUTHEFORD, Robert 64.
RUTLEDGE, RUTLIDGE, Andrew 14, 27; Edw. 5,
   13; Hugh 5, 13, 73; John 13, 49; Reason
   87; Thomas 61, 63, 65.
RUZELEY, Henry 44.
RYAN, Benj. 98; Benj. Jr. 98; James 17;
   John 80, 95, 98; Lacon 80, 97; Thomas,
   79, 101.
SABB, Morgan 66, 68; Thos. 6, 16, 66, 68.
SAILER, George 58; Isaac 54; John 53, 59;
   Richard 58, 59.
SAFFOLD, William Sr. 103.
SAKKER, Samuel 80, 97.
SALISBURY, Andw. 52.
SALKES, Henry 34.
SALLEY, John 67, 70.
SALTER, John 79, 98, 101.
SAMMET, Conrod 68.
SAMPEL, SAMPLE, John 87; Nathl. 54.
SAMS, William 8, 19.
SAMUEL, James 58.
SAMWAYS, Henry 18; William 14, 27.
SAMYZER, William 14.
SANDEFIN, Wm. 52.
SANDERS, SAUNDERS, Geo. 50; James 44, 54;
   John 8, 20; Joseph Jr. 17; Peter 6;
   Richard 70; Thos. 86; Thos. Martin, 34;
   Wm. 52, 53, 103; Wm. Sr. 44. See SAUNDERS.
SANDERSON, John 83.
SANDFORD, Philip 58.
SANDIFORD, William 18.
SANDLE, John 69; Peter Sr. 66, 70.
SANSUM, John 14.
SARGENT, Wm. 95.
SARRAZIN, Jonathan 5, 14, 27.
SARVISE, John 55.
SASS, Jacob 14, 27.
SATTERWHITE, Bartell 95; John 95.
SAUNDERS, Nathl. 40, 41; Peter 15; Roger
   Parker, 21.
SAUSEY, David 64.
SAVAGE, Daniel 63; Jere. 5, 14; Nathan 32,
   37; Saml. 77, 89; Thos. 5, 14, 27; Wm.
   14, 101.
SAVINEAU, Nathaniel 16.
SAXON, Benj. 93; Charles 82, 94.
SAYLOR, David 14, 27; Jacob 66, 72.
SAYWER, John 81, 100.
SCHAD, Abraham 34, 38.

SCISON, William 102.
SCOTT, Alex. 31, 37; Alex Jr. 35; Archb. 7, 18; James 36, 57, 76, 84, 86, 97; John 5 (2), 14 (2), 18, 27, 31, 37, 77, 89; John Jr. 5, 14; Jos. 19, 31, 37; Jos. Sr. 63; Josiah 60; Moses 37; Robert 32, 37; Saml. 77, 89, 95; Thos. 21; Wm. 5, 14, 31, 35, 50, 52; Wm. Jr. 5, 14, 27.
SCOTTOW, SCOTTOU, Samuel 14, 27.
SCOTTWINS, Thomas 43.
SCREVEN, Benj. 30, 35; Elisha 30, 35; Thomas 7, 17.
SCROGGS, John 102.
SEABERMAN, Jacob 64.
SEABROOK, Benj. 8, 19; John 19; John Jr. 19, Jos. 8, 19; Jos. Jr. 8, 19; Thos. 34.
SEAGLER, George 71.
SEAT, William 69.
SEAUGON, William 51.
SEGLER, John 91.
SEAWRIGHT, George 71, James 86.
SEDGE, Isaac 51.
SEE, Abraham 71; Nicholas 71; Wm. 71.
SEGWALD, SIGWALD, Christian 14, 27.
SELF, John 34.
SELLARS, SELLERS, John 58; Thomas 99.
SEMPLE, James 31, 36.
SESSIONS, Absolam, 43; Edward 43; John 34; Solomon 34.
SEUSTRUNK, Henry 52. See SUSTRUNK.
SEVERANCE, John 6, 15; Thomas 15.
SEYMOUR, Isaac 14.
SHACKELFORD, William 34.
SHAFFER, Francis 21; Jacob 21.
SHANDLEY, Thomas 64.
SHANES, John 100.
SHANK, Matthew 83.
SHANKLIN, Thomas 84.
SHANNON, Thomas 55.
SHARP, James 14, 27, 54; Martin 90; Wm. 102.
SHAVER, Andrew 56.
SHAW, Daniel 59, 79, 80, 98, 100; John 48, 97; Pott, 14; Thomas 89.
SHEECUTT, Abraham 63.
SHEERER, SHERER, SHEIRER, SHURER, Francis, 79, 94; Hugh 57; Paul 68.
SHEETS, Christopher 14, 27.
SHEILDS, James 42.
SHENE, Alexander 34, 38.
SHENKLER, William 83.
SHENTROBSER, John 98.
SHEPHEARD, SHEPHERD, SHEPARD, Charles 20; George 8, 21; James 78, 91; Matthew 14; William 35.
SHIDER, SHIDERS, John 69, 73.
SHILLING, Henry 70, 73.
SHINGLER, Simon 67, 69.
SHIPES, Jacob 98.
SHIPLEY, George 66, 72; John 102.
SHLAGEL, Bernard 34.
SHOEMAKE, John 43.
SHOEMAKER, Valentine 66, 68.
SHORT, Hugh 70.
SHREWSBERRY, Ed. 14, 27; Stephen 5, 14.
SHRINE, John 29, 32, 38; Wm. 34, 38.
SHROPSHIRE, Walter 49.
SHUBRICK, Thomas 5, 14.
SHULLER, SHOOLER, SHAULER, George 66, 68; Nichl. 66, 70.
SHUMAN, Martin 65.
SHUTTERLING, John 5, 14, 27.
SIGLER, David 99.
SILEY, John 46.

SIMMONS, Benj. 7, 18; John 21; Keating 16; Maurice 5, 14, 27; Semeon 37; Silas 37; William 53.
SIMON, SIMONS, Anthony 9, 22; Jesse 36; John 37, 52, 69; William 101.
SIMPSON, Daniel 95; Hugh 83; James 56; Jas. Gilchrist, 21; John 83; Sam. 94, 101; Thos. 67; Wm. 51, 56, 66, 68, 79, 100.
SIMS, SIMES, Benj. 52; John 79, 96; Nathan 77, 88; Robert 93.
SINGLE, Frederick 90.
SINGLETARY, Benj. 48; John 18; Michael 49; Richard 17, Thomas 45.
SINGLETON, Bracey 14, 27; John 8, 20, 34, 44; Joseph 47; Matthew 44; Philip 42; Richard 30; Thomas 5, 14, 27.
SINGUEFIELD, Francis 80, 97.
SINKLER, Danl. 22; James 9, 22; Peter 9, 23.
SISSON, Frederick 81, 100.
SKAVEN, Philip 46.
SKINNER, Chas. 48.
SKIRVING, James Jr. 8, 20; Wm. 9, 21.
SLADE, Henry 18.
SLAGEL, _____, 71.
SLANN, Andrew 21; Joseph 21; Peter 21.
SLAPPY, Casper 71; Geo. Jr. 71; Geo. Sr. 71.
SLIGER, Martin 51.
SLIKER, George 51.
SLISSE, Jacob 72; Ulrick 72.
SLOAN, James 85.
SMALL, Christopher 36.
SMART, James 65; William 29, 32, 39.
SMILEY, John 20; William 8, 19.
SMISER, Jacob 20.
SMITH, Abra. 46, 51; Alex. 51, 60; B. 84; Benj. 6, 16, 88; Chas. 20; Christian 17; Daniel 91; David 14, 27; Drury 93; Edw. 16; Elijah 100; Ezekiel 77, 87; Francis 8, 20; Geo. 5, 20, 34, 67, 87; Geo. Jr. 5, 14, 27; Gerard 95; Handcock 101; Henry 6, 16, 21, 57; Hugh 50; Isaac 54; Jacob 81, 100; James 18, 34, 35, 47, 52, 57, 61, 64; John 14, 27, 42, 54 (2), 57, 59, 62, 65, 70, 93, 94, 95, 100, 101; John Jr. 35; John Sr. 30, 33; John Christian 7, 17; Joseph 9, 21, 58, 65, 90, 95; Josiah Jr. 5, 14, 27; Kitt 93; Lance 61; Malcolm 21; Matthias 63; Melchoir 68; Moses 52, 89; Nicholas 14; Patrick 50, 58; Peter 14, 20, 27, 59; Philip 8, 20; Roger 5, 14, 27; Robert 69, 73, 94, 102; Samuel 29, 32, 38, 103; Smallwood 81, 100; Stephen 52, 67, 71; Thomas 5, 8, 14, 21, 27, 29, 32, 80, 91, 101; Thomas Keeling (Reeling) 77, 87, 104; William 8, 9, 20, 21 (2), 44, 52, 58, 103; William Jr. 8, 20.
SMITHERS, Gabriel 88; Gilbert 77.
SMITHSON, George 5, 14, 27.
SMOKE, Thomas 71.
SMOTHERS, Christopher 98.
SMYTH, John 5, 14, 27.
SMYZER, SMYSER, Paul 5, 14, 27.
SNEAD, Henry 53; James 14, 27; Robt. 44.
SNEES, Cornelius 20.
SNELGROVE, Henry 72.
SNELL, Adam 66, 68; Henry Sr. 67, 69.
SNIDER, SNYDER, Hendrick 22; Paul 14, 27.
SNIPES, Philip 98; William Clay 8, 20.
SNOW, George 30, 36; James 31, 36; Nathl. 31, 36; Thomas 30, 33; Wm. 31, 36.
SNOWDEN, Joshua 63.
SOMARSALL, William 5, 14, 27.
SOMMERFORD, Abram 57.

SOMMERS, SOMMER, Francis 72; Henry 72; Hymphry 5, 14; John 8, 21; Nicholas 72.
SOMMERVILL, SUMMERVILLE, Geo. 49; Hugh 49.
SCRUGS, John 97.
SOUTHWELL, Edward 70.
SOWERHAVEN, Henry 68.
SOWN, John 81, 100.
SPARKS, SPARK, Charles 40, 41; Danl. 40, 41; Jesse 96; John 91.
SPEARS, SPIARS, Abraham 80, 98; Chas. 46; William 29, 33, 85, 103.
SPEED, John 40, 41.
SPEIR, Robert 97.
SPENCE, Andrew 71; James 71; Robt. 72.
SPENCER, Geo. 64; John 80, 97; Labastion ? 14; Sabastian 27.
SPERDUE, Adam 99.
SPIDELL, SPIDLE, Abraham 5, 14, 27.
SPIGHT, Moses 40, 41.
SPINNEY, George 66, 68.
SPISEGAR, SPICESEGAR, John 14, 27.
SPIVEY, Francis 48; John 43; Wm. 49.
SPOON, William 21.
SPRADLIN, Charles 55.
SPRAGGINS, Nathaniel 77, 88.
SPRATT, John 84.
SPRING, Aaron 38; John 68; Robt. 32, 38.
SPRINGER, Casper 64; Thomas 101.
SPRUEL, John 43.
SPURLOCK, Drury 47.
STABLER, _____, 71.
STACEY, Edward 17.
STACKS, James 30, 36.
STACKHOUSE, William 35.
STAFFORD, Edw. 65; John 64; Joshua 65; Richard 65; William 62, 65.
STAKE, Jacob 72.
STALEY, Peter 69.
STALLIONS, John 57.
STANALAND, Jacob 34.
STANDARD, William 42.
STANLEY, Benj. 70, Joshua 70.
STANLEY, Ezekiel 58.
STANYARNE, John 18; William 18, 19.
STAPE, Lewis 64.
STARE, John 98.
STARK, STARKS, Douglass 46; Henry 66, 68; Jeremiah 95; Robert 80, 97; Thomas 45, 79, 94, 95; Wm. 49.
STARLING, Joseph 18, William 18.
STARNES, STERNES, Ebeneezer 78, 89, 96.
STARRAT, Thomas 30, 33.
STATLER, STATLER, John 14; Martin 52.
STEAD, William Jr. 17.
STEDAM, Zachariah 101.
STEDMAN, STEADMAN, Henry 79, 96; James 5, 14, 27; John 85.
STEEL, Aaron 76, 84; Alexander 84; Arch. 59; Isaac 84, 86; John 51, 78, 91; Joseph 63; Samuel 92; Thomas 37.
STEEN, STEENE, James 80, 102; John 80, 103; William 102.
STENT, John 18; Paul 18; Samuel 5, 14, 18, 27; William 66, 68.
STEPHENS, David 20; James 86; John 34; Joseph 20; William 95.
STEPHENSON, STEVENSON, David 58; George 84; James 84; John 5, 14, 27, 55.
STERLING, Isaac 70.
STEVENS, Daviel 63, 65; Ebenetus 88; Geo. 63; Jacob 8, 20; James 21; Jervis Henry 7, 17; Josiah 88; Thomas 21.
STEWARD, John 89; William 88.

STEWART, STUART, Alex. 57, 90; Andrew 5, 14, 27; Daniel 7, 17; Hugh 54; Isaac 86; James 8, 17, 20; John 29, 32; Joshua 90; Robert 85; Thos. 14, 27; Wm. 34, 58, 87, 90.
STICKMAN, John 91.
STIFFELMYER, Stephen 68.
STILES, Benjamin 7, 18.
STILLINGS, George 36.
STILLMAN, Augustine 14.
STIMSON, Enos 95.
STINWINDER, George 66, 72.
STITT, William 29, 32.
ST. JOHN, Audeon 5, 14, 27; James 14.
STOBO, Richard Park 7, 18.
STOCKER, Matthew 99.
STOCKMAN, STOKMAN, English 90, Engle 91.
STOCKTON, Newberry 56.
STOKES, Thomas 54; William 48.
STOLL, William 14, 27.
STONE, Benj. 7, 18, 22; David 63; James 96 (2), John 93; Joshua 44; Robt. 87; Saml. 14; Thos. 50; Wm. 14, 95.
STORR, Peter 14, 27.
STORY, Chas. 45; John 45.
STOUTENBURGH, William 62, 64.
STOUTENMYER, Martin 68.
STRADFORD, STRATFORD, Richard 51, 60.
STRAIGHT, Christopher 52.
STRAIN, John 56, 85; John Sr. 56; Thomas 84, 86; William 84.
STRANGE, Chas. 47; Edmond 52; Michael 52.
STRAWBRIDGE, Robert 50.
STREATER, James 6, 16.
STREET, Benj. 52; Richard 41.
STRICKLAND, James 5, 14.
STRINGER, George 86.
STROBHART, Jacob 65; John 65.
STROBLE, Daniel 5, 14, 27; Gasper 17.
STROCK, John 68.
STROMAN, Bolrer 69; Jacob Jr. 67, 69; Jacob Sr. 67, 69; John 69, 73.
STRONG, James 55.
STROTHER, William 41, 45.
STROUB, John George 72.
STROUD, John 47; Joshua 42; Wm. 55.
STRUB, John 72.
STUKES, William 5, 14, 27.
STUZZENGER, STUZENGGER, John 80, 98.
SUBER, George 78, 91; John 78.
SULLIVAN, SULIVAN, Daniel 89; John 20; Stephen 22.
SULLIVANT, Hampton 43.
SUMMERALL, SUMERAL, Henry 70; Jacob Sr. 97; Jesse 70.
SUMMERS, John Adam 72; John Adam Jr. 66; Adam Sr. 66, 72.
SUMTER, Thomas 44.
SUN, Mathias 71.
SUSTRUNK, Casper 69. See SEUSTRUNK
SUTTON, Jasper 44; Richd. 47; Robt. 31, 37.
SWADELL, William 49.
SWAN, SWANN, John 58; Samuel 46, 56; Stephen 64.
SWANSON, David 14, 27.
SWANZEY, Robert 87.
SWEARENGAIN, SWEARINGHAM, John 98; Jos. 76, 84; Vann Jr. 98; Vann Sr. 99.
SWEET, Anthony 30, 33.
SWEETEN, George 35; Lewis 47.
SWIFT, John 17.
SWIGHARD, Jacob 67, 71.
SWIGHTENBERG, John 72.
SWIKARD, George 72, John 72.

127

SWILLY, Nicholas 46.
SWINDFORD, John 95.
SWINTON, Alex. 37; Hugh 5, 14, 27; Wm. 21.
SYFRID, Adam 69; Alex. 69.
SYLVESTER, Asberry 48.
TAEK (TACK?), William 16.
TAGGERT, John 102.
TAHLER, Jacob 62, 64.
TAKINGS, William 59.
TALBIRD, Henry 61, 63.
TALLMAN, John Richard 14, 27.
TAMERLINSON, Wm. 49.
TAMPLETON, James 57.
TAMPLAT, TAMPLATT, Elisha 16; John 34; Joseph 35; Peter 6, 16.
TAPLEY, Key 47.
TARBURT, John 91.
TARR, William 101.
TART, Nathan 7, 18.
TATE, Jesse 102; Richard 88; Saml. 66, 68; Thomas 57; William 80, 102.
TATUM, Joseph 52.
TAYLOR, Abraham 99; Andrew 85; Bellington, 47; Champness 97; Christopher 29, 32, 39; David 14, 27; Jacob 45; James 45, 68, 73; John 46, 51, 79, 101; Jonathan 96; Peter 23; Reuben 98; Samuel 86; Thomas 46, 51, 63; Ward 98; William 37, 54, 91, 92.
TEAGUE, Elijah 79, 96.
TEBOUT, TEABOUT, Tunis 61, 63, 65.
TEMPLETON, David 94; Robert 94.
TERRELL, TERRILL, Joshua 42; Wm. Jr. 40, 41.
TERRY, John 53; Joseph 47; Stephen 55.
TETER, William 102.
TETSTONE, Henry 70.
TEW, George 5, 14, 27.
TEYSOR, Richard 31, 37.
THACKER, Joel, 86.
THARIN, Daniel 14, 27.
THEILER, Jacob 71.
THEUS, John 19; Randolph 29, 32, 39; Simeon 34, 39.
THOMAS, Anderson 54; Charles 103; Daniel 80, 102; Daniel Sr. 54; Edward 7, 17; Evan 101; James 54, 80, 81, 89, 99, 102; John 43, 90; Col. John 79, 100; Joseph 89; Nehemiah 89; Robt. 58; Saml 97; Stephen 14, 27; Trusham 42; William 40, 41, 54, 97.
THOMSON, THOMPSON, Abraham 78, 89; Adam 50; Alex. 55; Arch. 57; Charles 78, 89; David 50; George 32, 37; Hugh 46; James 8, 19, 57, 62, 65, 83; John 6, 14, 27, 37, 55, 56, 57, 79, 100, 103; Joseph 42, 78, 90; Joseph Sand 22; Lewis 68; Matthew 76, 84; Moses 53; Nathan 46, 59; Nicoles 51; Robt. 88, 104; Samuel 86, 100; William 30, 35, 48, 49, 64, 66, 83, 95.
THORN, Philip 14, 27.
THORNLEY, Robert 37.
THORNTON, Thomas 88.
THORP, Samuel 63.
THREEWITS, Joel, 45; John 52.
THURSBY, James 42.
TICKTELL, John 69.
TIDWELL, TIDWILL, John 51; Priestly 50; Robert 54.
TIKETT, Isaac 96.
TILGHMAN, Elisha 35.
TILL, Nichl. 69.
TILLET, James 79, 100.
TILLMAN, TILMAN, TILMON, Frederick 97, 99; George 80, 97; Lewis 81, 99; Wm. 45.

TILLY, TILY, David 68; James 68.
TIMBERMAN, Philip 89.
TIMMON, TIMMAN, TIMMONS, Conner 35; John 20, 37; Lewis 14, 27.
TIMOTHY, Peter 14.
TIMROD, Henry 6, 14, 27.
TIMS, Amos 46.
TINDALL, TINDAL, Robert 54; Samuel 35.
TINER, Caleb 84.
TINES, Samuel 68.
TINSLEY, Isaac 94; James 93; Manoah 93; Philip 93.
TIPPLING, James 58.
TIPPIN, Joseph 63.
TITCHCOAT, John 46.
TOBLER, John 80, 98.
TODD, Archibald 87; John 20; Richard 6, 14, 27; Thomas 34.
TOLAND, James 49.
TOLLESON, John 53.
TOMBELTON, John 51.
TOMKINS, Stephen 41.
TOMLINSON, George 32, 37; John 45; Richd. 48; Samuel 47, 59; Wm. 46, 59.
TOMPLATE, Stephen 34.
TOMSTER, Joseph 53.
TONNEY, Charles 70.
TOOMER, Anthony 6, 14, 27; Henry 63; Joshua 6, 15.
TORRANS, John 6, 14, 27.
TOUCH, William 14, 27.
TOUSSIGER, James 5, 14, 27.
TOWLES, John 77, 88; Joseph 88; Oliver 97; Stokley 88.
TOWNS, John 102.
TOWNSEND, Andrew 8, 19; Daniel 19; John 80, 103; Paul 6, 14, 27; Repentance 58; Stephen 6, 14.
TRAFT, George 71.
TRAMEL, TRAMMELL, Daniel 102; Thomas 101.
TRAPIER, Benj. 29, 33; Paul Jr. 29, 32, 39; Paul Sr. 29, 32, 39.
TRAPP, Wm. 53.
TRAVALER, Henry 101.
TRAVISE, Daniel 54.
TRAYER, George 71; Godfrey Jr. 71.
TRESCOT, Edward 14, 27.
TREZVANT, Theodore 5, 14, 27.
TROUP, John 5, 14.
TRUSLER, William 6, 14, 27.
TRYWEAK, Othneil 35.
TUCKER, Benj. 29, 32; Daniel 29, 32, 39; James 71; John 69; John Jr. 70; Joseph, 69; Thomas 5, 14, 27; Wanner 53; William 53, 66, 72.
TUFFEL, John James 89.
TUFTS, Simon 5, 14, 27.
TUKE, John 14, 27.
TUNDERBURG, Henry 55.
TURK, John 85; Theodosius 96.
TURLEY, Peter 50.
TURNBULL, John 84; Joseph 76, 84.
TURNER, Absolom 97; David 97; Drury 37; Edward 97; George 103; Gilbert 95; James 55; John 14, 51, 52, 78, 90; Samuel 86; Thomas 84; Wilkinson 57; William 97.
TURNEY, Charles 83.
TURPIN, Joseph Jr. 14, 27.
TUIT, Benj. 77, 89; Richard 77, 89.
TUTTEN, Peter 86.
TWEEDY, TWEEDEY, Robert 53; Wm. 93.
TWERNER, James 72.
TWINER, Alexander 46.

128

TWITTY, Henry 103.
TYDIMAN, Philip 6, 14, 27.
TYGERT, William 90.
ULMER, Adam 62, 64; Frederick 69; John 67;
  Peter 64; Philip 62, 64.
UNDERWOOD, Geo. 49.
UNGER, George 71.
UTISEY, Isaac 17.
UTZEY, George 69.
VALCAR, Peter 65.
VALENTINE, William 14, 27.
VALK, Jacob 6, 14, 27.
VALTON, Peter 14, 27.
VANDERKORST, VANDERHORST, Arnoldus 6, 15.
VAN BEBBER, VAN BEBBEN, Jacob 62, 64.
VANEY, Samuel 15.
VANHORN, Benjamin 90.
VANJANT, Jacob 78, 89.
VAN MARGINHOFF, John 8, 20.
VANN, Edward 97, 98; John 97.
VANVELSIN, Francis 23.
VARLIN, John 20.
VARNEN, James 79, 101.
VARNER, John 76, 84.
VASSEKS, James 98.
VASSER, James 80.
VAUCHIER, John 62, 64.
VAUGHN, Evan 38; Henry 47; Wm. 92.
VAUX, William 29, 32, 39.
VEITCH, John 21.
VENABLES, John 56.
VERBEE, John Sr. 47.
VERDIMAN, William 95.
VERJEN, Ejeniah 94.
VERNER, Jacob 18.
VERNON, Henry 47.
VEREE, VERREE, Joseph 6, 14, 27.
VERREEN, Jeremiah 34; William 29, 33.
VESSELS, Shadrach, 91.
VIDEAUX, VIDEAU, Peter 7, 16.
VILLEPONTOUX, Benjamin 6, 14, 27; Francis
  22; Paul 37; Zachariah Jr. 6, 16.
VILLER, Michael 72.
VINCE, Richard 70.
VINCENT, Jesse 102.
VINEAU, John Lewis 64.
VINEYARD, John 14, 27.
VINEGART, Mathias 71; Michal 72.
VINING, Thomas 42.
VOLENTINE, John 92.
WACKTER, Martin 71.
WADDLE, Abel 42; Joseph 59.
WADE, George 45; John 99.
WADELL, John 91.
WADKINS, Samuel 43; William 42.
WADLETON, Edward 78, 91; William 78, 90.
WADLINGTON, James 95; Thomas 79, 95.
WAFER, Francis 90.
WAGGONER, Hance 55.
WAGNER, John 6, 15, 27.
WAINWRIGHT, Richard 6, 15, 28; Samuel 6,
  15, 28.
WAIR, Samuel 54.
WAITE, WAIGHT, Abraham 7, 18; Abraham Jr.
  18; Isaac 61, 63; Isaac Jr. 18; William
  63, 65.
WAKARD, William 91.
WAKEFIELD, James 6, 15, 27; John 14, 27.
WAKER, Henry 90; Matthias 91.
WALCOTT, Abraham 63.
WALDROPE, James 97; John 92, 97; Michael,
  93.
WALES, Thomas 86.

WALKER, Alexander 54, 55; Benjamin 22;
  Hezekiah 80, 98; James 56, 88; John 46,
  52, 54, 77, 88; Joseph 52; Philip 46,
  55 (2); Richard 55; Robert 22, 55;
  Robert Jr. 55; Samuel 99; Tundy 81, 92;
  William 88, 91.
WALL, Bird 51; Howell 65.
WALLACE, James 59; John 59 (2), 94;
  Robert 77, 89.
WALLER, Benjamin 15, 28.
WALLEY, John 35.
WALLING, Thomas 53.
WALLIS, James 50.
WALLS, Benj. 63.
WALLZER, Gabriel 64.
WALNOCK, Joseph 18.
WALSH, John 28.
WALTER, Jacob 17; John 17; John Allyn, 7,
  17; Richard 7, 17; Thomas 6, 16.
WALTON, John 88; William 6, 15, 27.
WARD, John 8, 15, 20, 28, 36; Joshua 6, 15
WARDLAW, Hugh 77, 87; John 77, 86, 104 (2)
  Joseph 77, 88, 104.
WARE, George 93; Henry 77, 89, 98.
WARING, Benjamin 7, 17; John 6, 15, 27;
  Lott 99; Morton 7, 17; Richard 7, 17;
  Thomas 7, 17; Thomas Jr. 7, 17;
  William 81, 100.
WARLEY, Jacob 6, 15, 27.
WARNOCK, Chas. 48; Samuel 6, 14, 27.
WARREN, George 21; Hugh 103; John 8, 20.
WARICK, Nocholas 53.
WASHING, Gasper 6, 15, 27.
WATERS, Philemon 78, 89.
WATIES, William 29, 33.
WATSMAN, John 100.
WATSON, Arthur 81, 100; David 56; George
  31, 37; Hugh 21; James 56; John 15, 54,
  56, 81, 100; Lewis 100; Michael 81; Sam,
  46; Wichall 100; William 56, 58.
WATTS, WATT, James 85, 87; John 31, 37, 96;
  Reuben 36; Samuel 76, 86; Thomas 86.
WAY, Aaron 67; Samuel 70.
WAYNE, William 6, 14, 27.
WEARE, WEAR, John 16, 52; William 54.
WEATHERFORD, John 42.
WEAVER, WEEVER, Aaron 100; Nichl. 66, 70.
WEBB, Andrew 87; Benjamin 22; James 87;
  Jesse 65; John 6, 15, 27; Samuel 49;
  William 8, 20.
WEBBER, John 20.
WEED, Reuben 76, 83.
WEEDINGMAN, Christian 102.
WEEKLEY, John 62, 64; William 64, 70.
WEEMS, James 86; Thomas 76, 85.
WELCH, James 63.
WELKIN, William 103.
WELLS, Elijah 102; James 96; John 8, 20,
  22, 38, 53, 96; John Jr. 15, 27; Matthew
  20, 88; Richard 47; Samuel 18; Thomas 85;
  William 18.
WELSH, David 86; John 15; Wm. 49.
WELST, Thomas 81, 100.
WEMBERLY, Abm. 49.
WERLEY, Melchior 6, 15, 27.
WERNAL, William 70.
WERNN, Jacob 72.
WERSHING, Gasper 53.
WESBERRY, WESTBERRY, John 48; Wm. 36, 48.
WEST, John 56; William 99; Wm. Sr. 81;
  Wm. Jr. 81, 100.
WESTCOT, WESCOT, David 53; Thomas 19.
WESTFIELD, John 40, 41; Robert 41.

129

WESTON, Plowden, Powden, 6, 15, 28; Wm. 63.
WETSTONE, Henry 66, 68.
WEYMAN, Edward 6, 15, 27.
WHALEY, Arch. 19; James 20; Thomas 19.
WHARTON, Samuel 95, 96.
WHEELER, John 44.
WHILDEN, Elisha 15; Joseph 15.
WHIPPY, Joseph 19; William 19.
WHITAKER, James 45, 60; Richard 50, 60; Willees, 47, 60; William 45; Wm. Jr. 50, 60; Wm. Sr. 60.
WHITE, Alexander Sr. 85; Andrew 85; Anthony 30, 36; Anthony Jr. 31, 36; Anthony Martin 29, 32, 39; Arthur 47; Blake Seay 16; George 6, 15, 31, 35, 45; Henry 37, 55; Hugh 56; Jacob 15; James 98; John 6, 15, 19, 51, 56, 85, 102; Joseph 56, 94; Nathan 99, Samuel 15; Sims 6, 15, 27; Thomas 6, 15, 21; Wm. 51, 56, 84.
WHITEFIELD, Luke 30, 33; Matthew 9, 22; William 35.
WHITEHEAD, Nazeres 50.
WHITEL, Borris 100.
WHITESIDE, WHITESIDES, Edward 15; Hugh 54; John 15; Thomas 6, 15.
WHITFIELD, George 86.
WHITMAN, WHITEMAN, Jacob Sr. 66, 68.
WHITMORE, John 81, 92; Joseph 81, 92.
WHITNER, Jacob 49.
WHITNEY, Lebbeus 15, 28.
WHITTONE, Ambrose 92.
WHITWORTH, Abraham 37.
WHITTER, James Sr. 18.
WIER, James 15, 27.
WIGFALL, Elias 6, 15; John 7, 17; Joseph, 6, 15.
WIGG, Hilderson 63; William Hazzard 61, 63, 65.
WILD, WYLD, John 70; Thomas 69.
WILDS, Abel 40, 41, 43; John 42, 43.
WILEY, WYLEY, WYLY, WYLLY, David 85; Henry 85; James 55; John 44, 60; Samuel 47, 60; William 46, 55, 59.
WILFOR (WILTON?), Thos. 103.
WILKINS, Benjamin 6, 14, 27; James 14, 27, 55; John 64; Samuel 64, 65; Wm. 14, 27.
WILKINSON, James 57, 58; John 90, 96; Morton 9, 22.
WILKS, Samuel 37.
WILL, Philip 14, 27.
WILLARD, John 96.
WILLIAMS, Ase 70; Britten 67, 71; Burgas, 42; Charles 76, 77, 83, 89; Daniel 22, 50, 95, 96; Ezekiel 67, 71; Frederick 71; Hardy 69; Henry 46, 70; Hopkins 78, 95; Isaac 96; James 93, 94, 95, 97; James Green 15, 28; James Thomas 63; Jeremiah 91; Jesse 31, 36; Joel 52; John 47, 71, 83, 95, 97; John Mortimer 6, 14, 27; Jonathan 43; Joseph 49; Lud 80, 98; Maurice 19; Micaijah 29, 32, 39; Nimrod 78, 96; Philip 9, 22; Providence 95; Reuben 98; Richard 81, 100; Robert 6, 14, 48; Thomas 52, 102; West 42; William 35, 48, 79.
WILLIAMSON, Andrew 76, 86; David 20; James 42, 58; John Garnier 64; Joseph 34; Rowland 53; Shadreck 43; Thomas 42, 94; William 6, 15, 42, 58.
WILLIMAN, WILLEMAN, Christopher 6, 15, 27; Jacob 6, 15, 27.
WILLINGHAM, Edward 67.
WILLS, James 78.

WILSON, WILLSON, Alexander 20, 30, 33; Brazel 52; Charles 35, 91; David 31, 36, 44; Henry 20; Hugh 19, 59, 93; James 20, 53, 55, 56, 57 (2), 59, 88, 89, 90, 103; Jehu 8, 21; John 15, 19, 21, 30, 33, 51, 83, 95, 103; Michael 85; Nathaniel 84; Robert 86, 101; Robt. Jr. 32, 36; Roger 44; Russel 99; Samuel 84; Thomas 29, 32, 39, 58, 77, 84, 88, 104; Thos. Jr. 34, 39; Wm. 6, 15, 27, 30, 36, 44, 52, 76, 79, 86, 88, 95 (2), 104; Wilson 34, 38.
WILTON See WILFOR
WINBOURN, Damery 57.
WINBUSH, Samuel 76, 85.
WINCHESTER, William 96.
WINDESS, Barnabass, 37.
WINDHAM, Amos 42.
WINES, Samuel 42.
WINGOOD, Charvil 6, 15.
WINKLER, Lewis 64.
WINN, John 45; Richd. 50.
WINNINGHAM, Henry 68.
WINTER, John 30, 35; Robert 30, 35.
WISE, Geo. 89; John 47, 98; Sam, 41; Saml. 40, 44, 60; Thomas 47; William 70.
WISEMAN, Hugh 90; Robert 92.
WISH, Benj. 6, 15, 27.
WISNER, Jacob 50.
WISSE, George 72.
WISSENTUNT, Nicholas 59.
WITHERS, WITHRS, Jacob 77, 88; John 29, 32; Richard 9, 22; Saml. 96; Wm. 6, 16.
WITHERSPOONE, WEATHERSPOON, David 31, 37; Gavin 31, 32, 37, 38; James 31; James Jr. 37; James Sr. 37; John 31, 32, 37, 38, 45; Robert 31, 37.
WITSELL, John 88.
WITTEN, Peter 16.
WITTER, James 6, 15, 27; John 18; Thos. 18.
WOFFORD, WAFFORD, Wm. 79, 101; Col. Wm. 79, 101.
WONDERLY, David 65.
WONEMAKER, Jacob Jr. 69, 73.
WOOD (WEED?) Reuben 83.
WOOD, WOODS, Benj. 68; Edward 19; James 47; Jeroham 59; John 14, 16, 27, 35, 70; John Sr. 54; Joseph 16, 42, 82, 93, 97; Peter 96; Saml. 57; Solomon 98; Thomas 90; William 34, 76, 86, 101.
WOODALL, William 95.
WOODBERRY, Daniel 34; John 29, 32, 38; Jonah 30, 33; Richard 35.
WOODERSON, John 47, 59.
WOODLEY, Richd. 55.
WOODSON, Benjamin 102.
WOODWARD, John 45; Thomas 45, 47.
WOOLFE, Christian 68; David 73; Jacob Jr. 68, 73; Jacob Sr. 67, 69, 73.
WOOTERS, Jacob Sr. 48.
WORD, Thomas 93.
WORKMAN, John 59.
WRAGG, John 6, 14, 15, 27 (2); Joseph 29, 32, 39; Samuel 29, 32, 39.
WRAY, Alexander 65.
WRIGHT, Abraham 94; Alexander 17; George 48; Henry 57; Jacob 96; James 14, 15, 27 (2); John 6, 16, 78, 89; Samuel 20, 52; Thomas 48; William 47, 90, 102. See RIGHT.
WYATT, John 14, 27; Solomon 97.
WYCHE, Drury 45; John 52.
WYMORE, Jacob 67, 69, 73.
WYMPIE, Henry 52.

YARBOROUGH, James D. 8, 21; John 51, 52.
YATES, Joseph 15; Thomas 78, 95.
YEADON, Richard 15, 28.
YEARG, John 71.
YELDEN, Robert 85.
YOHN, John 70.
YOU, Thomas 6, 15, 28.
YOUNG, Adam 59; Benj. 29, 33; Francis Jr. 21; George 6, 15, 28; Henry Sr. 67, 70; Hugh 55, 82, 93; James 81, 84, 93 (2); Jesse 102; John 16, 58, 83, 95; Joseph 95; Matthew 85; Robert 84, 94; Thomas 6, 15, 67, 71, 97; Wm. 31, 37, 51, 96.
YOUNGBLOOD, Peter 20.
YUNGINGER, Simon 72.

ZAHN, ZOHN, Jacob Christopher 66, 68.
ZCHNDER, Philip 69.
ZIGLER, Jacob 67, 68.
ZIMERMAN, Bastian 69; Michael 69.
ZINN, Heronimus 70.
ZORN, Henry 69; Nich. 69.
ZUBLY, David 80, 98.

www.ingramcontent.com/pod-product-compliance
Lightning Source LLC
Chambersburg PA
CBHW070553170426
43201CB00012B/1826